THE
ACORN HOUSE
COOKBOOK

Arthur Potts Dawson has been cooking for twenty years and has worked
with all the big names – the Roux brothers, Rowley Leigh, Rose Gray
and Ruth Rogers. It was while working as Head Chef at the River Café
that he first began what was to become a lifelong commitment to using
organic products from local suppliers. He went on to restyle Petersham
Nurseries, relaunch Cecconi's, and to work as executive chef for Jamie
Oliver's Fifteen Restaurant.

In 2005 Arthur co-founded 'Eat Green', an initiative that has created a
number of sustainably-aware urban restaurants, including Acorn House.
Arthur is passionate about the variety of food on offer in towns and cities
and created a menu of 'Modern London' cuisine for Acorn House that
exemplifies the diversity of the city in which he was born. Eat Green has
just launched their most recent project, the Water House Restaurant,
which opened in February 2008.

The Acorn House Cookbook is his first book.

THE
ACORN HOUSE
COOKBOOK

Good Food from Field to Fork

ARTHUR POTTS DAWSON

with Susan Fleming

Foreword by Jamie Oliver

HODDER &
STOUGHTON

First published in Great Britain in 2008 by Hodder & Stoughton
An Hachette Livre UK company

A CIP catalogue record for this title is available from the British Library

ISBN 978 0 340 95460 7

Design by David Lane

Printed and bound by L.E.G.O. S.p.A.

In a strategy of sustainable development, this book is printed in the
European Community by L.E.G.O. Spa on Munken Premium Cream 80 gsm
paper, made in Italy following FSC standards, ensuring sustainable forest
management.

Hodder & Stoughton Ltd
338 Euston Road
London NW1 3BH

www.hodder.co.uk

To my children,
Aron Maze and Tuula Cherry,
you are the future.

CONTENTS

Autumn

An overabundance of fruit and vegetables, all of which have soaked up the sun of summer...

Winter

Cold days, nights by the fire, warming comfort foods, and the promise of spring to come...

FOREWORD

Arthur Potts…hmmm…what can I tell you about Arthur Potts?

Well – first and foremost – he is a good man. I first met him in 1997 and, like me, he was a fair bit peachier and a bit of a whippersnapper back then. We worked together at the River Café – certainly a place that made a big impact on both of our lives. It was a place where I think we both grew a lot as chefs and gained a lot of confidence. We've been good friends since those days and have always kept track of each other.

I'm happy to write this foreword for Arthur not just because he's a mate, but also because he's a great cook who is incredibly clever with flavours. To me, Arthur encapsulates the new generation of proper chefs: chefs who obsess about great flavours, true simplicity, and have the ability to rewrite menus daily because they're truly at the mercy of their local suppliers.

The point I want to make here is that Arthur works around the food, the food doesn't work around Arthur. How many times have you been to a Michelin-starred restaurant and found yourself eating asparagus tips, peas or broad beans from God knows where in the middle of an icy cold winter?! What is that all about? That's not a clever cook. But Arthur Potts is a clever cook, and there's plenty of evidence of that right here in this book.

Obviously every chef wants a busy restaurant, but I know what makes Arthur happy is having a busy restaurant full of regular customers. I think his customers return time after time not just because the food and the service are great but also because they buy into the whole ethos of where his food comes from and how he deals with any waste. The success of the restaurant only proves that people do care about these things and I think this is only going to grow.

I'll admit that when I first met Arthur I thought he was a bit of a hippy. He was always worried about the leftovers from the restaurant getting turned into staff lunches, where the food we served was coming from and whether it was sustainable and local... all of that 'ultra-green' stuff.

But bloody hell! How things have changed over the last ten years. Finally the rest of us have caught up with Arthur. Looking after our planet and thinking about stuff like carbon footprints, pesticides and Fairtrade — for our own farmers as well as foreign farmers — is now the kind of stuff that gets talked about every day.

So at a time when everyone's jumping on the green bandwagon (myself included), I couldn't be prouder of Arthur writing this book. In my view he's the original 'Green Chef'. In this book, you'll read incredible recipes to die for, get hints and tips on cooking and also learn about things you can do in your everyday life to become that little bit greener.

Hats off to you, Arthur — you did it! It's a great book, a great message, and all your friends and family couldn't be more proud. And, most importantly, mate, you deserve it!

Jamie O xxx

INTRODUCTION

I am a chef and, perhaps surprisingly, I am a 'green' chef. I have been nurtured by the catering industry for over twenty years, since I was sixteen, but I have been green for much longer. Thanks to my mother and father, I have been green all my life, and some of my earliest memories involve eating brown rice, turning off lights not being used, taping up old shoes before buying a new pair, putting vegetable trimmings in the compost bin, and knowing what was 'good' and what was 'bad' food. I still try to lead as ecological, ethical and green a life as possible, both personally and professionally.

I am green at home in North London. I buy and cook fresh foods, use water frugally, source ethical products, compost all my organic waste, and refuse before I recycle. Even my three-year-old son Aron knows which bin to put the plastic and paper in. The ethos of Acorn House, our restaurant in King's Cross, London, reflects these green principles: we buy sustainably (so no air-freighted food, no fish from endangered species), cook simply and seasonally, take responsibility for everything that comes in and out of the building (what is known as 'accountability'), ensuring ingredients are local, organic and/or Fairtrade, and dispose of our waste in an environmentally friendly way. We also make our own compost from the restaurant food waste, and use it as soil in which to grow vegetables, fruit and herbs. We're not quite self-sufficient as yet – I am experimenting with the concept of urban sustainability – but who knows…

We also train our staff at Acorn House, so that when they move on (only after three years, I hope), they take our green ideas with them. And this is one of the major reasons for writing this book, to have those ideas disseminated even further afield. This is primarily a cookery book though, for cooking is my stock in trade. My cooking is like any other chef's in the sense that we produce what we have been taught, what we have learned from other cooks and cuisines, and, most importantly, what we like. Happily, I am cooking exactly what I like to eat, but I differ radically from other restaurant chefs in that, rather than jostle for culinary accolades and stars, I'm trying to lead in another direction, a green and sustainable one. This has only come about by combining my personal life with my professional one.

The food I describe here — and I list what I buy and what I like to eat every month — is good, seasonal food, consisting of ingredients that have been sourced sustainably (so cutting down on food miles), that have been grown or reared humanely and healthily (so without the aid of chemicals), and that are cooked simply and, usually, minimally, so that the essential nature of the food remains, and few nutrients are lost. As well as including individual recipes, I have also offered quite a few less precise thoughts on how you might cook and eat what is best that month. It's a form of green blueprint, which will help you — without the aid of glossy pictures — to design and create your own version of a dish or meal. All these ideas will demonstrate the ease with which ecologically sound and healthy food can be sourced and prepared. The food focuses on sustainability, availability and affordability (with, admittedly, the occasional expense), all the while adhering to ecological ethics. I wanted to reflect real food in an increasingly unreal world.

I'm no environmentalist (although I have found myself becoming an accidental expert in green restaurants and other green areas), but in this book I wanted to share what knowledge I have. So, interspersed with those seasonal recipe and food chapters are tips concerning the seasonal eco garden, in which we could grow some of our food, and chapters that I hope will allow people to recognise how closely linked food, eating and the environment are. Food is basic to our society, to our survival, and it has a cyclical nature, a natural life-cycle from seed to compost. The journey was once a simple one, but it has been over-complicated by decades of monoculture, over-production and over-consumption.

As a consequence, we must recognise, *right now*, that we have to do something to reverse, or at least halt, the damage we are doing to our soil, to our food and water supplies, to our air, to our planet. We need to revolutionise the way we think about food production, and we need to pioneer a consciousness of the massive amounts of waste involved in producing, cooking and eating food (the restaurant industry is particularly guilty in this instance). We need to compost organic waste to supplement the overworked soil (in which to grow that food), and we need to do so both individually and together. There's an old saying that the family that eats together will stay together. I say that the community that composts together will survive together. For survival really is the issue now...

The stress we are putting on resources and environmental systems such as water, land and air cannot go on forever, especially as the world's population continues to increase. A widely used and accepted international definition of sustainable development is: 'development which meets the needs of the present without compromising the ability of future generations to meet their own needs'. Globally we are not even meeting the needs of the present, let alone considering the needs of future generations. Our current demands are costing the Earth.

At the heart of this book is the fundamental desire to do what I believe to be right, to be part of the environmental solution rather than part of the problem.

I feel that there is currently a shift towards the green point of view, and in this book I'd like to help that shift along by encouraging a new and green revolution. We can all help, if we work together, but if the government was to put as much weight behind a green revolution as the Industrial Revolution of 200 years ago, the British could be world leaders in saving the planet. Imagine a 'Great Green' Britain. Idealistic perhaps, but idealism is where revolution starts, and revolution (in all its senses) is a good thing. We have nothing to lose, the Earth has everything to gain...

Arthur.

SPRING

*When the world comes back to life,
and all the new plants are
young and green...*

The first equinox of the year, usually 21st of March, celebrates the renewed life that comes with spring. The smell of freshly cut grass on Hampstead Heath in spring is one of my fondest memories. Growing up where I did meant that I lived an urban lifestyle, but one that was, and still is, crossed with a strong awareness of the seasons.

March signifies a new beginning for me, and it also marks the first month of spring in this book. The green fingers of daffodils just showing above the soil are an indication of the hope that March brings. The most prominent ingredients coming on to the market now are the green leaves that our ancestors would have been so pleased to see after months of winter staples. Whether bought from suppliers, or foraged, these include spring greens, stinging nettles, alexanders, wild garlic, seakale and many delicate spring herbs. Most of these are available all year round now, but I like to stick to them seasonally, as my body tends to need greens at this time of year. After the fasting of February, March is a month for 'cleansing' and waking the body up. Seasonal greens, with their bitter, sharp freshness and their high quantities of vitamins and minerals, are just what I need.

In April, the cherry tree in front of our house on Woodland Rise was always the first on the street to blossom, which made me feel very special. There's a lot happening in April: it's actually a month full of anticipation, with fruit tree blossoms and young vegetable shoots appearing that will need to be nurtured until the summer months. However, there are also some sprouts and shoots which reach their peak around now, and I'm thinking about things like rhubarb, seakale, purple sprouting broccoli, asparagus (see May) and the famous — usually wild — mushroom of spring, the morel. I love the idea that these have lain in the ground, throughout the whole winter, growing slowly, waiting for the warm weather to entice them out.

April is also not a bad month in the markets, as they are now starting to fill up with some very fine products from the Continent. I am a European romantic, and I love buying stuff from Europe. I can never resist the opportunity of buying the slightly earlier varieties of peas and broad beans grown in the Mediterranean sun (and of course they are all delivered by LPG vans, see page 131)…

But nothing compares to the sense of connection with the Earth when I pick the first broad bean in May out of my own sustainably composted soil. Watching the spring vegetables arrive — the leafy greens, sprouts and shoots of March and April, the peas and beans of May — is the clearest sign to me that the winter months are past. The pale greens and delicate whites, the sweet scents and spring perfumes seem to allow my body to emerge from its months of hibernation, fasting and cleansing.

Apart from my own peas and broad beans, my favourite vegetable is asparagus, and the stuff I buy comes from one small farm in Norfolk: it only lasts four weeks, but it is really special. I can't get enough of it, and I suspect that because of climate change, and the loss of the old-fashioned art of asparagus growing, it will continue to be a romantic — and expensive — delicacy.

In spring, I don't use lengthy cooking techniques, as the vegetables are still delicate and young, and require only quick and simple recipes.

Arthur's Spring Growing Tips

I save all my tin cans, rinse them, and punch a hole in the bottom. I put my compost in, plant a couple of seeds, and wait to see what happens! To remind me what I've planted, I tend to grow tomatoes in tomato cans, and peas in my chickpea cans...

The size of the plant is dependent on the size of the can and how much space the roots have, so you're not going to get a giant plant growing on your windowsill, but you might still get a good yield.

Hedgehogs, frogs and thrushes all like to eat slugs and snails, so you should encourage them in your garden. Hedgehogs like dense hedging, frogs like water, and thrushes are quite keen on handy 'anvils' for their snail-shell bashing. A thrush cracks hers on the top of my stone Buddha's head!

Peas build up nodules of nitrogen on their roots, so when I have harvested all the pods, and the plant is dying back, I leave the roots in the soil so that the nitrogen feeds and enriches it naturally.

I collect every scrap of organic waste – be it household, old flowers, veg peelings, even tea-bags – and put it on my compost heap. At our restaurant we have designed the 'total rotter': a hot composter that quickly produces humus for our vegetable beds.

What I buy in March

Vegetables
Alexanders, artichokes (globe, Jerusalem), broccoli (calabrese, purple sprouting), cabbages (green, white), carrots (spring), cauliflower, celeriac, celery, chard, chicory, endive, horseradish, kale, leeks, lettuce, mushrooms, onions, parsnips, potatoes, pumpkins, seakale, spinach, spring greens, spring onions, stinging nettles, swede, turnips

Fruit
Apples (stored), rhubarb (forced), nespole (loquats)

Fish
Mackerel, pollack, sea bass, sea trout

Shellfish
Cockles, crab (brown, cock), mussels, oysters (rock), prawns, scallops (hand-dived only)

Game
Hare, wild rabbit

Fungi
Morels

How I eat in March

I find my body needs waking up after the winter, and I can't wait to savour those fresh, usually bitter, tastes of spring's light green vegetables. The only products the supermarket or shop will have that are truly seasonal are spring greens and perhaps purple sprouting broccoli, while other types of greens and less usual herbs will only be found in farm shops and farmers' markets, for many are localised and probably wild. March is really a month in which you should cultivate the friendship of a forager (ask at your local market, or go online), for he or she will be able to get hold of things like nettles, alexanders, lovage and wild garlic.

What I feel about most of these green leaves of March is that they are 'additives' rather than principal ingredients – but they contribute flavour, colour, texture, interest, and lots of vitamins and minerals. For instance, there are still a lot of winter roots around – celeriac, pumpkins, potatoes, turnips, beetroot (the latter is on my menu all year round) – which will be happy to have a relationship with March's greens.

Spring greens, the ones you will be able to buy in the greengrocer, are very young cabbages, but without the heart of fully mature cabbages, and they are actually more like kale. They taste sweet, though, and are really good in a stir-fry. Their sweetness is also used in a Chinese culinary 'trick'. Spring greens are chopped into the smallest shreds, then deep-fried, topped with some soft brown sugar and salt, and served as 'seaweed'.

Cooking spring greens is easy. Trim off outer leaves, if you want, to get to the sweet heart (but the dark leaves are good for you), then chop and drop into boiling, salted filtered water for about 8 minutes. Drain and use as a green veg, perhaps with some butter and lots of black pepper, as the base of a ribollita (see page 142), or you could mix them with cooked potato for a bubble and squeak. You could also play with lots of stir-frying ideas. Sometimes I fry some garlic in a little oil, add some Dijon mustard and the blanched greens, and cook for about 5 minutes. I have also pan-fried juniper, pancetta, thyme and honey with spring greens. Both combinations are fabulous with pork chops. You can lend an Asian slant, by frying off fresh root ginger, chillies, garlic and soy sauce, then adding the spring greens.

Stinging nettles are one of the new greens of spring that our ancestors would have relied on. They played a prominent role in my childhood: spending school holidays with my father, I always seemed to be cutting down great swathes of nettles that were taking over the garden. Now I'm finding that having some nettles in gardens is a good idea: they are great for biodiversity, as many butterflies and insects love them, and they are really good for you too, as they are rich in Vitamin C and iron. I love nettles now, but hated them when I was child; apart from being stung by them, my mother once made me nettle soup when I was sick. I refused to eat it, and got better very quickly…

NETTLE BEWARE

Nettles need soil rich in phosphates, and they flourish where men and animals have left their refuse, their droppings, their bonfires, their graveyards. (In fact you can tell where deserted houses/villages are in the countryside by the colonies of nettles still surviving in the immediate vicinity.) The plant may be very cleansing in our diets, but it is also an efficient 'cleanser' of the soil it grows in, absorbing anything and everything in it. So you must be very careful about any nettles that you eat, checking that there is nothing unpleasant near where they are growing, like a sewage outlet, a motorway or an old dump. Nettles in markets usually come from certified organic growers (but do check); mine come from my parents' garden.

Nettles have to be picked with care — as on previous page, of course, but wear gloves as well! They should always be cooked. I use them in a wonderful risotto (see page 23), and as 'chlorophyll', a green colorant, in my home-made pasta recipe (nettle chlorophyll was actually used in the Second World War to dye camouflage fabric!). Many people use spinach or parsley to make green pasta, but I think these produce a slightly watery result. Nettles, however, blended to a purée, give a fabulous texture as well as colour, almost like satin or velvet, smooth and luxurious (due to some gelatinous quality in the plant, I think). Use approximately a handful of nettle purée to replace one of the egg yolks in the basic recipe. Blanch until soft enough for you to pinch them, about 4-5 minutes, then drain, squeeze and purée (I use my daughter's mouli).

You can use this nettle pasta to make tagliatelle, lasagne, tagliolini, whatever. I like to make ravioli (see page 43). As a filling, you could take some alexanders leaves, fresh rocket, some new-season parsley and a touch of tarragon. Chop together and mix with some fresh ricotta, nutmeg, salt and pepper. Make an accompanying sauce with some of the other vegetables available this month (see below).

Another wild edible plant at this time is alexanders, which tastes a bit like celery, and which was forgotten about when new varieties of celery were cultivated in the 19th century. It is one of the first green plants to poke through the snow in early spring. It is an umbellifer, which is the parsley family (be careful, some of them are poisonous), and the leaves and young shoots, the stems, seeds, flower buds and roots are all edible.

You can eat the peeled stems of alexanders like asparagus, but I eat them raw with cheese. I also chop them up and use in a lovely spring minestrone soup instead of celery. A spring potato-based soup could also be made lighter with some of our spring greens. Cook the soffrito as described on page 142, but using parsley and alexanders stalks and onion instead of the classic onion, carrot, celery and leek. Add your potatoes, with nettles, alexanders (stems and leaves) and/or lovage, plus stock. Leave it chunky, garnishing the top with chopped alexanders or lovage leaves, or young blanched nettle tips. A combined nettle and alexanders soup would be delicious, cleansing, and full of vitamins and iron.

I always welcome salads at this time of year, so use some of the new spring growth raw as an extra leaf: finely chopped alexanders leaves would be good with celeriac blanched in strips as for rémoulade. Cooked alexanders stalks would be good with a roast celeriac salad. If you then added some smoked eel or mackerel... (An even better addition would be some little bunches of seakale, but see April.)

Wild garlic grows in huge patches in dark and damp places all over Britain. In fact you can always tell where wild garlic is growing by the pervasive smell of garlic! The flowers, which are white and star-like, are very strong in flavour, much more so than the leaves. The first (and last) flower I tasted raw blew my head off! Try to find young leaves as they are more tender and less powerful in flavour. The leaves and flowers would be great in a soup or sauce. A favourite of mine is chopped wild garlic leaves in a sauce for ravioli (perhaps nettle ravioli with an alexanders filling, see below!), lightly cooked with a bit of butter and grated Parmesan.

Lovage is a herb with leaves like celery, which taste like a cross between celery, yeast and curry. The seeds are edible as well, but both leaves and seeds should be used sparingly as they are so powerful. It will grow happily in any herb garden, but perhaps towards the back, as it is so tall.

Artichoke & Purple Sprouting Broccoli Soup

I love this soup, which is rich and elegant, even though it's basically a poor man's soup, simply made from stock, vegetables and cheese... Change the cheese if you prefer.

For 6

2 medium globe artichokes, cooked and peeled down to the hearts
12 heads purple sprouting broccoli
2 litres double chicken stock (see page 266)
1 garlic clove, peeled and halved
6 oblong slices ciabatta bread, toasted
200g Parmesan, freshly grated
sea salt and freshly ground black pepper
extra virgin olive oil

Cut the cooked artichokes into thumbnail-sized pieces. Trim and wash the broccoli. Bring the stock to the boil in a pan and put in the broccoli. Cook for 6 minutes or until soft.

Rub the garlic over each piece of toast, and place a toast in each soup bowl. Put 3 pieces of artichoke on top. Sprinkle with a handful of Parmesan, and put 2 pieces of the drained broccoli on top. Ladle out some of the stock to just cover the rest of the ingredients: it should slosh about in the bowl. Check the seasoning, and finish with some good olive oil

Stinging Nettle & Potato Risotto

Just after having sung the praises of stinging nettles, here is the risotto made velvety by the introduction of nettle purée. Using a good wine for this will make all the difference: so rather than spending a little on a lot, spend a lot on a little.

For 6

1.5 litres vegetable stock (see page 267)
light olive oil
150g butter
1 medium onion, peeled and finely diced
1 medium leek, white only, finely diced
1 head celery, finely diced
420g vialone nano risotto rice (use arborio if you can't find)
500ml medium dry white wine
150g medium potato, peeled and diced
150g young nettle tips, prepared (watch your fingers!), blanched and chopped
150g Parmesan, freshly grated
sea salt and freshly ground black pepper

Heat the stock in a pan and keep it simmering. In a thick-bottomed saucepan, heat enough of the olive oil to cover the base, along with 100g of the butter. Add the onion, leek and celery, and fry until soft but without colour, about 20 minutes. Add the rice and stir until the rice becomes opaque. Then pour in the wine and stir until the liquid has been absorbed.

Add the potato cubes and enough hot stock just to cover: as the liquid disappears, keep adding more ladlefuls of stock, stirring all the time.

After 15 minutes cooking, add the chopped stinging nettles. Stir and cook for another 8 minutes or until the rice is cooked to your liking. Finish with the grated Parmesan, the remaining butter and a little salt and pepper to taste.

Smoked Mackerel, Celeriac, Parsnip & Chive Salad

I love smoked mackerel, it's really good for you, and mackerel is one of the more sustainable fish. I have it on my menu every day. Pick the dandelion leaves from your garden or local park: don't worry, when you start to look, they're everywhere. Pick the smallest leaves, and make sure you wash them really well.

For 4

400g celeriac
200g parsnips
1 bunch dandelion leaves, washed well
4 smoked mackerel fillets
about 4 tbsp house dressing (see page 270)
2 tbsp snipped chives

Peel the celeriac and parsnips, working quickly with the former as it will go brown.

Cut the celeriac into 10cm-thick discs, and the parsnips into thumb-sized pieces. Blanch in a pan of boiling filtered water until just before soft, about 8 minutes. Strain, reserve, and allow to cool.
Preheat the grill. Just before serving, grill the celeriac for that charcoaly effect. Cut the celeriac discs into quarters.

Divide the ingredients between 4 plates: a piece of parsnip, then celeriac, then dandelion leaves, then mackerel, then repeat in a higgledy-piggledy fashion until everything is used up. Drizzle some house dressing over each plate, and finish with some snipped chives.

Brochette of Prawns & Scallops, with Seakale, Spring Carrot & Spinach Salad

Buying your fish carefully, from a trusted supplier is best. I buy sustainable paradise prawns (bred without the use of antibiotics, pesticides or additives), but these are quite rare, so you could use freshwater crayfish tails or additional hand-dived scallops instead. If you don't want to use both prawns and scallops, you could replace the latter with button mushrooms on the rosemary skewers.

For 6

6 long rosemary sprigs
18 hand-dived scallops, cleaned
18 large raw prawns, the size of your thumb, shelled, tail on, gutted
sea salt and freshly ground black pepper
light olive oil

Seakale, Spring Carrot and Spinach Salad
2 bunches spring carrots, trimmed
600g seakale
500g spinach
½ recipe bagna cauda (see page 272)

For the salad, wash all the vegetables, and cook individually (as follows). Put the carrots in a pan of cold, salted filtered water and cook until just tender, about 25 minutes. Cook the seakale in a separate pan of boiling, salted filtered water for 2-3 minutes maximum. Spoon out the seakale.

Add the spinach to the boiling water, cook for 3-4 minutes, then drain. While the vegetables are still warm, arrange on individual plates, then pour some of the bagna cauda dressing over.

Meanwhile, prepare the rosemary 'skewers' by stripping off most of their leaves, leaving a little frond at the top. Scrape the stems down with the back of a knife, as the outer coating is a little bitter. Skewer the fish — scallop, prawn, scallop, prawn, scallop, prawn.

Preheat the grill or a cast-iron ridged skillet or griddle.

Season the brochettes, brush with a little olive oil, and grill, turning occasionally, for about 6 minutes in total.

Put the brochettes on top of the warm vegetable salad, sprinkle with a little more dressing, and serve.

Flourless Peppered Chocolate Cake with Ginger Ice-cream

The recipe for this cake has been perfected in the Acorn House kitchen by my sous-chef, Clare Mitchell. You won't need all of the ginger syrup for the ice-cream, but it will sit happily in the fridge and is great for dipping your finger into!

For 8

180g unsalted butter, plus extra for greasing
a little cornflour, for dusting
240g good-quality dark chocolate (61% cocoa solids)
6 medium eggs, separated
70g caster sugar
about ¾ tsp freshly ground black pepper
a pinch of fine salt
icing sugar, for dusting

Ginger Syrup
375g caster sugar
750ml filtered water
350g peeled fresh root ginger, finely sliced

Ginger Ice-cream

850ml double cream
225ml milk
2 vanilla pods, split
1 cardamom pod, crushed
7 medium egg yolks
310g caster sugar

Start the ice-cream the day before by making the ginger syrup. Bring the sugar, water and ginger to the boil together in a large saucepan, reduce to about 500ml, then remove from the heat and leave to infuse overnight.

The next day, make the ice-cream custard. Put the cream, milk, vanilla and cardamom in a pan and bring to the boil. Put the egg yolks and sugar in a bowl and whisk until thick and pale. Pour half of the hot cream mixture on top of the egg yolks and stir vigorously, then pour that mixture back into the same pan the cream came from. Lower the heat and stir, patiently, for 15-20 minutes. As the mixture begins to thicken, pour it into a bowl sitting over ice — this will stop the temperature going too far and overcooking the eggs.

Leave to cool and then add ginger syrup to taste. Turn the mixture into an ice-cream machine and churn until ready, or freeze in suitable containers, mixing every now and again.

For the cake, preheat the oven to 150°C/Fan 130°C/Gas 2. Butter, cornflour and chill eight 10cm (width) 5cm (deep) circular baking tins or moulds, placed on a baking tray.

Melt the butter and chocolate together in the top of a double saucepan, or in a bowl over a pan of hot water (a bain-marie).

In a separate bowl, whisk the egg yolks and caster sugar together until light and fluffy. Add the pepper and the chocolate mix and fold together carefully — you don't want to knock any of that air out. Taste for pepperiness. It should be quite hot, but remember that cooked pepper increases in heat...

In another bowl, whisk the egg whites and salt to stiff peaks. Carefully fold a quarter of the whites into the chocolate mixture, then add the remainder in three batches, folding carefully each time.

The fluffiness of the cake depends on the fluffiness of the mixture at this stage. Fill the prepared baking tins to within 1.5cm of the top. Place the baking tray and tins into the preheated oven and bake for about 20 minutes (no less, or the shape will not hold). Remove from the oven and leave to cool a little before using a sharp knife to loosen the little cakes from their tins. (This slight cooling helps to keep the edges straight.) Serve the cakes warm on individual plates, with a scoop of ginger ice-cream and a dusting of icing sugar.

What I buy in April

Vegetables
Agretti (see more details below), alexanders, asparagus, beetroot, broccoli (purple sprouting), cabbages (green, red, Savoy), carrots, cauliflower, celery, dandelion, horseradish, kale, leeks, lettuce, nasturtium leaves, nettles, onions, potatoes, pumpkins, radishes, rocket, seakale, spinach, spring greens, spring onions, watercress

Fruit
Rhubarb, nespole (loquats)

Fish
Mackerel, pollack, sea trout, skate

Shellfish
Cockles, crab (brown, cock), mussels

Game
Venison, wood pigeon

Fungi
Morels

How I eat in April

The sprouts and shoots in April are very fresh and very young, and because of this, I cook — if necessary — with great care. You can murder a bunch of seakale or a stem of purple sprouting if you cook it just a fraction too long, and then I think you would lose some of the quality that April can bring. In fact I would go so far as to call April the month of steaming, gentle frying and light boiling. 'Kettle blanching' might be a better description — just pouring boiling filtered water from the kettle over a vegetable in a colander. But the concept of 'blanching' is interesting too in that a number of the April sprouts and shoots will have been 'blanched' in their actual growing process: cultivated seakale, for instance, is covered over to keep the shoots white, as are some asparagus plants; the young rhubarb available at this time of year is 'blanched' as well, grown in the dark to retain the pale pink of the young stalks, giving it the name 'champagne'. (Technically speaking, this is actually 'forcing', rather than blanching.)

'New' or young vegetables are also available, things like cauliflowers, leeks, some chicories, agretti, spinach and even nettle and dandelion leaves. I eat these, simply blanched and dressed with soy sauce and extra virgin olive oil to make a wonderful warm salad or an accompanying vegetable.

Rhubarb is one of my favourites at this time of year. I try to buy from producers in what is known as the 'rhubarb triangle' — an area between Bradford, Wakefield and Leeds. Forced rhubarb is grown indoors and harvested by candlelight. Someone told me you can even hear it growing! In keeping with my 'cleansing' theme of February and March, rhubarb is high on the list of appropriate foods, given its diuretic properties.

I cut the tender stems of rhubarb into finger lengths, put into a pan, and just cover with filtered water. Sprinkle sugar in to taste, but not too much (you can add more later if it's too sour), as the tartness is what I want. Add a sliced vanilla pod and/or a few cardamom pods, and poach it (10 minutes max) or bake in a medium oven (180°C/Fan 160°C/ Gas 4) for about 40 minutes. I try to retain the recognisable shape of the pieces, rather than reduce them to a mush. Then you can serve the rhubarb simply with a vanilla custard (see page 273), or use it as the basis for a crumble with some of the stored apples still around. Purée the rhubarb and mix it with whipped double cream for a fool (probably with a little more icing or caster sugar stirred through it). You could even try the pieces in an Eton mess, with a little broken meringue, or as a pavlova topping when summer berries aren't around.

If you purée your rhubarb and syrup, you can pour it into the bottom of a glass with some Prosecco on top to make a rhubarb Bellini. I use this same purée and syrup with some champagne as the basis of a rhubarb sorbet (see page 47), and serve it with star-shaped sablé biscuits.

Rhubarb makes a good chutney. Make a 'gastric' first, a classic French way of getting both sweet and sour flavours into a preserve. Put sugar into a thick-bottomed pan, and heat to melt and caramelise, then add lemon or lime juice, or vinegar (red wine would be particularly good with the cold venison, page 32). Cut the rhubarb into large pieces, and put in the pan with large chunks of cinnamon stick (so you can fish it out), dried chilli and star anise, some diced shallots, a bay leaf, some mustard seeds if you like, and salt. Cook down until sticky, and then keep in the fridge. This very basic idea is for a chutney to use straightaway, rather than keep for months (not a luxury I can really afford).

Seakale grows around the coastlines of Britain and Ireland, is quite rare, and is illegal to gather in the wild (all you would-be foragers). It is now cultivated to a degree, and blanched, to keep the stalks white and tender; good greengrocers and delicatessens are stocking it in season. Seakale produces shoots and, if left to nature, huge leaves. It is the bunched shoots/stems that you want, though, and I only buy them when they are a lovely, pale creamy yellow, not torn or discoloured in any way. I am now trying to grow seakale in my garden (come and see me in three years, I might have a good crop by then).

I tie the shoots together and drop them into slightly salted, boiling filtered water and cook for 4–5 minutes. Be careful not to overcook. Pull out of the water and drain, and eat it simply. Seakale is delicious with just about every type of seafood, especially lobster and crab; because it is a sea vegetable, its saltiness is partnered with sweetness (rather like the basil of Liguria, see page 97). If you mix that vegetable sweetened by the sea with something from the sea, you have a marriage made in heaven. See my crab and seakale salad, page 35. I flake smoked mackerel over the top of my seakale, with some capers, French beans and some herb mayonnaise. Nasturtium leaves add a nice bite. To me seakale sums up what April is, delicate and fresh, to be eaten nice and simply.

I cut 10cm long pieces of purple sprouting broccoli, and gently blanch them until tender. I use those stems in many different ways: straight up with oil and lemon as a salad, inside a frittata or omelette, mixed with French beans and peas for an accompanying garnish for fish or meat. It's great in soups (see page 22 for one example), and it's really good for you, as it's full of antioxidants. I love cooking it soft, chopping it up, and rolling it through some penne pasta with grated Parmesan and butter. And it's really good with *bagna cauda* (see page 272), or cold anchovy mayo left in the fridge from last week.

Baby gem lettuces are around at this time. Cut in half, wash well, and put in a pan with a little filtered water, light olive oil and garlic, and poach/sauté. Serve with some poached fish, clams or prawns, or crispy bacon.

Whenever I see morels, I take the opportunity of buying them, as they are so delicious. The most famous of spring mushrooms, they are expensive, but definitely worth it (second only to ceps or porcini for me). Clean them minimally with a brush (I blow on them to get the dust off), and then pan-fry with butter, diced shallots, thyme, salt and pepper. They are good with pork chops, a piece of venison or a wood pigeon breast (my favourite). Agretti is a bushy type of grass, which looks a bit like large chives. It's also known as *barba di frate* (monk's beard). I grow it in my garden all the time, it grows wherever I sprinkle it, and I bought my seeds from an organic online shop. It has a crunchy texture and is high in Vitamin C, but don't look for any miracle on your taste-buds! Steam it lightly, and dress with extra virgin olive oil, lemon juice and garlic, or add it, chopped, to a risotto. I blanch it and use it in salads, and serve it with spaghetti because the two are very similar in shape.

COOKING MUSSELS

Mussels are brilliant in April, but make sure you cook them properly. A lot of people put them into a hot pan, piled on top of each other, and then blast them with heat. What happens is that the ones on the bottom of the pan dry out quickly, and are well overdone by the time the ones on the top have steamed open. I use a really large, flat-bottomed pan, start from cold, and do it in batches (even if serving 6 or more). Put in the pan some raw onion, a little raw garlic, some parsley stalks, butter and a little white wine. Add enough mussels to cover the bottom, cover the pan, then, and only then, put on the heat. The mussels will all pop open at the same time (discard any that remain closed), and they will be cooked to juicy perfection, not one overcooked. Scoop out that portion, and start cooking another, adding more butter, wine and some flavourings if necessary.

Why not try shallots instead of onions, good Somerset cider instead of white wine, and you could play around with spices (turmeric, cumin, you have a go). I would cook cockles, also good now, in the same way.

Watercress Soup

Try this recipe with stinging nettle tips too. Both are really good for you, but my kids love the watercress one.

For 6

250g watercress
100g butter
400g onions, peeled and chopped
6 garlic cloves, peeled and chopped
200g potatoes, peeled and diced
1.5 litres chicken or vegetable stock (see pages 265 and 267), hot
sea salt and freshly ground black pepper
100g crème fraîche

Wash the watercress. Melt the butter in a large saucepan and fry the onions gently until translucent. Add the garlic and potatoes and cook gently for 2 minutes. Add the hot stock, bring back to the boil, and simmer for 30 minutes.

Throw in the watercress, and then liquidise until smooth.
Season and serve with crème fraîche on top. Good with crusty bread.

Spaghetti with Mussels

I used to cook this at the River Cafe, and it is an unashamed borrowing from *River Café Cookbook Two* by Rose Gray and Ruth Rogers. It is to die for...

For 6

4 tbsp light olive oil
3kg mussels in shell, cleaned (discard any that remain open)
3 garlic cloves, peeled and chopped
1 small dried red chilli, crumbled
2 tbsp chopped oregano
150ml good dry white wine
1kg ripe tomatoes, skinned, seeded and chopped
sea salt and freshly ground black pepper
3 tbsp roughly chopped agretti (or parsley)
400g dried spaghetti
extra virgin olive oil

Heat half the light olive oil in a large saucepan with a good, tight-fitting lid. Add the mussels in one layer (see above), cover and cook briefly in batches over a high heat until they all open. This should take about 5 minutes. Discard any mussels that remain closed. Drain, retaining the liquid. When the mussels are cool, remove from the shells and chop. Reduce the liquid by half, strain and add to the mussels.

In another large pan, heat the remainder of the light olive oil and add the garlic, chilli and oregano. Cook briefly until the garlic begins to colour, then add the wine and reduce for a minute. Add the tomatoes and cook, stirring to prevent sticking, for 15 minutes, until reduced. Add the mussels, juice, salt, pepper and agretti (or parsley). Keep warm.

Cook the spaghetti in a separate large pan of boiling, salted filtered water until *al dente*, then drain. Add to the mussel sauce, and mix. To finish, drizzle over some extra virgin olive oil.

Fresh Crab, Seakale & Dandelion Salad

Try to buy a big fresh live crab, and cook it yourself: put in a pan of cold filtered water and bring up to the boil, then turn the heat off and allow to cool. Drain, then get all the meat you can out of the crab. Mix the brown and white meat in one bowl, this dish needs both.

For 6

1 large cock crab, cooked and picked
sea salt and freshly ground black pepper
extra virgin olive oil
juice of 1 lemon
1 large fresh red chilli, seeded and finely chopped
50g dandelion leaves, trimmed and washed
50g rocket leaves, picked and washed
30g 'micro' salad leaves (such as bull's blood), washed
2 bunches seakale, trimmed and blanched for 3 minutes
a handful each of chopped chervil and chives

Put the crabmeat in a bowl with some salt and pepper, about 2 tablespoons of olive oil, a squeeze of the lemon juice and the red chilli. In a large bowl, put the salad leaves, seakale and most of the chervil, and gently toss together with a little olive oil and lemon juice. Season this too.

On a serving plate, put a little of the salad and then a little of the crab, and repeat this three times to create a layered salad. Finish with some chopped chives and the remaining chervil. Drizzle with olive oil and serve.

Roast Venison with Beetroot, Crème Fraîche & Horseradish Salad

The simplicity of this dish should entice you into cooking venison. Get the butcher to roll the saddle for you. He will probably wrap it in some sort of larding – pork fat, caul fat (best), prosciutto, bacon – just to keep it moist, as the cut is so dry. If you have any left over, serve it cold with something like rhubarb chutney (see page 30).

For 6

1 boned saddle of venison, about 3kg, larded (see above)
1 onion, peeled and finely chopped
2 carrots, peeled and finely chopped
3 celery stalks, finely chopped
5-6 sprigs thyme

Beetroot, Crème Fraîche and Horseradish Salad
1.5kg fresh beetroot, cooked, skinned and sliced
3 bunches rocket leaves
300g crème fraîche
200g fresh horseradish, peeled and finely grated
2 tbsp red wine vinegar
sea salt and freshly ground black pepper
extra virgin olive oil

Preheat the oven to 240°C/Fan 220°C/Gas 9. Put the venison in a roasting tray with the vegetables and thyme underneath (which stops the meat scalding on the bottom), and put into the preheated oven. Sear for 10 minutes, then reduce the oven temperature to 180°C/Fan 160°C/Gas 4, and cook for another 15 minutes. This will produce pink venison, which is how I would eat it, but take it a bit further if you like.

Meanwhile, for the salad, arrange the cooked beetroot and rocket on a serving dish. Mix together the crème fraîche, horseradish, vinegar and some salt and pepper. Pour this over the salad, then drizzle with olive oil.

Rest the meat for about 5 minutes, and put the vegetables back in the oven to carry on cooking. Cut the meat into nice 5cm-thick slices, and serve 3 or 4 slices per plate, with some of the cooked veg and the salad.

Apple Pie

Although spring is hardly the time for fresh apples, it's great to use some of the stored apples, which are quite fluffy now. I've chosen an apple pie, as it's so very British (best with clotted cream), and we couldn't take it off the menu at Acorn House. The short pastry is very special, because I put a touch of fresh vanilla in it.

For 6

Pastry
150g unsalted butter, plus extra for greasing
30g icing sugar, sifted
½ vanilla pod, split
250g plain flour, plus extra for dusting
a pinch of fine salt
1 medium egg, lightly beaten

Filling
2 Bramley apples
6 small dessert apples
½ cinnamon stick
1 cardamom pod
½ vanilla pod, split
50g caster sugar (or to taste)

Frangipane

65g blanched almonds
65g unsalted butter
65g caster sugar
1 medium egg
½ tbsp Calvados

For the pastry, in a food processor or mixer, cream the butter, icing sugar and the vanilla seeds (retain the empty pod for vanilla sugar) until there are no lumps. Sift in the flour and salt and only just combine. Scrape down the sides of the bowl. Add the egg, and mix until just combined. Do not overwork. Refrigerate for at least 2 hours.

For the filling, peel, core and chop all the apples. Put in a pan with the other ingredients and cook gently, with the lid on, until the pieces of dessert apples are soft but still a little chunky. The Bramleys will have 'melted'.

For the frangipane, blitz the almonds in the food processor until finely ground. Cream the butter and sugar together in the food processor or mixer. Add the egg, ground almonds and Calvados and mix well. Preheat the oven to 180°C/Fan 160°C/Gas 4, and grease and flour a 25cm pie tin.

Cut the pastry in half, and roll half out for the base. Place into the prepared pie tin, line with baking parchment, and pour in some baking beans. Bake blind in the preheated oven for about 10 minutes. Remove and allow to cool. Remove the beans and parchment.

Spread the frangipane evenly over the pie base, and pour over the cooked apples. Roll out the remaining pastry and place over the top of the filling. Spike a few holes in the top to allow steam to escape, and then seal the edges with your fingers or a fork. Bake in the same temperature oven for 15–20 minutes. Serve warm with clotted cream, custard (see page 273), or whatever you like.

What I buy in May

Vegetables
Artichokes (globe), asparagus, beans (broad), broccoli (calabrese, purple sprouting), cabbages (green), carrots (spring), cauliflower, chard, horseradish, lamb's lettuce, lettuce, melon, mushrooms, nettles, orach, onions, peas (including sugar snaps), potatoes (new), radishes, rocket, samphire, seakale, sorrel, spinach, spring greens, spring onions, watercress

Fruit
Rhubarb

Fish
Black bream, crayfish (freshwater), mackerel, pollack, sea trout, trout

Shellfish
Cockles, crab (brown, cock, spider), cuttlefish, lobster, mussels, scallops (hand-dived only)

Game
Rabbit, wood pigeon

How I eat in May

Broad beans are enjoying the beginning of their brief season in my garden now, and fresh peas are around too. I eat them both, pod and all, when young. When I have to buy them, the pods are bigger and tougher, and I remove the peas and beans. Later on in the season, when they become a bit leathery, pop the broad beans out of their shells and eat only the vividly green centre. Put the shells on the compost heap (as well as the pods).

What I do when broad beans are in season, is take a handful, pod them and blanch the beans for no longer than 3 minutes in boiling, salted filtered water. I would do the same with a handful of peas: pod and blanch them. Blanch a handful of sugar-snap peas as well (home-grown, not Kenyan), and put the beans, peas and sugar snaps in a bowl. While still warm, dress with extra virgin olive oil, lemon juice, salt and pepper. This is a fantastic warm salad that would serve two (if you're very hungry) or four (with other salads or some protein). Then you can play around with it...

To this salad, you could add a torn herb of choice — mint, basil or, my favourite, lemon thyme. Blanched asparagus can be added to the legume mixture, as can baby new potatoes, boiled until they just retain some crispness. This would expand the dish to feed four or six people. The salad could happily be finished off with a handful of your own home-grown sprouts. Fenugreek would also be particularly flavourful (see page 197).

A slightly more sophisticated dressing for the bean and peas could be made with natural yoghurt mixed with a little white wine vinegar or sherry vinegar, and flavoured with toasted crushed fenugreek seeds (or curry leaves or celery seeds).

The salad can also serve as an accompaniment to fish. Cook good fillets of Marine Stewardship Council (MSC) approved organic salmon in a little light olive oil in a hot pan, skin-side down, for 3 minutes (but depending on thickness). Or mackerel fillets would be good too – 2 minutes would cook them. Serve on top of the warm vegetables.

Or as an accompaniment to meat. Fillet of lamb – one fillet to serve two – could be gently fried in light olive oil or butter in a pan until done to your taste. Slice on the diagonal and serve on top of the vegetables. Mint would be a good addition to the salad here, and I am a great fan of Dijon mustard with lamb.

Make a basic risotto (see page 143) and, at the last minute, add the blanched bean and pea mixture before dressing it.

For a pasta sauce, cook a soffrito base (see page 142), and then add the raw broad beans, peas and sugar snaps. Cook for a few minutes, and then add vegetable stock to cover (probably about 120ml). Cook for a few more minutes, then add up to 50ml double cream. Cook until quite thick, then add freshly grated Parmesan to taste. Add your cooked pasta of choice (I like pappardelle best), and mix. Serve with some more freshly grated Parmesan.

To make a great spring frittata, cook a soffrito base (see page 142) in an ovenproof pan. Add the raw broad beans, peas and sugar snaps and fry for a minute. Add beaten egg (2 eggs per person) mixed with a little double cream to the pan, sprinkle with freshly grated Parmesan, and put into a medium oven (180°C/Fan 160°C/Gas 4) for about 10 minutes.

Asparagus, Broad Bean & Pea Soup

The most seasonal of soups, apart from pumpkin soup in the autumn, this is how I like to introduce spring into my menus.

For 6

2 medium onions, peeled and finely chopped
light olive oil
250g podded broad beans (big ones), blanched and shelled
250g asparagus stalks, chopped
250g podded fresh peas
1 litre chicken or vegetable stock (see pages 265 or 267), warmed
100g cooked pasta, chopped if large or long (a great way to use leftover pasta)
sea salt and freshly ground black pepper
freshly grated Parmesan
extra virgin olive oil

Fry the onions in a little light olive oil in a pan until just golden. Add the broad beans, asparagus and peas, and stir to coat with oil, about 3 minutes. Add the warmed stock and bring to the boil, then simmer for 10 minutes. Bring back to the boil, add the pasta (chopped spaghettini is good), and cook for a couple of minutes.

Season to taste, and serve with some grated Parmesan and extra virgin olive oil sprinkled over the top.

Ravioli of Summer Herbs & Ricotta

I love making ravioli because it makes me feel like a child again, throwing flour everywhere, playing with shapes — round, square, big, small, with fluted or straight edges. It's good to make them with someone else: I've made them with Italian grannies, 2-year-old boys, and almost everyone in between.

For 6

250g fresh pasta dough (see page 269)
60g young herbs (chervil, mint, basil, parsley)
freshly grated nutmeg, to taste
125g ricotta cheese
60g Parmesan, freshly grated
sea salt and freshly ground black pepper

To serve
60g butter, melted
25g flat-leaf parsley leaves, chopped
freshly grated Parmesan

Roll the pasta into two sheets, thin enough so that you can just see the colour of your palms through them. Keep covered when not working with them. Wash and cut the herbs into small pieces, and place in a bowl. Grate in some nutmeg to taste, then mix in the ricotta and Parmesan. Season well.

Arrange one pasta sheet on the work surface. Place tablespoonfuls of the herb mixture at 2.5cm intervals on the pasta. Spray (use a clean plant mister) between the piles of mixture with filtered water; this is better than brushing, as it prevents the pasta from becoming too gluggy. Cover with the second sheet of pasta, and press down between the mounds.

Make sure there is no air left in each, as heated air expands, and will blow a hole in your ravioli. I always make square ravioli, as there is no waste. Press on the edges of the pasta to seal.

Place the ravioli into a large pan of simmering filtered water for 3 minutes, until they bob back to the top. Serve with melted butter, the parsley, some more nutmeg and grated Parmesan.

Smoked Eel, Samphire & Horseradish Salad

Eel is held in such high regard by the *bon viveurs* of this world, that I have to include it in this book. It has the most amazing texture, rich and gelatinous, and it is brilliant smoked. It's an expensive product, which I hope will keep it sustainable.

For 4

500g fresh samphire (or French beans)
300g smoked eel, cleaned and sliced
1 large bunch rocket leaves
150g fresh horseradish, peeled and finely grated (watch your eyes and nose, it's strong!)
50ml red wine vinegar
sea salt and freshly ground black pepper
extra virgin olive oil
juice of 1 medium lemon

Cook the samphire (or beans) in a pan of boiling, unsalted filtered water for about 3 minutes. Drain well.

Arrange the cooked samphire (or beans), smoked eel and rocket on serving dishes. Mix together the horseradish and vinegar, and season to taste. Pour this dressing over the salad, then drizzle with olive oil and lemon juice. Serve.

Pea & Mint Torte, with Asparagus, Broccoli & Sun-dried Tomato Salad

This is a great dish for vegetarians, but meat-eaters can add some prosciutto.

For 6

115g unsalted butter
215g Parmesan, freshly grated
250g spring onions, chopped
3kg fresh peas, podded
2 tbsp chopped mint
4 tbsp chopped basil
150ml vegetable stock (see page 267)
sea salt and freshly ground black pepper
300g ricotta cheese
4 tbsp double cream
4 large eggs

Asparagus, Broccoli and Sun-Dried Tomato Salad
3 bunches asparagus
1 head calabrese broccoli
100g sun-dried tomatoes, reconstituted
extra virgin olive oil
6 tbsp sunflower seeds, toasted

Preheat the oven to 190°C/Fan 170°C/Gas 5. Use 15g of the butter to grease a 25cm round spring-release cake tin, then dust with 15g of the grated Parmesan.

Melt the remaining butter in a pan, add the spring onions, and fry gently until soft, about 3 minutes. Add half of the peas, mint and basil and all of the stock. Season and then cover and cook gently for 5 minutes. Remove from the heat and allow to cool a little. Put half of this mixture into a food processor with half of the ricotta and cream, and blend quickly. Add the rest of the ricotta and cream, and while blending, add the eggs one at a time.

Remove the mixture to a large mixing bowl, season, then fold in the remaining peas and herbs and most of the Parmesan. Spoon into the prepared tin, sprinkle with the remaining Parmesan, and then bake in the preheated oven for 45 minutes. When cooked, it should be firm in the centre and pulling away from the sides.

Meanwhile, prepare the salad. Blanch the asparagus and broccoli in a pan of boiling filtered water until just soft, about 6 minutes, then drain well. Drain, then chop the sun-dried tomatoes. Arrange all the vegetables and tomatoes on a serving dish, drizzle with olive oil and top with the seeds.

Let the torte rest for 5 minutes, then lift and release on to a large serving dish. Serve in wedges, with the salad.

Rhubarb Sorbet

Juniper and cardamom are two of my favourite secrets, because people can't quite get them on their palate. 'What's that flavour? I know it, but...' Their influence on a dish is haunting. This sorbet is a little play on the traditional relationship between juniper and gin. If you are ever in Tuscany, try and get some local juniper berries as they are superb. You could use some champagne instead of some of the water for a very special sorbet.

For 6

1kg forced rhubarb
250g caster sugar
250ml filtered water
50ml gin
5 juniper berries

Put all the ingredients together in a non-reactive aluminium saucepan, cover and cook until soft, but without any evaporation. Turn off the heat and allow to cool.

Purée the mixture in a food processor. Check for sweetness, adding a little more sugar, if necessary. Pour into an ice-cream machine and churn until pink and fluffy, or freeze in suitable containers, mixing every now and again. (More of a granita than a sorbet but still delicious.)

Serve with whatever you like. I serve it in the restaurant with biscotti, or you could make your own sablé biscuits.

PRODUCING
FOOD

WATER

Everything on Earth needs food and water. With a rapidly increasing world population, supplies of both are under threat. I think we must be careful, and swiftly turn to sustainable ways of producing food and conserving fresh water in order to survive into the future.

Water is essential for all life forms — the human body, for instance, is composed of nearly two-thirds water — and life on Earth only became viable because of the presence of water. Human food — animal and plant — is also reliant on water. Water covers over 70 per cent of the Earth's surface. Nearly 98 per cent of it is in the oceans, and is salt. Fresh water makes up the rest, over two-thirds of which is frozen in the polar ice caps and glaciers. Think about that...

The Sea & Seafood

All life on Earth began in the sea, more than three billion years ago, and the sea is still a mystery to us. We may have gained control of the land, flown to the Moon and identified distant stars, but we still cannot claim to have got to the bottom of the sea (literally). The sea is the last great unexplored frontier on Earth.

The sea provides food for all forms of life, from microbacteria to krill and plankton, from shellfish to whales (the largest sea creatures, which feed on one of the smallest). Man has fished the sea for food since the earliest times, but the sea contributes to our well-being in other vital ways too: marine plants provide the oxygen we need (as do land plants), and the sea helps to regulate temperature, without which life on land would not be sustainable. I feel we should take more care of the sea. We should stop polluting it, mining it, stripping it of life. We are also causing it to warm up, part of what is called the greenhouse effect or global warming (see Box). All this has an effect on the marine life which the sea produces, and which we have always relied on for food.

When sailing in the Mediterranean, I saw plastic bags, bits of netting and lumps of wood floating by. I've seen at first hand that we are using the sea as a dumping ground for much of our waste, most controversially sewage. It amazes me that we continue to do this, when so many other cleaner and more useful systems of disposal are available (composting, biomass and anaerobic digestion, for example, see pages 256, 255 and 263). This pollution of the sea poisons the fish and can poison us in turn. I once caught a sea bream off the English south coast and, as I was cleaning it, there was an unmistakeable smell of raw sewage; I had obviously been fishing near an unseen sewage outlet.

And we have all heard about levels of mercury in tuna, swordfish and marlin. Thought to be contained in airborne pollution from fossil-fuel burning, mercury and other metals find their way into the oceans, into small surface fish, and then into larger predatory fish. Metals are 'conservative' pollutants (unlike organic waste such as sewage, which is subject to bacterial decay), and can build up in animal tissue – which is what is causing the problems with fish like tuna. Oil spills, run-offs of agricultural chemicals from the land, and many other industrial pollutants inflicted on the sea by man affect every stage of marine life, from larvae to full-grown fish or shellfish, and can and do kill them and can render them unsuitable for us to eat. I'm afraid that seafood, however delicious and good for us, is something to be wary of these days. We have to be sure of where it comes from, how it was caught, and who is supplying it.

Over-fishing is the other threat to the production of food in the sea. Cod is a classic case in point. In the 1500s, the explorer Cabot and his men were said to have scooped cod out of Newfoundland waters in baskets; by 1994, Canada closed the Grand Banks fisheries because, although Canadian cod was not quite biologically extinct, it was certainly extinct in commercial terms. Centuries of over-fishing – catching both too many young fish (not allowing them to mature) and too many sexually mature fish (preventing them from reproducing) – had compromised stock maintenance. Stocks of larger predatory fish such as tuna and swordfish have been severely diminished by over-fishing as well, and the catch is becoming younger and smaller. Whole species of fish are disappearing, and to be truly ethical and sustainable, we have to be very careful about what we choose to buy at the fishmonger's counter.

Modern fishing practices such as trawling also destroy sea-bed habitats, endangering or depleting bottom-dwelling fish, and nets kill and waste millions of tonnes of by-catch – unwanted fish, seabirds, turtles, sharks and dolphins (roughly a horrifying one-third of the total world catch). And because stocks of surface fish – cod and herring – have been reduced so much, fishermen are now hoovering up fish from much deeper water. These fish live, grow and mature slowly, and are therefore extremely vulnerable to over-exploitation. Stocks would take many years to recover (if indeed stocks are sustainable; I don't think they are). The orange roughy, which I ashamedly ate in New Zealand, doesn't reach sexual maturity for 20–30 years, and in those southern waters, once a prime source for this species, the original numbers have been reduced by at least 80 per cent (quotas have now been introduced).

It seems extraordinary to me that we have managed to damage and deplete the sea and its life so much in so short a time. It is a unique resource, and we may have to depend on it for food in the future, if we cannot nurture the land sustainably. We must look after our seas.

Arthur's Notes

I often go shellfish foraging along the Essex coast, near Colchester, and I have a great photograph of me with cockles and mussels, even seaweed! Do, however, check carefully that the water in which the shellfish grow is clean, as they are filter feeders (see page 56).

The sea is hugely powerful, and we must quickly think of ways in which to utilise it (a wave farm in Cornwall, opened in 2007, represents a start). I truly believe that if we could utilise the power of the sea properly, we would never have to worry about energy or fossil fuels again.

We can all nurture a small plot of land, care for it and feed it, so that it can feed us safely. It is impossible to nurture a small plot of sea, so we can never be sure...

I've been cooking for twenty years, and over the past ten, I've seen a huge change in the way that fish has been arriving to me: the size, the shape, the coloration, the state of health (parasite infestation). And now, I'm afraid, all I am serving at the restaurant is mackerel.

I do not eat or serve turbot, wild salmon, cod, monkfish or tuna.

Fresh Water & Freshwater Fish

I have fished in some of the most beautiful freshwater lakes in the world, from the South Island of New Zealand to the northern lakes of Norway. Freshwater fish has always been a major source of human sustenance. But global warming, pollution and other agencies – mainly man-made – have had a desperate effect, and these fish are no longer available to the same extent as they once were. And fresh water itself is running out: the Aral Sea in Russia, once the world's fourth largest freshwater lake, is now dry; many rivers in Australia do not exist any more; and groundwater in ancient aquifers (reservoirs of water thousands of years old) is being pumped out, and is not able to be replenished.

What is most worrying of all is the possibility of global warming melting the polar ice caps, which hold so much of the world's fresh water. If these melt, they will flow into the sea, and become salt water. We will have lost the majority of our planet's fresh water as a consequence. And today, of course, there is the suggestion that environmental wars could break out between neighbouring countries over the vital resource that is fresh water. We may be moving inexorably from the oil wars of the 1990s to the water wars of the 2030s...

Arthur's Notes

I always drink filtered London tap water, and have done all my life. You can fit a filter to your mains supply (as I have), or you can use a filtering jug.

It takes approximately 300 times more energy to produce a litre of bottled spring water than it does a litre of tap water. The price of bottled can be 1000 times more than that of tap water...

If you do buy a small plastic bottle of water to carry with you, try to find one that is compostable (made from corn). Fill this up every day with filtered tap water, rather than buy new, and when you've finished with it, put it on the compost heap.

Research should be aimed at finding plant foods that are less water needy. The Israelis are cultivating a cactus that they have persuaded to provide fruit, known as koubo, for eleven months of the year.

Desalination plants might seem to be the answer to a lack of fresh water, and Australia – the driest continent on Earth – is exploring this currently.

However, the process uses a great deal of energy, and also produces a lot of salt...

If water cost more, I dare say you'd soon see a positive decline in individual usage... The cost of water, in Britain alone, is going to go up so rapidly that we have to get used to using less – and NOW.

I think we should put more pressure on the people who manage our water to manage it better...

Aquaculture

Aquaculture or fish farming is considered by many to be one way of replenishing food stocks of fish. The world's demand for fish is increasing — due to rises in population and, in the West, to the need for healthier protein — and aquaculture will probably become a major contributor.

Apparently one in five fish sold worldwide is farmed, and the value to countries' economies is enormous. But there are some huge disadvantages environmentally, let alone in terms of flavour and texture. A farmed salmon lacks the muscle tone of its wild, hard-swimming relative, and often its diet makes the flesh grey and insipid — so they have to colour it, and dye the pellets pink... Other worries include:

• Farmed fish are fed on pellets made from fishmeal. It is estimated that as much as 5kg of wild fish needs to be rendered into fishmeal to produce 1kg of farmed fish. There is little eco logic there...

• Farmed trout and salmon (and presumably other species) escape regularly to the wild and dilute the genetic makeup of the wild stock by interbreeding. This might, for instance, interfere with the wild salmon's ability to find its way back to its home waters.

• Escaped fish also transmit disease, such as sea lice, to wild fish, which can have a considerable impact on the survival of salmon and trout fry in particular.

• Nutrients such as ammonia produced by waste food and fish faecal matter in farm cages are released into the sea, where they can have a devastating effect on other marine life.

• Warm-water prawns are farmed in man-made ponds, which have been shown to deplete freshwater supplies, and to have a hugely detrimental impact on mangrove forests (which provide breeding grounds for fish and help clean the water) and to contribute to coastal erosion.

• Fresh-water crayfish farms proliferated in the UK for a while, but the fish that farmers chose to use was the American signal crayfish. These immigrants escaped, then predated on and diseased our native species, which has now all but disappeared.

However, there are some rays of hope. A proportion of the baby eels or elvers which return from the Sargasso Sea each year to their native European rivers are caught and then fattened, which takes the pressure off the wild population. Lobster fry are being farmed in hatcheries, and then released into the wild. Although farmed shellfish such as oysters, scallops and mussels can be contaminated if the water quality is not optimum – they are filter feeders, and obtain every bit of their nutrition from the water in which they live – the majority of shellfish farmers are well aware of the problems, as are their buyers, and strict codes of practice control the market. I think we can happily and ethically buy and consume most native and local shellfish.

Organic fish farms are now increasing, and you can find organic salmon, trout and even cod. The fish are given more space, which cuts down on the sea-lice problem, and builds more muscle, thus texture, and are fed higher-quality feed. Although this inevitably increases the price, I think it is well worth it. In Scotland, a salmon farm in Loch Duart, although not organic, is producing salmon that are sold for sushi. The salmon are farmed by a rotational fallow system, thus minimising sea-bed pollution. Near to the salmon pens, they also farm seaweeds which help clean the water, and sea urchins which, being omnivore, clean algae and any salmon waste from the sea bed. (Both seaweed and urchins are sold for sushi as well.) Seaweeds, of course, are extensively farmed in Japan, mostly what the Japanese call nori, and we call laver (made into laverbread in Wales), and we should really remember that there are a number of edible seaweeds, yet another food (and a very healthy one) which salt water provides.

It is in the east that the most enlightened systems of aquaculture are practised. Here in the west we farm mostly monoculturally – one species only – but in China and Asia, they are farming polyculturally. For instance, four species of carp are grown together, which all feed on different ingredients in the pond. Nothing is wasted, there is no competition, and protein is produced extremely efficiently. As a result, aquaculture has emerged as a leading source of animal protein in China.

China also has many other systems, which integrate agriculture and aquaculture. One is the mulberry dike-fishpond system, in which mulberry trees are grown on the side or dike of a fishpond, and the leaves are fed to silkworms. The detritus from the worms – excreta and pupae – fall into the pond, feed the fish, and add to the richness of the pond mud, which is later used as fertiliser for the mulberries (a very natural and eco cycle). In other parts of Asia, fish are introduced to the waters of rice paddy fields; this has been shown to increase rice production, possibly because fish excreta increase soil fertility, and the fish also help in the control of weeds and pests.

It would be difficult to replicate this rice-paddy idea in the UK, but it could well be possible in Spain and Italy, say, where rice is grown. However, the basic concepts of agri-pisciculture (as it is known) are well worth exploring in order to help us produce more fish for food, and to do so more sensibly, usefully and ethically.

THE LAND

Thirty per cent of the Earth is land, but we use only a small proportion of that percentage, both to live on and to grow food. As a result, the land is overworked. In the future, with population increase, we shall be forced to produce larger amounts of food from that same land, and unless we find intelligent alternatives, I'm afraid that much the same thing is going to happen with the land as with the sea — we are working against it rather than with it.

Once early humans gained control over food animals and learned how to grow plants to feed those animals and themselves, they would remain in one place, rather than wandering as nomads, and cohere into a society. They would need to collaborate in order to till, to plant, to oversee crops, to harvest, store and cook. This may be simplistic, but the land and all it can provide lies at the heart of what we think of as civilisation, and it gave us our laws. Early man would have appreciated the land — religions were based, after all, on worship of the natural cycles that provided food — but today we have come so far from a proper respect for and understanding of the land, its structure and its provisions, that we are in danger of losing it.

The Soil

Soil is one of the world's most important natural resources, and, along with air and water, forms the basis for life on Earth. Without soil, there would be no plants, which would mean no food for animal or man — and indeed little oxygen, for plants absorb the gas CO_2 (as do the oceans) through photosynthesis and give us oxygen. Soil also plays a major part in the natural recycling of water and other nutrients.

Soil forms an almost complete skin over the Earth, apart from where it is broken by oceans and other bodies of water, and by mountains, where soil does not readily form. Soil is ground-up rock in essence, rock that has broken down through time, through the action of sun, ice, rain, wind and weather in general. Apart from the minerals present in the rock particles, soil also contains water (depending on climate), air and organic matter — which is rotted and decomposed vegetable and animal remains. Those remains are home to many billions of tiny soil organisms (there are more in one teaspoon than there are people in the world, some claim). These organisms feed on and break down the decaying organic matter, thus releasing nutrients, and create pores in the soil, which allow air, water and tiny roots to permeate through the soil. Earthworms do this too, although obviously on a larger scale. They too eat plant remains and many of the micro-organisms, along with mineral particles in the soil; the material they excrete after digestion is of a good texture and rich in nutrients. They also improve the structure of the soil through their burrowing and casting. Worms are the soil's personal assistants…

The skin of the Earth that is soil can vary in depth and constituents, but what farmers and gardeners call topsoil, the nutrient-rich top layer containing organic matter, is very thin, usually about 20cm only. It is this topsoil in which plants can be easily grown, which can be damaged by pollutants, and which can be washed or blown away, literally. In the simplest sense, soil is held together by moisture and by the roots of plants, and if there is little rain and no plants — and rainfall depends to a great extent on the largest of plants, trees — then the soil will disappear. This is what is happening in many parts of the world currently: great swathes of the tropical rainforest are being cut down to enable local people to grow food crops in the rich leaf-mould soil beneath the trees, and this is destroying the natural balance, changing climate and causing soil erosion, which in many cases is irreversible.

Soil is so essential, yet so fragile a resource, that we have to do everything in our power to protect it and to replenish it. Many people and organisations are trying worldwide to prevent the cutting down of trees and overworking of scant soils in the Third World, and to improve the quality of soil in drought-stricken, therefore soil-poor, countries. We can do this too, on a domestic scale. Good farmers know that food plants leach nutrients from the soil, so they take steps to give those nutrients back, so that the soil is ready to nurture the next crop. If we all transformed our organic kitchen waste into compost, this could be added to our garden soils, which would amplify the topsoil, and enrich it, ready for our own next crop. If this domestic initiative were adopted by families, by groups of neighbours, by communities large and small, by big businesses, even nationally, all over the world, we would be helping hugely to reverse the damage we have done to the soil on Earth.

I LOVE TREES!

Without trees we wouldn't be here; they are essential to life. Trees breathe in carbon dioxide (CO_2) from the atmosphere, and store it as carbon in the wood. They exhale a waste product called oxygen, which is quite important for us. They provide shelter, they hold the soil together, they create soil with their fallen leaves, they provide food, they absorb pollution , and they cool the Earth down. They provide warmth, but every time you burn wood you release its stored carbon, affecting the carbon/oxygen balance of the atmosphere. As our trees disappear, so too will the quality of our air, our soil and sustainable life on this planet.

Food from the Land

Plant life is the basic food produced by the land, and plants feed humans, animals, insects and most other creatures. Many animals in turn feed humans, thus plants are doubly important to us.

The essential starter kit for plant life consists of five elements: air, water, soil, sun and pollination. Plants grow from seeds, but a germinating seed will not develop without soil. The better the quality of that soil, the greater the potential of that seed. A seed can only utilise what it is given, and I think a bad seed grown in good soil would be much better off than the reverse. The good seed grown in good soil, with the right amount of sun and water, and the attentions of a pollinating insect at the right time, will become the healthy plant. You eat this, and what's left over you use in compost or give to your chickens or pigs. They benefit in turn, and their eggs and/or meat will deliver back the best nourishment (the natural cycle).

However, in the pursuit of maximum rather than optimum product, our foods have been compromised — and continue to be so, due in part to the huge power of the supermarkets and the cheap food culture. In the UK, after the Second World War, farmers were told to increase yield from the land to feed the population. To do this, it was necessary for the farmers to specialise and concentrate on one single product (monoculture), which meant they gradually lost sight of the old system of mixed farming (rotating crops and breeding different types of animals).

With mixed farming, the rotation of crops disrupted the life-cycle of single-crop pests; with monoculture, or intensive farming, these pests returned and pesticides had to be used. With mixed farming, the fertility of the land would have been replenished naturally (by manure, compost, letting fields lie fallow, and the growing of forage crops); with the greed and speed of monoculture, chemical fertilisers had to be used. (In fact, the reliance on chemicals began just after the war when nitrates left over from the arms industry were used to fertilise land.) The same applies to intensively reared animals such as cattle, pigs and poultry: to enhance production, fertility-boosting drugs, antibiotics and growth hormones were once routinely given. (They may not be permitted now in the EU, but who knows what has been given to imported food animals?)

The chemicals used in intensive agriculture remain in the soil, or filter through to the water table: as a result, we can ingest them through the plants or animals produced from that soil, and through our drinking water. There are arguments at the highest level about whether we can be affected by agricultural chemicals, but if they can kill a moth or caterpillar, they must involve some harm to humans. Medical advice is to wash any fruit or vegetable, but in some cases, the chemicals are systemic, meaning they are in the tissue of the plant. I wouldn't want to feed that plant to my children, would you? And, frighteningly, although toxicologists can efficiently investigate single substances such as pesticides, they are unable to test them in combination; and a toxic cocktail is what we all might have in our bodies after several decades of eating intensively farmed food and drinking contaminated water.

The only answer would seem to be to buy and eat organic food, but the organic question is a bit tricky for me. I have been eating organic food for my entire life, I feed organic food to my children, my family and friends, and the principles of organics have led me to the beliefs that rule my life and my career and are encapsulated in this book. If I sound a little dubious, it's because I am a little disappointed with the direction in which organics has been moving. I've always taken organics for granted — it's the oldest, the most natural, the only way to grow and rear, the best — and now it has been made to appear as if it has resurfaced and been brought back to life as something cool, modern, a bit trend-setting. I'm suspicious of this attitude: where there's a trend these days, there's someone ready to make money from it, and I don't want organics to suffer from an over-exposure it didn't really need.

That said, I believe that organics is the most natural and harmonious way of feeding people. The principles of organic farming, initiated by the

Soil Association in 1946, are based on the connection between healthy soil, healthy food and healthy people. A soil that is healthy (with lots of organic compost) will nurture plants and animals without recourse to artificial or chemical interventions to make them healthy or grow. So no fertilisers, insecticides, growth-promoters or antibiotics are used in organics. And, as opposed to the practices of intensive agriculture regarding the 'well-being' of animals – chickens kept in horrendous battery conditions, veal calves and pigs in pens too small for them to turn around in – animal husbandry is important in organic farming, for animals and birds that are free-range, fed well and naturally reared.

It's not just domestic animals that benefit from organics, it's wildlife in general. Insecticides may aim to kill the caterpillar, but they kill pretty much everything else in sight, and when they are not used, insect, mammal and bird life returns, as does the all-important biodiversity. With organic farming, there are more spiders, more frogs, more birds, more butterflies and more bees (to pollinate your plants). Farmers are obliged to farm in a different way, once they aren't ruled by chemicals and monoculture, and can return to sensible and intelligent farming, rotating crops and companion planting (see page 68). This too adds to the biodiversity of the land.

The principles of organic farming are anything but new: once organic was the only way we gardened and grew our food. (If you talked to an Italian about organic food, he wouldn't know what you meant, as their land has always been farmed and their food grown without the aid of chemicals.) The tenets of the organic movement today are, basically, preserving soil fertility, animal welfare and using fewer chemicals. We shouldn't have to think in terms of moving forward into an organic mind-set, we should be moving back to our original ways of doing things. I'm not denying that there have been huge technological and scientific advances in the food production arena, but we should be using them to enhance the traditional agricultural practices and skills that were already in place.

But there is another major question about producing food from the land, which involves the protein we crave. We have discussed fish, but producing meat protein means huge swathes of prime agricultural land (70 per cent worldwide) is used to grow grain to feed animals. To achieve 1kg of meat requires up to five times that weight of grain feed, which seems crazy, when that grain (and the land on which it grows) could be feeding people much more productively and usefully. (And soya for animal feed is often grown on land cleared from what was once tropical rainforest.) Water too is an issue, and apparently to produce 1kg of beef can take up to 100,000 litres of water – whereas you need much less to produce 1kg of wheat.

We in the west are the largest (sometimes literally, for too much protein can contribute to obesity) consumers of meat with our high-protein diets. However, many fast-developing countries such as India and China, whose cuisines were traditionally more carbohydrate and vegetable based, are now enthusiastically coming into the market for meat (and fish) proteins. How are the limited land and water resources going to cope? Will intensive farming increase rather than decrease as a result? Although personally I am a keen meat and fish eater, perhaps vegetarianism is the answer…

BAD CHI…

Each day, it has been claimed, every one of Britain's ten million cows is responsible for pumping out 100–200 litres of methane, a greenhouse gas which is contributing to global warming. Rear-end emissions were thought to be the main culprit, but it's actually caused more by belching cows, sheep and pigs (and, oddly, moose in one report). Research is being undertaken to find a diet that will result in less flatulence, and meadow plants like bird's-foot trefoil and high-sugar rye grasses are being investigated.

All animals produce faeces, but when animals for food are intensively reared, there is so much more to cope with. Once this organic matter would have either been broken down naturally, or used to enrich the land as manure. Nowadays, most of it runs off as slurry, polluting both groundwater and soil. I think farms rearing animals should employ practices that are quite common now, such as desiccation or anaerobic digestion (see pages 262 and 263).

GROWING
YOUR OWN

I was brought up a London boy with country roots, and 'growing your own' is ingrained in my thinking about food. I grow my own vegetables and herbs, and am starting to cultivate fruit, in a small plot at home in North London and in an even smaller plot behind Acorn House. The trick lies in altering one's preconceptions about growing food, and thinking green, thinking organic, thinking small, thinking laterally (and sometimes vertically, see page 76)…

We all need to eat, and to my way of thinking, to do so sustainably we need to start moving away from industrialised agriculture towards an individual and bio-diverse gardening philosophy. As a society we should be thinking more in terms of market gardens, allotments and community gardens than of monocultural prairies of wheat, rape or cabbages. As individuals, we could be growing a potentially significant part of our own food needs, in pots, window-boxes, roof-tops, backyards and gardens. Apart from anything else, growing our own food is fun, and can reconnect us with skills and pleasures that we seem to have lost in the twenty-first century.

This community thinking is part of what has become known as permaculture: short for *'permanent agriculture'*, its principles have expanded to encompass the idea of a 'culture' that is permanent. Permaculture and its ideas are based on a sustainable form of agriculture used by early indigenous peoples, in which food crops are closely integrated into natural cycles. Although the majority of the emphasis is still on agriculture, on how to grow food, permaculture today also tackles how to build houses and create communities, in a way that works with nature and minimises environmental impact at the same time. Permaculture is about designing an all-round ecologically sound way of living.

On a smaller scale, permaculture involves what is known as a 'mandala', a word in Sanskrit meaning 'circle' or 'centre'. Mandala garden designs feature plants radiating out in a circle from a central source of nutrition or water (an oasis is, in essence, a mandala based on water). I created a mandala garden in Spain some years ago, on a piece of waste ground near the restaurant where I was cooking. I dug a hole or well, into which I put the organic waste from the restaurant. I planted banana trees around the well, then radiating beds of other plants and crops, varying their heights so that all of them could share air, light and shade, according to need. Walkways allowed easy access to beds and the central well. By watering the well, and feeding it, plants on the periphery, via their roots, were able to access water and nutrients. As long as the well is fed, the garden sustains itself. I revisited it recently, and it's gone wild, but it is still greener and lusher than its surroundings – and I think that some of my tomatoes have reseeded themselves, season after season.

The Eco Garden

Since the Second World War, the way we garden has changed dramatically. Wartime gardens were used entirely practically to grow food, and this way of thinking persisted for a decade or so afterwards. Thereafter, certainly since the 1950s, the garden came to be seen more as a place of relaxation, an 'extra room' for the home, and attitudes to garden usage and garden purpose completely changed. Instead of vegetable plots, we now have lawns and patios on which to play and socialise. Flower or vegetable beds, if they exist, are filled with peat and exotic imported plants bought at garden centres, and these are sprayed with chemical pesticides and herbicides and fed with fertilisers from a bottle.

I don't agree with this at all. I would rather work with nature than try to tame it. I always have several 'rules' in mind, which are: feeding the all-important soil naturally; keeping growing plants safe; growing appropriately with an awareness of biodiversity; using only sustainable materials; and avoiding water wastage. I have successfully designed and run a permaculture mandala, and feel this is the best way of producing food without much water.

If you make your own compost from organic waste (see page 256), this can be dug into the soil when it's ready, and that would probably obviate the need for adding any other type of topsoil (which is in very short supply now, and very expensive, quite justifiably). Composting would also help to prevent the obliteration of some of our ancient peat bogs (plus the plants and wildlife that live there), which are being depleted for the gardening industry. This peat, when added to garden soil, adds bulk and organic matter (it is formed from an accumulation of decomposed plants), and helps the soil retain its moisture. Your own compost can do all this just as well, if not better. It will also feed the soil, thus you won't have to use any artificial types of food for your plants — although I do have a few extra ideas up my sleeve (see below).

Instead of buying bottles of toxic chemicals to control pests — which inevitably affect the natural balance of the garden (they kill those all-important micro-organisms in the soil, for instance) — I encourage predators such as ladybirds, lacewings or hoverflies to do the work for me. All three of them, as adults and/or as larvae, prey on many of the insects and grubs that do the most damage in the garden, such as aphids and caterpillars. I invite them into my garden (and birds, and spiders, and frogs): all I have to do is provide food, give them shelter, and avoid the use of pesticides. The pests themselves are the 'food', but I leave a fifth of my garden wild, with weeds, grasses and other natural plants, such as nettles, in which they can hide from their own predators. Growing some plants there which are rich in pollen and nectar, such as members of the daisy family and some of the flowering herbs (ladybirds particularly like dill and fennel) would provide more food. Some of the pests like my flowers and herbs better than they do my vegetables so remain in the wild corner: blackfly coat some white daisies, and leave my vegetables alone. It's part of what is called 'companion planting' (see Box), and it is biodiversity supremely at work, with the wild part of the garden drawing off some of the pressure from the rest of the garden, and happily fighting most of your battles for you. It would also be an organic garden. For all that, I still can't guarantee that your rocket or your roses will be completely aphid-free, but you will be tackling the problem in a much more natural and symbiotic way.

COMPANION PLANTING

Companion planting is an ecologically friendly way of managing your garden, an organic system in which plants do most of the work. It is based on the principle that by planting certain plants close to one another, their natural properties can help with pest control and actually boost growth. Aromatic plants are the most common, so think herbs mostly.

For instance, Mexican marigolds have roots that emit secretions and aromatic leaves that discourage aphids and slugs. So plant them near your potatoes, pumpkins, squashes and tomatoes. Carrots should be grown along with garlic, chives, rosemary and sage; their scent disguises the smell of carrots, therefore confusing the carrot root fly. Cabbage white butterflies and their caterpillars are not keen on mint or rosemary, so grow those herbs with members of the cabbage family (but watch out for mint's invasive roots). Garlic can protect your raspberries from aphids, and coriander will keep aphids away from most vegetables – and coriander's flowers also attracts bees, another plus.

I know the climate is changing, but I still like to grow what is appropriate — to the season, to the climate, to the habitat, to the soil. I could grow exotic grasses or palms in my sheltered garden at home, but I don't want to, I would prefer native species, whether in the cultivated or wild part of the garden. These would attract insect and other life: butterflies (they love nettles!) and particularly bees, which play such an important part in the pollination of flowers, vegetables and fruit. None of these would fancy a palm tree or exotic flower that originated in the West Indies... This modern trend for non-native plants and manicured gardens is actually depleting our native species: in 2007 hedgehogs and sparrows — once familiar inhabitants of even the most resolutely urban garden — were included in a list of wildlife in danger, in the UK Biodiversity Action Plan. It's simply because they can't find anything to eat in our modern gardens.

I want us to return to the days when we didn't have access to those instant blooms or plants bought at garden centres, but had to work for them: taking cuttings, grafting (in both senses), sowing, potting and thinning. Then we would have a renewed awareness of the natural growing seasons again (as we should in the food-buying area, something we are losing due to the supermarket phenomenon). As I speak, my son is planting iris bulbs, and I can't wait to see his face when they come up in spring...

Many of the attributes of the modern-day garden are actually not at all ecological. Patio 'deckings' and garden furniture are often made of wood from unsustainable sources, and for me they cover up soil that could be used much more productively. (Look for the FSC — Forest Stewardship Council — symbol to be reassured that wooden furniture is sustainably sourced.) Fences are something we are keen on, but they too use wood, which needs painting with chemical preservatives (you could actually use linseed oil). Why not consider planting a hedge instead? It will take time, but it will provide good privacy as well as benefiting wildlife. Lawns are much loved all over the world, but to keep them well-manicured, bright green and smooth requires hard work, as well as damage to the environment: think of the amount of water a lawn requires, and a motorised lawnmower is said to produce as much pollution in an hour as forty cars. Unless you possess acres of lawn, I would suggest you stick to the old mechanical lawnmower — it's also good exercise!

Saving water — as well as soil — may well be one of the most important concepts in our thinking not too far into the future. In every garden, not only the eco garden, we should be organising run-offs from roofs, sheds and greenhouses into water butts. We should be reducing the amount of household water we use, and saving it for re-use (you can buy gravity hoses, which can bring cooled bath water down to containers in the garden). But to save water that is already in the soil — whether dew, rainfall or actual watering — you should always mulch your well-composted beds. I use grass cuttings, straw and leaf-mould (which you can dig in later), as well as twigs and organic rubbish that I don't want to use on the compost heap. You can also use pebbles, bark chipping (but check the origin) or pine cones. This layer not only prevents evaporation, but also keeps the weeds down!

Rudolf Steiner, founder of the Biodynamics movement, the oldest form of organic practice (he also founded the teaching method my son is learning), said that 'gardens are nutrition for the senses'. They certainly can be that, but I would love to see eco, biodynamic, organic, permacultural gardens producing good and safe nutrition for our bodies as well. The gardens of Britain together cover an area roughly five times the size of London. If all those gardens used organic compost, and gardened ecologically, that would be such a huge step forward in creating a sustainable country.

Many bee species throughout the world are declining or have become extinct. This is due to land-use change (house and road building, hedges ripped out to cater for monocultural crops), resultant loss of habitat, intensive farming and its agricultural chemicals, disease (a mite is responsible for decimating colonies of honey bees worldwide), and possibly climate change. In one scientific study, the decline in bee populations was matched by an equal decline in certain wildflowers through northern Europe. If this pattern continues and is replicated, the 'pollination services' we have always relied on and taken for granted could be severely at risk, and with it not just the wildflowers we enjoy in the countryside, but our food!

In the UK, crops such as apples, pears and berries are entirely dependent on pollinating insects such as bees for fruit production. Insects pollinate over 80 per cent of crops in Europe, and about one-third in the USA, where honey bees pollinate more than ninety cultivated crops, including avocadoes, cucumbers, watermelons, citrus fruit and almonds. The economic value of pollination is said to be £20–50 billion per year, and an astonishing one-third of the food we eat, from vegetables to oils to meat from animals that graze on pollinated forage, is reliant on pollination.

A strong argument, I think, for having a wild part of your garden, with lots of nectar-containing flowers, and for growing plants that honey bees and bumble bees like. For if we have no bees, we have no pollination, no plants, no food...

Arthur's Notes

You can actually buy little 'houses' for ladybirds and lacewings, made from sustainable woods, in which they can nest, propagate and shelter.

To make a very effective natural fertiliser, I put nettles from the wild part of the garden in some collected rainwater in a bucket. Leave for a couple of weeks, and then drain over your chosen plants. (The nettles can then be composted.)

I actually grow Russian comfrey, which I rot down in a tube to make a sticky black glue. I mix this with water, and use as a fertiliser. It's brilliant.

Instead of cutting the lawn, if you have one, completely down, allow it to grow about 3–5cm high during the summer. This saves on watering, prevents brown patches, and is lovely to lie or sit on (although not so good for playing cricket, I must admit). I leave the edges of the lawn uncut where they grow around my garden pot plants, which helps to keep them moist as well.

One problem with a water butt is that rainwater can bring down leaves and other matter from the guttering. One way of preventing this is by putting some sort of filter over the end of the pipe: an old nylon stocking or leg of tight would be perfect. But don't forget to clean and replace this every so often.

From my two wormeries, I am getting wonderful worm water and 'gardeners' gold', which is worm cast. I use this sparingly when I plant out seedlings, and this is just the kick-start they need.

As soon as I started my eco garden at home, it was visited daily by a posse of local cats, who thought the newly turned soil a wonderful lavatory. There are quite a few non-eco products available to keep them at bay, but it occurred to me that most of these cats are probably used to a litter tray at home... So I introduced a litter tray, which has been used a couple of times. We shall see how successful it will be...

Container Growing

I think one of the most important things about gardening in general, and eco gardening in particular, is recognising how much you can do in a limited environment — a small garden, a smaller backyard, a window-box or a flowerpot. The entire garden behind Acorn House, for instance, consists of containers, in an area no bigger than two skips. This garden is, in fact, the concrete roof of the room in which we keep the wormeries and desiccator. It's typical London, a potentially wasted space. But I built oblong boxes out of storm-felled trees, and filled them with good soil and rotted-down compost. They line three sides of the area, one against a sunny wall, up which I grew climbers such as cannellini beans this last summer.

I've used old olive oil cans as well, which look great, and hold a good few vegetables and herbs. From these containers, I have managed to produce enough food for me to take home and feed my family twice a week, and one night I supplied enough beans for sixty guests at the restaurant. I apply these principles at home too: my apple tree — a variety dating back to the seventeenth century — is planted in my old rubbish bin, full of my restaurant rubbish (compost). It's highlighting the success of the system by delivering me delicious apples.

Any small garden can have containers, large or small, along a fence or hedge, or up on a surface — pots of plants on top of a wall will help act as a screen and would be much better than a fence. Hanging baskets and window-boxes are other obvious ideas, and to me all these could much more usefully contain herbs, fruit and vegetables, rather than the ubiquitous geranium. Think of having culinary herbs just outside the kitchen door or window: the softer, less hardy basil and mint. I couldn't think of anything nicer than having mint handy for fresh mint tea every day, but keep it in a container by itself, or it will strangle its neighbours. Tougher and hardier herbs such as rosemary and thyme, sage too, will do well in more exposed positions.

I am also growing vegetables in small containers: there's rainbow chard, fennel, cavolo nero, sweetcorn, tomatoes and chillies. Some varieties of vine tomatoes would be good in hanging baskets. I'm planting a variety of grape vine that will happily climb out of the pot and along a trellised wall to provide shade for some of my more delicate plants. As for fruit, you could consider strawberries. It's quite a chore picking strawberries at ground level; in a window-box they are at chest level or lower.

The ultimate and quickest container growing at home is sprouting pulses, grains or seeds (see page 197).

Arthur's Notes

In October, I am preparing for frosts by laying down two poly tunnels to protect herbs and lettuces through the winter months.

You can buy a gel that helps retain water in hanging baskets, which are always particularly thirsty. But I would use worm cast, even in pot plants in the house.

Try to choose galvanised or glazed pottery pots, as these will retain water better than terracotta.

In my large halved whisky barrels, I have slated my mint off from the other herbs to prevent it taking over. Slide in a large roof slate to cut the container into quarters or halves, and this stops the mint roots spreading.

Allotments

Allotments have a long history in Britain. The 1887 Allotment Act was introduced to enable the poor who lived in poverty-stricken inner-city slums to have access, for a reasonable rent, to a small parcel of land on which to grow food. By the First World War, there were around a million allotments in the country; during the Second World War, the Dig for Victory campaign encouraged everyone to cultivate a plot for food (vegetables replaced flowers in London's Kensington Gardens, and sports fields and parks all over the country were dug up). From the high at that time of 1.5 million, the number of allotments in the country diminished in the 1960s to around 600,000, and nowadays only about half of those still exist.

This lack of interest gradually developed when the post-war consumer boom began (growing food was what the older generation did), and led to councils selling off allotment land to developers from the 1960s onwards. However, in the 1990s, allotments started to become trendy, and local authorities, who are obliged by law to provide fifteen allotments per 1000 households (difficult when land is at a premium) are now beginning to cut their long waiting lists by offering plots a quarter of the traditional size.

It seems to be younger people who are now interested in having an allotment, and there are increasing numbers of women as well (for the allotment culture was once dominated by older men). This new interest probably stems from a need to save money, but I imagine that many — they're my generation, after all — want to be certain that their vegetables and fruit are organic. Allotments fulfil many other needs too: they are sociable, and encourage a sense of community; people are out in the open and taking exercise (half an hour of digging burns 200 calories); children can play safely within sight of their parents (and they can help too); and if you're fed up with your never-ending runner beans, you can barter them with a neighbour for something different! Most importantly of all, the allotment-grown veg and fruit just taste better.

Allotments should be supported. Farmers' markets should allow some space for allotment produce.

Community Garden Projects

Because of what I am doing, I have become involved in an arena much wider than my home life, Acorn House and its garden. I have been asked several times recently to advise whole communities — largely through the intervention of local authorities — about communal eco gardening and green living, both of which I care a lot about. This concept I truly believe can bring like-minded individuals together into groups — a street, say, or an estate or a village — and working in tandem, they can achieve amazing things ecologically.

Permaculture (see page 65) might be exemplified by just one of the directions in which my eco mind has been turning. There are many council estates throughout the country, where going eco or green is the last thing many residents would think they could do, but it could so easily be possible. For example, housing estates are usually composed of tower blocks, vertical as opposed to horizontal communities. If you were to look at the top of one tower block from the air, you would see that its 'footprint' is not large in a spatial sense — no more than that of two to four terraced houses with about twenty people living in them (obviously integral to the original concept). However, in a carbon footprint sense, these tower blocks are creating much more environmental impact through emissions — they might house up to 400 people in twenty floors, say — and, most importantly, they are creating much more rubbish. That rubbish should be utilised.

I am already involved in this way on an East London estate: two or three people collect the rubbish of the vertical village, then, on space specially set aside by the estate managers and the council, it is sorted, re-used, recycled and the organic content macerated and composted. The compost is used in a garden created from a concreted area next to a green area, both of which were prone to vandalism. Within weeks of the project starting, there was a 50 per cent take-up: retired people, stay-at-home mums and even the kids themselves wanted to get involved. They are now aiming to grow vegetables to be shared within the community, and planning to plant some fruit trees. Not only has the project given some pride back to a community, I think it has empowered them as well. It may seem sociologically simplistic, but attitudes changed once the garden began: people are communicating, children are playing, and everyone has much more confidence in where they live.

There are many places within communities that can be utilised similarly. My ideas even extend as far as the disused tops of some of those same tower blocks. Properly fenced, they could hold a garden along with the composting systems themselves, even some beehives and/or chicken coops (at least the bees have got a good runway, which they need). And for the gardener, think of the view! The vertical community would be working in tandem, and if they were all of the same mind, many hundreds of people would be living in an eco-friendly way – and having fun at the same time. If I could do that on every estate in East London, say – the composting, the recycling, the reducing, the refusing, the community awareness and the coming together of people – think of the potential. Then I could take it to West London, North London... Then we could lobby the government to ensure that such practices could be the norm on all estates throughout the country. The greening of London is only the start.

A LESSON IN ECONOMICS

I recently interviewed some kids on a London estate for Channel 4. When their local youth club closed down, they had nothing to do, and nowhere to go for the seven weeks of the summer holiday. I told them my ideas on community composting, etc, and asked what they would grow if I gave them some soil. One child said she'd grow carrots, another said oranges. The third, a tycoon in the making, rather sheepishly whispered that she wanted to grow a money tree. 'If you grow an apple tree,' I said, 'that'll be your money tree. You could collect your apples and sell them at the market around the corner every year.' 'Wow!' was her response, and then she and her pals conducted me round the estate, suggesting where we might keep chickens, and where the vegetables or fruit might be protected from the wind or safe from vandals.

SUMMER

*The sun shines (we hope), plants
sweeten and mature, and we
go on holiday...*

The summer solstice, in middle to late June, celebrates the longest day of the year, and I remember the long summer days of my youth in Dorset, cycling, camping, watching the swallows arrive, and the shooting stars blazing across the sky at midnight.

There is a period between spring and summer (three-quarters of the way through May to Midsummer Day in June) that is known as 'early summer', and this is virtually a separate season for gardeners. In early summer, there is none of the ripeness that characterises the later summer months, and none of the slightly more mature, even 'readiness', of July and August. Everything in early summer still carries the paler greens of spring. But don't be fooled, few of the vegetables and none of the fruit are ready yet.

The secret, I think, of June's success is the long hours of daylight, because plants love it. Following on from the rains of the spring months, grass grows particularly lushly, and this is great for the new lambs and other livestock. The trees, fruits and vegetables are all growing on, to be enjoyed later in the summer, but there are still a number of treasures that we can pluck and enjoy now.

July is the month I've been waiting for. Winter has been gone a while, but we still haven't had a true sense of produce until now. This is when the farmers' markets start to prove their worth, with a huge choice of sun-ripened vegetables, herbs and fruit. I take advantage of this bounty as much as I can. This is a time of glut, so I turn some of this excess of produce into jams, chutneys and pickles for the larder, purées and soups for the freezer.

By August, the sun has delivered richness and sweetness to the vegetables and fruit throughout the first two summer months, but now they are starting to lose their youth, and some are getting bigger, more mature, and their flavours richer and more confident. I love the colours of August, they're deeper, darker, and they give me a sense of wealth without a penny in my pocket...

August is holiday time and hosepipe ban time, and it's usually still sunny and hot, so you need to remember to water well. Summer crops of lettuce and other leaves, and those wonderful beans, need lots of moisture on their roots. Late summer or early autumn crops such as tomatoes, squashes and sweetcorn will also need a lot of attention so that they can ripen fully and sweetly before the good weather runs out in the next couple of months.

Arthur's Summer Growing Tips

As the summer starts, I am always aware of water, so mulching is very important. This stops the roots dying because of lack of water, and you won't have to water so much. In my home garden, I use grass clippings, but you can use bits of old bark or straw. In my son's sunflower pot, we use marbles, which look great and he loves it.

I try to introduce a couple of worms into each of my flowerpots. They provide aeration, and also help the soil stay damper, which is great if you forget to water.

If I have to, I water the garden at the end of the day when the sun is down. Water applied during the day may just evaporate, and if the sun's rays hit water on the leaves, they can be scalded or burned.

I buy environmentally friendly, biological clothes detergent and washing-up liquids in bulk, filling the plastic containers up at my local supplier. Sometimes, though, I have a container left over, and I cut the top section off, and place it, cap removed, over ripening fruit such as strawberries. This protects the fruit from pests, keeps it clean and acts as a miniature greenhouse, promoting growth. I make holes in the bottom part of the container, fill with compost, and use it to grow vegetables and herbs.

If you don't use the cardboard tubes from toilet rolls in your compost (as a 'brown', see page 257), save them for use in the garden. Cut in half, into two smaller tubes, fill with seeding compost, and plant herb or vegetable seeds. Store them tightly together in a tray, water as normal, and then when the seedlings are big enough, plant out in the garden, cardboard and all.

I run two of my own worm farms, and collect their worm casts. To me this is the gold dust of soil food, and I get free worm 'tea' which I mix with water for my plants. I just can't get enough of this wonderful stuff. I urge everyone to get a wormery, full stop.

I always grow plenty of basil in pots. I keep some in the kitchen for use in cooking, and some in the garden beside my tomatoes, as a companion plant (keeping white fly away).

I like to work with nature in my gardens, and always plant a seed for the soil, a seed for the animals, and a seed for me.

What I buy in June

Vegetables
Artichokes (globe), asparagus, aubergines, beetroot, broad beans, broccoli (calabrese), cabbage, carrots (old and new), cauliflower, celery, chicory, courgettes and courgette flowers, garlic, lettuce, peas (including sugar snaps), potatoes (new), purslane, radishes, rocket, samphire, sorrel, spinach, spring onions, watercress

Fruit
Blackcurrants, cherries (European), gooseberries, peppers, raspberries, redcurrants, rhubarb, strawberries, tomatoes, white currants

Fish
Black bream, brown trout, crayfish, grey mullet, mackerel, pollack, rainbow trout, sea trout

Shellfish
Crab (spider), cuttlefish, mussels

Meat
Welsh lamb

Game
Quail, venison (buck), wood pigeon

Flowers
Elderflower

How I eat in June

What excites me most about this month is that the Jersey Royal potato is here. This uniquely British potato — christened a 'fluke' when it was first discovered, in the 1880s — has the best taste of all potatoes, probably due to the fact that it grows near the sea, and is fertilised naturally by seaweed. The mild Jersey climate must also play a part. When Jersey Royals are around, I eat an awful lot of them... But all new potatoes are good now, like Pentland Javelin, Ratte and Pink Fir Apple.

Last June, my courgettes were fantastic, small and tender, and so deliciously sweet, I ate them raw like carrots. Aron loves them. I left a few to grow on throughout the rest of the summer, and they transformed into huge marrows: try baking them, stuffed with minted minced lamb. I also grow other summer squashes, which have a bit more flavour than marrows, such as flying-saucer patty pans and white-skinned courgettes. The list is endless. Also available at this time of year is a plant related to the thistle, the globe artichoke, which I must admit I am rather an expert at preparing. At one time I did nothing else in the kitchen, so much so that I thought of changing my name to Artie (thanks, Rowley)! — and I would be happy if anyone were to challenge me to a race...

Choose Jersey Royal new potatoes from the sacks, still covered with that unique soil (which I keep and put on my garden or window-boxes). To prepare them, I put them in a sink, turn the tap on, and massage them together to rub the soil off. I never use a peeler, scraper or brush. Once the potato is clean, cut away any blemishes, but they've been in the soil for so short a time, nothing much will have happened to them.

To cook Jersey Royals, boil them until the *al dente* point is just past. Crunchy is a no-no, soft is criminal, so you need to be very careful. This is why I tend, in opposition to much received wisdom, to cook them very slowly: I bring them up to the boil then turn them down and just tickle them with heat until the right stage is reached. This takes far longer than usual, obviously, but the window for mistakes is much reduced: if you accelerate the cooking, then you could miss that crucial minute or two between undercooked and overcooked. I don't use mint with them — this can overpower — but I do add a little salt.

To prepare Jerseys for a potato salad, I drain them through a colander, then put them on a flat tray, where they will take about 15 minutes to cool. I don't pour cold water over them to speed this process, as this would wash away a lot of the flavour from the skins. Then I make the simplest salad combination with the potatoes, with house dressing (see page 270), French beans, raw diced shallot and crunchy radishes.

Apart from potato salad, I also like taking really young potatoes, boiling them as above, and crushing them down rather than mashing them, when they will still have some texture. Use a heavy-duty whisk for this, stabbing at them with it, and then they are brilliant dressed with some extra virgin olive oil and chopped green chilli. I also like cutting young potatoes in half raw and sautéing them in a touch of light olive oil and butter until just cooked and still crunchy. Or I sometimes slice them perhaps 5mm thick, mix them with chopped tomato and fresh herbs, and roast them. All these potato recipes would be perfect with hot or cold lamb, or most grilled fish.

Summer squashes are, in general, the young versions of the squashes and pumpkins that grow on to become the winter varieties. They are soft skinned, and can be eaten, skin and all; on winter varieties, the skin has hardened for protection, so isn't usually eaten. In June you will be finding the very youngest and tenderest in farmers' markets — or picking them, if you are lucky enough to grow them yourself. They need the most minimal cooking, and I actually make a raw mushroom and courgette salad. You can roast them whole, grill, fry or coat in batter and deep-fry.

Courgettes are my favourite summer squash, and I love stuffing them. Cut them in half lengthways and use a teaspoon to take out the central core of immature seeds. This leaves a channel to stuff. Chop the removed core, then mix with fresh crumbly ricotta, some grated Parmesan, a spot of dried chilli and grated lemon zest and a few fresh breadcrumbs. Make this into small sausages and place in the channels. Bake in a moderate oven (180°C/Fan 160°C/Gas 4), drizzled with a little light olive oil, until the flesh is soft (the timing will depend on size). I was served this by the same lady who introduced me to her pesto recipe (see page 97), and I ate far too many. If you say something is delicious to an Italian cook, they take this as a request for more...

I tend to think of courgettes as being more of a vehicle for things, because to be honest, they are fairly non-committal in flavour. They are delicious sliced lengthways and char-grilled — but think about it, it's the char-grilling you are tasting really, rather than the courgette. Fry slices, to use in a frittata, perhaps fairly generously flavoured with grated Parmesan. Fry discs in light olive oil, drain and dry, then drizzle with wine vinegar and chilli for a fried courgette salad; or skewer discs with some protein or other veg and grill. Immerse slices or chip shapes in a good batter (see page 153), and deep-fry. Cut them in long slices and roast or, my favourite, cut into random chunks and roast with light olive oil, garlic and chilli: the odd shapes add texture, and the many points and cut faces get caramelised, adding flavour. Great with lamb and some fish.

Globe artichokes come big or small, and I like them both. In the UK we used only to get the large ones from France, but now the Italians are importing their small ones, and we are also growing them ourselves: look at your farmers' markets starting in late April for the Italian, June for the English... Artichokes can be prepared raw and then cooked, or cooked and then prepared. I tend towards the latter, as the veg are not quite so brittle or aggressive, and you lose much less product.

Large raw artichokes are trimmed of their leaves down to their crowns or hearts in the restaurant, but you can cook and eat them whole at home. Trim minimally, particularly of the leaf spikes, then boil in a court-bouillon until a sharp knife goes into the stem end, but with a little resistance. Take out, drain and it will be perfect. If you leave it until there is no more resistance, it will continue to cook when resting and will be overcooked. Remove the choke, and serve with vinaigrette or melted butter to dip the leaves in. Or remove all the leaves and then use the hearts.

For globe artichoke hearts or crowns, cook as above or cut down, then boil. Leave the heart whole (with a hollow where you cut out the choke) or cut into eight wedges. Serve the latter as part of a larger salad, or sauté with light olive oil, butter, a bit of young turnip and some radishes for a wonderful seasonal garnish. I was once flown to New York to cook on a boat for 110 people as they sailed round Manhattan. I did my artichoke crowns Roux Brothers style: upside-down crowns with chopped smoked salmon, crème fraîche and caviar in the hollow; this was topped with a poached egg and a perfect, wafer-thin slice of smoked salmon... Great for two, but a nightmare for 110! You could try something a little simpler in the hollow of the heart, serving it rather like a half avocado.

The smaller artichokes are even more fiddly to prepare than the large ones. You need to peel around the stem, then trim and cut them in half. Any choke, if formed, should be removed. They can be eaten raw in a salad, which is delicious, dressed with parsley and lemon juice. But what I do at the restaurant is tip the halved baby artichokes into a soffrito (see page 142), and sweat them down before adding some white wine, a bay leaf, some wine vinegar, and salt and pepper. Cover with a piece of parchment or greaseproof paper, and leave to cook for a few minutes. Serve them steaming hot. This dish walks out the door in June...

Chanterelle, Thyme & Summer Truffle Soup

Simple seasonality delivers this sophisticated soup, one that I wanted to share with you.

For 6

1kg chanterelles
150g butter
250g shallots, peeled and finely diced
2 garlic cloves, peeled and chopped
3 tsp picked thyme leaves
sea salt and freshly ground black pepper
1 litre chicken or vegetable stock (see pages 265 or 267), warm

To serve
6 slices ciabatta, toasted
50g Parmesan, freshly grated
20g summer truffle
extra virgin olive oil

Break the chanterelles open with your fingers, and brush them clean with a pastry brush.

Place the mushrooms and butter in a large, hot, thick-bottomed saucepan. Fry until most of the liquid has evaporated, then add the shallots, garlic and thyme. Continue to fry for a few minutes, and then season. After 5 minutes pour over the warm stock, and simmer for 8 minutes.

Put a slice of warm toast in each soup bowl, and sprinkle a little Parmesan on top, then some mushrooms, then some of the liquid. Slice fine slivers of the truffle over the top of the dish, and drizzle with extra virgin olive oil. Serve hot.

Artichoke & Parsley Risotto

Artichokes oxidise (discolour) very quickly when cut. To prevent this, break parsley stalks into water with a little salt and add the artichokes. This avoids the need for added vinegar or lemon juice which, although they too prevent discoloration, ultimately taint the delicate artichoke flavour.

For 6

1.5 litres chicken stock (see page 265)
8 young artichoke hearts
light olive oil
100g butter
1 medium red onion, peeled and finely chopped
1 head celery, finely chopped
1 tbsp chopped parsley
420g vialone nano risotto rice
50g Parmesan, freshly grated
1 small bunch rocket leaves, chopped
6 tbsp torn basil
sea salt and freshly ground black pepper

Heat the stock in a pan and keep it simmering. Slice the artichokes and reserve in parsley stalk water (see above).

In a thick-bottomed saucepan, cover the base with olive oil and melt half the butter. Add the onion and celery, and fry until soft with a touch of colour. Add the parsley and artichokes and cook, stirring, for 5 minutes. Add the rice and stir until the rice becomes slightly opaque. Add enough hot stock just to cover and every time the liquid disappears, keep adding some more, stirring all the time, for about 20 minutes, or until the rice is cooked to your liking.

Finish with most of the Parmesan, the chopped rocket, basil and the rest of the butter. Season to taste, stir together, and serve with a dusting of Parmesan.

Carrot, Beetroot & Rocket Salad

This has been my most popular salad yet. It's great when people are happy to be so simple.

For 6

500g large carrots, trimmed and peeled
50g butter
1 litre filtered water
1 tbsp caster sugar
4 sage leaves
1kg beetroots, boiled until cooked
10g cumin seeds, toasted and crushed
sea salt and freshly ground black pepper
250g natural Greek yoghurt
1 bunch rocket leaves
house dressing (see page 270)
2 tbsp chopped mint

Put the carrots, butter, water, sugar and sage into a pan, cover with a lid and bring up to the boil. Remove the lid and continue boiling to allow all the water to evaporate away, by which time the carrots should be cooked, sweet and buttery. Reserve, and when cool, cut into irregular shapes.

I don't peel my beetroots as the skin is so good for you. Cut them into irregular shapes as well, and arrange on a platter, along with the carrots. Mix the cumin seeds and some salt and pepper into the yoghurt, and drizzle this over the arranged vegetables. Then comes the rocket, a drizzle of the house dressing to taste, and a final sprinkle of the mint.

Seared Mackerel with French Bean, Cauliflower, Anchovy, Caper & Potato Salad

I have a pepper mill specially reserved for cardamom seeds, which I grind over the top of this mackerel to give it a unique flavour. What you do is crush the cardamom pod in your fingers, then empty the little black seeds out, put them in your mill, and grind away. (Or you can do this in a pestle and mortar, but because they are so oily, they stick.) They are very strong!

For 6

6 large fresh mackerel, filleted and pin-boned
freshly ground cardamom (see above)
a thumb-sized piece of fresh horseradish, peeled

French Bean, Cauliflower, Anchovy, Caper and Potato Salad
1kg new potatoes, washed
300g cauliflower, cut into florets
sea salt and freshly ground black pepper
300g French beans, topped and tailed
12 salted anchovy fillets
20g salted capers, soaked in filtered water for 30 minutes
house dressing (see page 270)

For the salad, cook the potatoes gently in a pan until perfectly cooked (see page 84). Drain well. Put the cauliflower into a large pan of boiling, salted filtered water and cook for about 4 minutes, then add the beans and cook until just soft, about another 6–8 minutes. Drain these well too.

Meanwhile, prepare the salted anchovies. Rinse them under cold running water to remove the salt. Lay skin-side down on the work surface, and gently remove the spines and the heads. Pat dry and use immediately. To prepare the salted capers, drain well after soaking and pat dry.

Arrange all the salad ingredients on a large serving dish. Sprinkle with the house dressing.

Lay the mackerel fillets on the work surface, flesh-side up, grind some cardamom over, and then finely grate on the horseradish. Season lightly with salt and pepper. Pan-fry, skin-side down, over a medium heat for about 8—10 minutes, which should cook the fish all the way through. Turn over for a further minute or two, then arrange on top of the salad.

Lemon Tart

This is a tart made on the same principles as the apple pie in spring, using the same frangipane filling. You could omit the frangipane if you liked.

For 4

½ quantity apple pie pastry (see page 37)
frangipane (page 38)

Lemon filling
finely grated zest and juice of 4 lemons
3 medium whole eggs
4 medium egg yolks
175g caster sugar
150g unsalted butter

Preheat the oven to 180°C/Fan 160°C/Gas 4, and grease and flour a 25cm tart tin.

Roll the pastry out, place into the prepared tart tin, line with baking parchment, and pour in some baking beans. Bake blind in the preheated oven for about 10 minutes. Remove and allow to cool. Remove the beans and parchment. Spread the frangipane into the pastry case, and bake for another 10–12 minutes. Leave to cool.

For the lemon filling, put the lemon juice, whole eggs, egg yolks and sugar into a large saucepan and, over a low heat, whisk until the eggs have broken up and the sugar has dissolved. Whisk in half the butter and cook until you have a runny curd consistency. Add the rest of the butter and the lemon zest, and whisk until thick. Remove from the heat, allow to cool, then pour on top of the frangipane in the pastry case.

When this is cold, I glaze the lemon curd topping under a grill. Some people use a blowtorch, but I hate the flavour this gives. Just make sure your grill is hot, and you'll be fine.

What I buy in July

Vegetables
Artichokes (globe), aubergine, beans (borlotti, broad, French), beetroot, broccoli (calabrese), carrots, cauliflower, chard, courgettes, cucumbers, fennel, garlic, horseradish, kohlrabi, lamb's lettuce, lettuce, onions, pak-choi, peas, potatoes (new), purslane, radishes, rocket, samphire, shallots, sorrel, spinach, spring onions, turnips, watercress

Fruit
Apricots (imported), bilberries, blackcurrants, blueberries, cherries, gooseberries, loganberries, peppers and chillies, raspberries, redcurrants, rhubarb, strawberries, tomatoes, white currants, wild strawberries, worcesterberries

Fish
Black bream, crayfish, mackerel, pollack, river trout, sea trout

Shellfish
Crab (brown, hen, spider), cuttlefish, lobster, scallops (hand-dived only)

Game
Rabbit, wood pigeon

Flowers
Elderflower, lavender

Fungi
Chanterelles, chicken of the wood, field mushrooms, summer truffles

How I eat in July

July sunshine helps to fix the natural sugars in both my vegetables and fruit. Courgettes, tomatoes and green beans, for instance, are all succulently sweet at the moment. I like to keep everything raw or semi-cooked: I eat washed radishes and carrots, fresh and crisp, with a chickpea hummus; I serve my family a tomato salad, dressed simply with the best extra virgin olive oil and torn basil; at the restaurant, I lightly grill fennel with a piece of fish; and at home I make my pasta fragrant with a topping of my home-made basil pesto. My whole family enjoys the healthiness of juiced young beetroots, carrots and celery.

I scoff as much soft summer fruit now as I can. This is when British strawberries are perfect, and is what I shall concentrate on here. They played a large part in my childhood: I remember sticking my fingers through the wire cage my parents had put around our strawberry patch, my frustration at not being able to get at them as obvious as that of the predatory blackbirds. But in July we also have raspberries, blueberries, redcurrants, blackcurrants and gooseberries, and I use most of these in the same way as I suggest for strawberries — except perhaps the gooseberries and blackcurrants, which are a bit tart. As I write this, my taste-buds are remembering as a child reaching into our blackcurrant bush, and eating the fruit, some sweet, some sour. I had a love-hate relationship with them, but I always went back for more.

First of all, take your strawberries (buy lots of punnets when they are at their cheapest). They should be soft and sweet-smelling. Wash gently in cold water, dry on absorbent paper, then hull, pulling and twisting out the green top (if it doesn't come out easily, the berry is not ready). Never use a knife to cut the top off, which is so wasteful. Then work quickly, as washed strawberries won't last...

Macerate whole strawberries in balsamic vinegar with a sprinkling of freshly ground black pepper — the vinegar just a further flavouring step along the classic route of strawberries and pepper. Another twist on this is using the pepper in a flourless chocolate cake (see page 26), and serving the balsamic crushed strawberries with it.

Strawberries and other soft July fruits go perfectly with cream- and egg-based desserts. I like to make a basil pannacotta, which I serve with sliced fresh strawberries. (Once I made a lavender pannacotta, but it wasn't much of a success, not sitting on the palate well. But I pick the lavender from my mum's garden, and hang a stalk or two in my car to stop it smelling like a car!!)

Make a pavlova, and top it with fresh strawberries and cream. My best pavlova was an accident, and I have never been able to reproduce it. I was cooking in the French Alps, in an electric oven, and I allowed 8 hours for my pavlova. While I was ski-ing happily, the electricity went off, as did the oven. When I returned at the requisite time to take the pavlova out, the oven was stone cold — but the pavlova was perfect, having cooked on in the residual heat, and I have no idea of the length of time involved. You could use broken pavlova (or meringue), fresh strawberries and cream, with some strawberry coulis (see below), to make an Eton mess.

Make a strawberry jam or conserve. Put the fruit whole in a pan with sugar, some lemon juice (for a touch of pectin) and a split vanilla pod. (You could add a little liqueur if you wanted.) Cook until just beginning to break down, minutes only, then cool and store in the fridge. This will only last a couple of days, but it's a definite means of making a glut last just a little bit longer.

That strawberry conserve can be used in a number of ways. On your breakfast toast or afternoon tea scones obviously, but you could also use it as the filling for a chocolate sponge, with some cream, and whole fresh strawberries on the top. Or you could use it as the base of a strawberry ice-cream. What I like even better is to make a strawberry ripple ice-cream. Churn a vanilla ice-cream (see page 273) until it's partially set, then add some strawberry jam. Allow it a couple of twists, so there are a few streaks of pink in the cream, and put into the freezer.

Savoury strawberries might sound strange, but I make a savoury risotto with strawberries, which Aron loves. Acorn House makes this risotto wickedly. Chopped and mashed strawberries are macerated in good-quality balsamic with some black pepper (no sugar), then that goes into a white risotto base (see page 143) about 5 minutes before the risotto is ready. With 30 seconds to go, you add a touch of butter, grated Parmesan and some more chopped fresh strawberries, which you just minimally warm through. It's intensely savoury, with a touch of sweetness and acidity too.

Drying strawberries is another way of possibly coping with a glut. It's a pity that they can't be frozen (as you can raspberries), but you can dry them as you might tomatoes (they do this in Italy in the sun). If you have some time, then cut perfect specimens in half, put on wire cooling trays and into a very low oven (110–120°C/Fan 90–100°C/Gas ¼–½) or put into a warm oven after you have finished cooking, and leave until they are the texture you would like. They intensify in flavour. If softish, use fairly soon; if dry, keep in a jar and reconstitute with filtered water or liqueur when you want to use them. Or make a strawberry powder, which is great for dusting over desserts.

Make a strawberry purée. Put strawberries in a pan and mash with a potato masher. You shouldn't need much sugar if they are ripe and sweet enough. You could add some vanilla seeds, or a touch of vanilla syrup instead (made from 1 litre filtered water, 800g caster sugar and 1 vanilla pod, heated and infused together). Set the purée with some gelatine to make a strawberry jelly. You can also strain the purée to make a strawberry coulis, a great accompanying sweet sauce for a variety of desserts. I made a wonderful dish at Gavvers twenty years ago with Michel Roux, which consisted of towers of butter sablé biscuits filled with strawberries and crème pâtissière, served with strawberry coulis and crème anglaise.

Put some of the plain strawberry purée into the bottom of a champagne glass and pour over some Prosecco or champagne for a strawberry

Bellini. For non-drinkers, use sparkling water. Use the same liquid — strawberry purée and sparkling wine — as the basis of a strawberry soup, to be served as a dessert. You could add a little orange-blossom water for another taste sensation. Serve a scoop of vanilla ice-cream in the middle. Perfect!

A POT OF BASIL

Basil is one of my favourite herbs, and it is characteristic of July. The best basil in the world comes from Liguria in Italy, and this is all to do with the topography of the province. The land dictates flavour. A narrow coastal plain rises to steep cliffs; clouds sit at the top of these cliffs, coming from the land behind, but prevented from going any further by the prevailing winds coming in from the sea. As a result the coastal plain enjoys what is almost a microclimate – salty, damp air, with lots of sun and heat – which is perfect for vegetables, fruit and herbs, especially basil and tomatoes, imparting a sweetness as well as a saltiness. The only other place I've encountered this is in coastal Andalucia in southern Spain, where I was alerted by the fantastic taste of the tomatoes. I looked to check, and I saw the sea – the Mediterranean breeze coming in from Africa – I saw the mountains behind Malaga, I saw the clouds holding back, and it was all explained.

I learned how to make basil pesto from Silvana Chiomento, the mother of a Ligurian friend, Max. She grew endless pots of the local small-leaved basil on her patio, and her pesto genovese used to come to the table with steaming bowls of freshly made, plump gnocchi. They were topped with some of her salsa rossa di pomodoro and some pesto, which recreated the tricolore, the red, white and green flag of Italy. With something like that to eat, I don't need white truffles or sparkling wine…

Tomato, Cucumber & Basil Soup

This is my play on gazpacho, which, when running a restaurant in Spain, I put on the menu. But there was no pleasing the Spanish, whose national dish is gazpacho, and everyone told me their own particular way of making it… So I took some advice on board, and this is what I came up with.

For 6

750g soft, ripe tomatoes
2 medium cucumbers
50g white onions, peeled
1 ciabatta loaf, cut in half
4 tbsp chopped basil
4 tbsp red wine vinegar
½ tsp smashed garlic
sea salt and freshly ground black pepper
extra virgin olive oil & light olive oil

In a large bowl, tear the tomatoes into fairly small chunks with your hands, making sure you squish and squash as you go. Chop the cucumber into similar-sized pieces, and finely dice the onions. Tear up half the bread, crust and all, into small pieces. Put all of these, plus the basil, into the bowl with the tomatoes, along with the vinegar, garlic, salt and pepper and at least 6 tablespoons of extra virgin olive oil. Just squeeze the whole mixture together, and reserve at room temperature for 3-4 hours.

Then put the mixture into a blender or food processor and blitz until smooth. Pour into bowls. I serve this at room temperature, as I think cold inhibits flavour. Drizzle a little extra virgin olive oil on top, with perhaps an extra basil leaf. Serve with the other half of the ciabatta, broken up and toasted in the oven with some light olive oil.

Prawn Caramelle

I was told by everyone who has eaten this that if I put it in my book, they would buy it. So here you are!

For 6

1kg whole large prawns (see page 185)
1.7 litres prawn stock (see page 268)
1 fresh red chilli, seeded and finely chopped
1½ bunches rocket leaves, chopped
sea salt and freshly ground black pepper
light olive oil
250g fresh pasta dough (see page 269)
60g butter

Break off the prawn heads, peel off the tails, slice down the top of the backs and de-vein. Keep all the trimmings for the stock, and chill the prawn flesh: you should have about 500g.

Make the stock and then reduce your 1.7 litres down to about 200ml, so that you have this sticky caramel, with a wickedly intense prawn flavour. In a food processor, or by hand and knife, chop all the prawn meat. Add the chilli and two-thirds of the rocket, season with salt and pepper, and then pour in half of the prawn caramel. This is quite sweet, and if you put too much in at once, it could be too powerful. Then in a pan, I fry a teaspoon of the mixture off in a little olive oil, just to check the flavour. Get it to your desired taste by adding more caramel if you want, or more seasoning, and reserve in the fridge.

Roll out a quarter of the pasta until you can just see the colour of your palms through it. Cut into 10cm squares. Put a little finger-shaped piece of the prawn mixture along the bottom of each square (I use a piping bag), spray lightly with water (use a clean plant mister), and roll upwards to create a fat cigar. Twist the ends just like you would with a sweetie paper, to make large boiled sweets (or small Christmas crackers). Repeat until the mixture is finished.

Cook these caramelle in a pan of slightly rolling, boiling, salted filtered water, until they pop up to the top, about 4 minutes.
To make the sauce, take a little of the remaining prawn caramel, and warm through, letting it down with a little of the pasta cooking water, then drop in the butter in small pieces. Roll around in the pan, and finish with some more chopped rocket. Put the cooked caramelle into the sauce to get them all saucy, and then tip into a serving dish. Serve immediately.

Char-Grilled Courgettes with Chilli & Mint

I cut my courgettes really thin here. I treat this dish as a light starter for anything else I am doing, and my friends are always surprised at its simplicity.

For 6

1.5kg small yellow and green courgettes
sea salt and freshly ground black pepper
4 fresh red chillies
3 garlic cloves
½ bunch mint
light olive oil
5 tsp Volpaia herb vinegar
extra virgin olive oil

Wash and trim the courgettes, then cut lengthways into 1cm-thick slices. Put in a colander, sprinkle lightly with salt, and leave for about 30 minutes, then pat dry. Cut the chillies in half, scoop the seeds out, and finely slice the flesh lengthways. Peel the garlic, and cut into thin slices. Remove the mint leaves from the stalks.

Preheat the grill or griddle. Char-grill the courgette slices – or use an overhead grill, or cast-iron griddle – until light brown and cooked. Reserve on a serving dish. Gently fry the garlic slices in a little light olive oil in a pan until golden brown. Drain and cool.

Sprinkle the chilli over the courgettes, then tear over the mint leaves. Sprinkle on the garlic slices and drizzle with the vinegar and extra virgin olive oil to taste. Season well.

Char-Grilled Lamb Chops, with Young Turnip, Artichoke & Tahini Salad

This salad would accompany almost anything, meat or fish, cooked very simply as the chops are here.

For 6

18 small lamb chops
sea salt and freshly ground black pepper

Young Turnip, Artichoke and Tahini Salad
36 young turnips, boiled until just soft
18 young artichokes, boiled, prepared and halved (see page 86)
6 tbsp Fairtrade tahini (sesame paste)
juice of 1½ lemons
6 tbsp mixed black and white sesame seeds
100ml extra virgin olive oil

For the salad, place the cooked vegetables in a serving bowl. In a smaller bowl, mix together the tahini, lemon juice, half the sesame seeds and the olive oil. Drizzle over the vegetables, mix with your fingertips, then arrange on serving plates. Sprinkle with the remaining sesame seeds.

Preheat the grill, if using. Season the lamb chops, and char-grill, grill (using an overhead grill) or pan-fry them until done to your taste. Serve with the salad.

Summer Pudding

The blackberries and blackcurrants here are essential for colour, as I love summer pudding with deep dark colours. If you have some of the fruit mixture left over, you could purée it and make a sorbet.

For 8

2 loaves ciabatta bread
250g strawberries
2 ripe peaches, stoned
250g blackberries
250g raspberries
250g blackcurrants
about 400g caster sugar
1 vanilla pod, split
½ bottle Valpolicella red wine

Have ready a large bowl of about 1-1.5 litre capacity. Although I don't like to use clingfilm, it makes the whole process easier here. Line the bowl with a double layer of clingfilm, leaving an overlap with which you can turn the pudding out.

Cut the crusts thinly off both loaves of ciabatta, and cut the bread into 1cm slices lengthways. Completely line the bowl with as little bread as it takes, leaving some for the top (which will become the bottom). Set on a tray.

Wash the fruit very briefly, and prepare minimally: cut the strawberries in half only if they're big, and cut the un-skinned peaches to the same size as the blackberries.

Put the sugar and vanilla pod in a large, thick-bottomed pan, and heat gently to the caramel stage when it will be a touch past light brown and very hot and sweet. Pour in the wine, and as it fizzles and steams, stir together to create a lovely sweet winey mixture. This action cooks out the alcohol, making it less aggressive.

As the caramel dissolves into the wine, put in the strawberries, peaches and blackberries, and 3 minutes later the raspberries and blackcurrants. I try to keep all the fruit with some sort of character, rather than having them turn into a mush. Cook until the mixture boils, then turn off, remove from the heat and leave to cool slightly, 10 minutes or so maximum.

Working while still warm, and using a slotted spoon, ladle as much fruit as you can into the bread-lined bowl, squashing and ramming it in to about 7/8 of the way up. Then I pour in some of the juices, enough so that it overflows (there is nothing worse than a white summer pudding), then I top with the remaining bread. Fold over the edges of the bread, tidy the whole thing up, and place a plate on top. Put a heavy weight on the plate — a mortar, a big jug of water, whatever. Leave for 24 hours in the fridge if you can, but at least prepare it in the morning for the evening.

Invert the pudding out on to a serving plate, using the clingfilm. Baste with a little of the juices left, particularly over any white patches. Any fruit left over will jar quite nicely, but I serve the fruit and juice on top of the summer pudding, with some thick oozy double cream or crème fraîche.

What I buy in August

Vegetables
Artichokes (globe), aubergine, beans (borlotti, broad, cannellini, French, runner), beetroot, borage, broccoli (calabrese), cabbage, carrots, cauliflower (romanesco), celery, chard, chicory, courgettes, cucumber, fennel, garlic, horseradish, kohlrabi, lamb's lettuce, leeks, lettuce, onions, pak-choi, peas, potatoes (new), purslane, radishes, rocket, salsify, samphire, sorrel, spinach, summer squash, sweetcorn, watercress

Fruit
Apricots (imported), blackberries, blackcurrants, blueberries, cherries, figs, gooseberries, greengages, loganberries, melons, mulberries, peaches and nectarines, peppers and chillies, plums (and Victoria), raspberries, redcurrants, strawberries, tomatoes, whitecurrants, wild strawberries, worcesterberries

Fish
Black bream, crayfish, mackerel, pollack, river trout, sea trout

Shellfish
Crab (brown, hen, spider), cuttlefish, lobster, prawns, scallops (hand-dived only), squid

Game
Rabbit, wood pigeon

Flowers
Lavender

Fungi
Ceps/porcini, chanterelles, chicken of the wood, field mushrooms, horse mushrooms, oyster mushrooms, parasol mushrooms, puffballs, summer truffles, trompettes de mort (horn of plenty)

How I eat in August

I love how I eat in August. There are plenty of fruits around, and I could live on peaches and nectarines — along with the first of the Victoria plums. The vegetables are great too, and the choice available allows me to change direction slightly, so I have chosen here to write about leaves and beans...

I eat salad leaves all year round, but there are so many to choose from at this time, that I have a completely different looking and tasting salad every day, perhaps by itself for lunch, or with some protein — a piece of mackerel, prawns or scallops — for dinner. The richer and darker leaves of August are coming in now too, things like spinach and chard, and these can be cooked in interesting ways as well. The slightly more mature vegetables, like borlotti and cannellini beans, can actually be used instead of protein, so August sometimes for me is quite a 'vegetarian' month. If you ate some borlotti beans cooked as I describe below — August in a pot — you probably wouldn't even notice that you hadn't eaten meat in your meal...

Take 2kg borlotti beans (or cannellini, big broad — or indeed fresh chickpeas or soya beans). Please note that they must be fresh, dried is quite different. Give them a quick rinse, then tip into a pan. Cover with filtered water, plus 5cm more. Add a couple of slugs of good wine vinegar, 6 or so glugs of light olive oil, 3 tomatoes, a fresh or dried chilli, 4-5 peeled garlic cloves and a bay leaf. Bring up to the boil, skimming off the froth as you go. Turn down the heat, and let it tick over for a good 1-1½ hours, or until you like their texture (I like them soft, but not mushy). You could do this in the oven as well (about 180°C/Fan 160°C/Gas 4), covered with parchment paper and foil, where it will take about 2 hours. (The all-round gentle washing of oven heat is less aggressive than stove-top cooking.)

Take a quarter of the cooked beans, along with the tomatoes, garlic and liquid and mouli them or put them through a ricer. Return this to the whole beans to thicken them. You never tip the liquid away. This would be a good bean dish by itself, great with bread, or an accompaniment to something like confit of duck. I cook cannellini beans in this way and serve them as baked beans for breakfast in the restaurant. People tend to ask if they are organic, and I say they are more than organic: they have been made by us, I know where they were grown, how they were cooked and that there isn't a trace of additives or preservatives...

You could alter the texture of the beans more radically, by puréeing a greater proportion of them — perhaps the whole lot — or by mashing them with a potato masher. Whole or smashed, you can make these beans into a soup, adding them to a soffrito (see page 142). You could add spices and herbs such as chilli or cayenne pepper, cumin and fresh coriander to make Mexican refried beans. Leftovers freeze well.

There are wonderful salad leaves in the garden and in the shops. Instead of me trying to define what you should use — although I've given a listing of my favourite combination in the mixed salad below — simply go to your farmers' market or supermarket, and buy what is the best on offer. Use lettuce leaves, some vegetable leaves (like spinach), wild leaves (there will be some dandelion and sorrel around), herbs, sprouts (see page 197), and add other ingredients to taste. I would use some raw vegetables (fennel, radishes, celery, etc), some seeds (sesame, sunflower, pumpkin), and some toasted nuts. You could add meat or fish, but if you wanted to remain vegetarian you could add some nutty tofu. I always like a hint of seaweed, some nori sheets cut with scissors at the last minute. Serve a good dressing with it (see pages 270-271).

There's some wonderful spinach around at this time. I started at the Kensington Place Restaurant when I was 16, and on my first day in the kitchen was put in charge of picking boxes and boxes of French spinach, which were taller than me (and I am six foot six!). At the end of 2 hours, I hadn't even finished one box — in fact I fell asleep with my forehead on the box — after which I did what we tend to do, put the smallest fiddliest leaves in the bin (the best ones!). The sous-chef was wise in the ways of juniors, fished them out, and made me do the job properly.

That experience hasn't soured my romance with spinach, and I love it (and see page 181 for how to wash and prepare it).

You could blanch your spinach (in lots of boiling, salted filtered water), or steam it. Served simply with butter, salt and pepper, it is delicious, and would make a wonderful base for a piece of fish. But, to be slightly more eco in my spinach thinking, I tend to put it in a cold pan along with some light olive oil, a few splashes of cold filtered water, some salt and pepper; the lid goes on, as does the heat, and the spinach will start to hiss straightaway. Give it a few minutes to evaporate the water, drain if necessary, then you can add some butter or double cream, some nutmeg, some fresh lemon juice and extra virgin olive oil, crushed fennel seeds, chilli oil or chilli flakes, pine nuts and raisins. There are a million ways in which you can dress up basically cooked spinach.

You can also use this basic spinach in other ways: in gratins with cheese and other vegetables, in soups (some chefs add spinach to their watercress soups to darken the colour), in risottos and pasta sauces. I use spinach for its chlorophyll, as I do nettles (see page 19), to make green pasta.

I cook plain green chard in the same ways as I do spinach, although it loses its colour more than spinach. Don't do anything to the wonderful ruby and rainbow chards other than steam them…

TOMATOES

Tomatoes are really magical. They can be creamy, sometimes tart, sometimes sweet, they are all the colours of the rainbow, they are soft, they are firm, you can fry them, bake them, eat them raw in salads. And don't forget the ketchup. They are one of the kitchen's most staple ingredients during the summer months, and because of that I almost didn't mention them! One of the finest marriages of flavour is the basil of Asia and the tomatoes of South America, coming together in some of the most classic of Italian dishes. Gimme spaghetti with tomato sauce and basil any day!

Beetroot, Vodka & Soured Cream Soup

The quantities here might surprise you, but you need to make it big for richness and character. I use Tabasco instead of pepper, as the pepper will show up in the soup, which needs to be really, really smooth in texture and colour. In fact, using Tabasco is the best way of replacing pepper if you are looking for that particular finish.

For about 8

1 head celery, chopped
1 large red onion, peeled and chopped
2 garlic cloves, peeled
125g butter
3kg red beetroot, washed and cut into large dice
1 cardamom pod, crushed
sea salt and freshley ground pepper
450ml vodka
2.5 litres chicken or vegetable stock (see pages 265 and 267), warm
500ml soured cream
Tabasco sauce, to taste

Gently fry the celery, onion and garlic in the butter in a pan until just colouring. Add the beetroot and cardamom and season with salt. Stir and cook until the ingredients start to stick to the bottom of the pan. Add half of the vodka and allow it to steam off the pan bottom. Add the warm stock and bring to the boil. Cover and simmer for 45 minutes or until the beetroot is soft to the knife. Remove from the heat and cool slightly.

In a blender or food processor, blitz the mixture in equal measures of liquid to veg, adding some vodka and soured cream each time, with Tabasco to taste. Pass through a fine sieve into a large container. Check the seasoning, and add the rest of the vodka and soured cream. Serve hot or cold.

Penne with Raw Tomato & Rocket

I always use soft and juicy tomatoes raw for pasta sauces. There is no need to cook them. The olives add a lovely deep flavour to the dish.

For 6

1kg ripe plum tomatoes
2 garlic cloves
sea salt and freshly ground black pepper
1 small dried chilli
150g salted capers, soaked for 30 minutes (see page 90)
200g black olives
2 bunches rocket leaves
900g penne
extra virgin olive oil

Cut the tomatoes in half. Squeeze out and discard the excess juice and seeds, and chop the flesh coarsely. Peel the garlic and squash with 1 teaspoon salt. Crumble the chilli. Rinse and dry the capers, and stone the olives. Roughly chop the rocket.

Combine the tomatoes with the garlic salt, chilli and capers. Season generously, add the olives and put aside for 30 minutes.

Cook the penne in a large pan of boiling, salted filtered water until *al dente*. Drain, and then stir the pasta into the tomatoes. Add the rocket, and finish with some good olive oil.

My Salad

I haven't specified quantities here. The ingredients are just an idea of what you can put together in a salad, which is so good for you and the family. This combination happens to be my favourite.

For as many or as few as you want

oak leaf, frisée and baby gem lettuces
radishes, trimmed
mung bean sprouts (see page 197)
sesame seeds, toasted
pumpkin seeds, toasted
shelled unsalted peanuts
Medjool dates, stoned and cut into gondolas
unsalted cashew nuts, toasted

To finish
nori sheets
organic, reputably sourced tofu (English is now good), cut into 1cm cubes
alfalfa sprouts (see page 197)
tahini dressing (see page 271)
extra virgin olive oil
light Japanese organic soy sauce

Wash the lettuce leaves and radishes well. Roll your nori sheets up like parchment paper, and cut with scissors, and you will end up with long crisp strips. They are so good for you.

Put everything in a bowl except the nori, tofu, and alfalfa. Pour in the tahini dressing, and toss. Sprinkle over the tofu cubes, then the nori, then finish off with the alfalfa. I quite like the alfalfa undressed, but for a touch of further richness, add a little olive oil and soy sauce.

Guinea Fowl Stuffed with Mascarpone & Sage, with Braised Young Carrot & Artichoke Salad

This recipe is perhaps a bit fancier than other recipes in the book — my French influences revealing themselves? — but it's well worth trying, as the flavours are fantastic.

For 6

3 guinea fowl
10 tbsp mascarpone cheese
finely grated zest and juice of 1 lemon
sea salt and freshly ground black pepper
6 slices prosciutto
24 sage leaves

Braised Young Carrot and Artichoke Salad
1kg young carrots, trimmed
800g young artichoke hearts (see page 86)
a handful of parsley stalks
light olive oil
3 garlic cloves, peeled and chopped
4 tbsp chopped fennel herb
2 tbsp chopped thyme
500ml vegetable stock, or to cover (see page 267), warm
extra virgin olive oil

For the salad, clean the carrots and slice them on the horizontal. Put the artichoke hearts in parsley stalk water (see page 86) to prevent them discolouring. Slice the artichoke hearts quite thinly just before cooking. Heat enough light olive oil to cover the base of a large thick-bottomed pan, and add the garlic. Just as the garlic starts to colour, add the carrots and stir for 1 minute. Add the artichokes, half the herbs and the vegetable stock. Cover with the lid and cook for 30 minutes or until soft to the touch. Take off the lid and cook for another 15 minutes to allow the liquid to evaporate. Finish with the remaining herbs and drizzle over some extra virgin olive oil. Check the seasoning.

Meanwhile, for the guinea fowl, fillet each bird, cutting the breasts carefully off the carcass. You should now have six breasts with thighs still connected. Take the bones out of the thighs as well. Ask your butcher to do this if you're not confident.

Season half the mascarpone with half the lemon zest, a little lemon juice, and salt and pepper. Place the slices of prosciutto on a flat surface, and spoon the mascarpone mix on to the widest part of the prosciutto slices. Roll each into a thumb-sized shaped parcel. With the breasts of the guinea fowl skin-side down, slide your thumb between the breast and skin to create a cavity. Put a sage leaf in this, and a prosciutto parcel. Cover over with the breast meat. Repeat with all the breasts.

In a little light olive oil, pan-fry the guinea fowl, skin-side down, over a medium heat for at least 12 minutes, before turning over and cooking for another 8 minutes. Add the remaining sage leaves to the pan now, and when the guinea fowl are cooked, put the rest of the mascarpone into the pan with the rest of the lemon zest and juice. Wait for the mascarpone to melt — stir a little — before serving.

Arrange the guinea fowl on individual serving plates, and drizzle with the pan juices. Serve with the salad.

Grilled Peaches with Rice Pudding

I make a mean rice pudding, and this one, baked in the oven rather than cooked on the hob, goes amazingly well with grilled peaches. For vanilla sugar, simply store a vanilla pod in a jar of caster sugar.

For 4

3 ripe peaches, briefly washed
50g vanilla sugar
100ml Amaretto (almond liqueur)
4 amaretti biscuits

Baked Rice Pudding
250g arborio risotto rice (or short grain pudding rice)
1.8 litres milk
1 vanilla pod, halved lengthways
about 50g caster sugar
2 medium egg yolks

Preheat the oven to 170–180°C/Fan 150-160°C/Gas 3–4.

Make the rice pudding. Mix the rice and milk in a large, deep, ovenproof baking dish. Scrape the vanilla seeds into the dish, and add the pods as well. Stir through, then bake in the preheated oven for about 2½ hours. Stir every 15 minutes or so.

Preheat the grill. Put the halved (stoned) peaches, rounded-side down, in a heatproof dish, sprinkle with the vanilla sugar, and grill for a few minutes, just to caramelise the tops. Keep the grill on.

Remove the rice dish from the oven, and add sugar to taste, along with the egg yolks. Stir together well. Arrange the halved peaches on top, again rounded-side down, and sprinkle with the Amaretto. Put back under the grill to cook the peaches a little more, about 5 minutes. Scoop out a peach half per portion with some rice, then crumble an amaretti biscuit on top of each. Serve immediately.

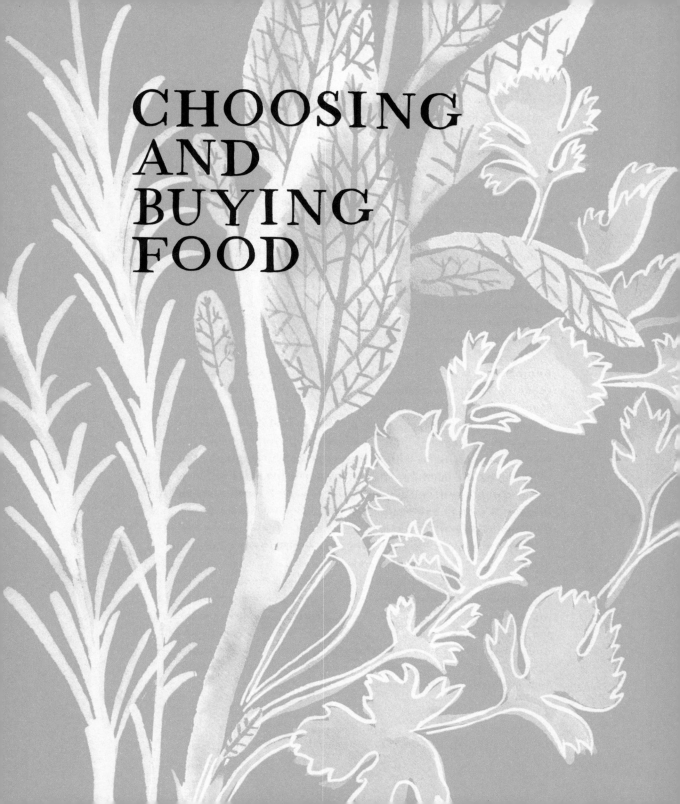

CHOOSING
AND
BUYING
FOOD

The perfect scenario for me for choosing and buying food ethically would run something like this. In the mornings the milkman would deliver me re-usable bottles of organic milk and apple juice (in an electric, rechargeable float). Once a week I would have an organic box of seasonal vegetables and fruit delivered (some companies also offer organic eggs and chocolate, and Fairtrade coffee). I would buy the little protein I need – meat, poultry, eggs and cheese – at good local shops, and for those special seasonal items I couldn't find easily elsewhere, I would go to my local farmers' market once a week. For anything else – food basics or household stuff – I would go online (and that too would probably be delivered by electric van). You can already see where I am coming from: my food shopping is basically seasonal, fresh, local and organic, it doesn't take up too much of my time, it doesn't involve me getting in my car (on the whole), I don't rely on only one source of supply, and it means very little packaging.

Another vital factor in that ethical food choosing and buying scenario is good, old-fashioned trust. It's the most integral issue in the restaurant industry, and is no less important to the domestic shopper. As a restaurateur, I have to trust my suppliers (and I do, I've worked with many of them for years), otherwise how would I know whether those carrots were organic or not? As soon as people come into the restaurant, they are putting themselves in my hands, trusting that I will be serving fresh, organic, Fairtrade food, as I claim to do. Whenever people come into your home, in a sense they too are putting their faith in you, trusting that you will serve them good, fresh, organic food – and that you will dispose of any waste in an ethical, responsible way.

WHAT TO CHOOSE

Choosing and buying good food is actually about common sense (as well as trust). If nothing else, I hope that this book will empower you to think about what you are buying before you part with your money.

I was going to have individual headings for 'fresh', 'local' and 'seasonal' foods, but the concepts are all too intimately related to separate out. If those foods are also organic, so much the better. I try to find Fairtrade products — which are increasingly available in good supermarkets — and I always choose foods that I like the look of, and that I think will do me and my family good.

Fresh, Local & Seasonal

'Fresh' so far as food is concerned is the key word, and I don't think anything else sums up so succinctly how you should be buying. It has got to be fresh: the fresher it is, the better it will taste, and the better it will be for you in a health sense. A fresh fruit or vegetable will be packed full of nutrients — and these would have diminished considerably if the plant had not been grown locally (perhaps driven from the other side of the country) or was not seasonal (perhaps flown from the other side of the world).

There are other advantages to fresh, local and seasonal produce. A vegetable or fruit will be cheaper when at the height of its season. I've actually seen tables outside houses in the country labelled 'Take me', when they have obviously had a glut of apples or plums! If you're buying fresh, locally grown and seasonal food, not only has the product not travelled far, so avoiding food miles (the environment-damaging distance usually involved in producing and distributing food), but you probably won't ever need to get in your own car. Altogether this means fewer emissions from delivery vehicles and yourself, less traffic on the roads and, if you walk, you get some exercise as well.

Buying locally can also help the local economy, perhaps keeping the wolf from the door of the farmer up the road (they have a difficult time these days), perhaps enabling a grower to carry on producing a rare variety of local apple or plum. By buying in the local community, you also might be helping preserve a job. An amount of money spent locally is worth more than double that to the local economy (it goes to local suppliers and employees). If that same amount of money were spent in a supermarket, it would be worth much less to the local economy, because the profits go elsewhere than locally (to pay distant suppliers and transport costs, or shareholders).

Fresh, local and seasonal is not so easy when you are buying meat and fish protein. However, unless the protein has been preserved in some way, who would want to buy meat or fish that was not fresh? Meat of course needs to mature a bit to be at its best, so fresh does not mean killed that day. But meat that has perhaps been reared locally, so you know where it comes from, how it has been reared (free-range preferably), what it has been fed on, and that it hasn't had to travel too far to an abattoir, would be the best (this is where organic comes in, see below). Buying meat locally means that you can probably get to know your butcher, who should know the provenance of all meat, and be able to tell you.

Fish is trickier ethically (see pages 50–53). The freshest fish is that which has just been pulled out of the water, but you're unlikely to experience this often unless you live by the sea. (Although many sea fish are actually frozen as soon as they come on board, which can be nearly as good.) Again, as with your butcher, get to know your fishmonger, and learn to trust him. It's worth it as fish is potentially one of the healthiest foods on the planet. However, as mentioned already, many pollutants of the sea can build up in fish tissue, and this can cause problems. Ask your fishmonger how and where the fish were caught. If they were from local day boats, there would be no fish miles involved; if they were line caught, there would be no net damage; if scallops were hand-dived, there would be no seabed dredging. Look for the Marine Stewardship Council (MSC) label, which will reassure you that the fish come from sustainable, well-managed fisheries.

QUALITY OVER QUANTITY

Good fish and good meat are expensive, and they have the right to be. They have been cared for and nurtured throughout their lives, and some beef cattle take over two years to mature: that's a lot of love and attention, and that costs money.

On the contrary, many chickens, veal calves and pigs are intensively reared in the most terrible conditions in order to create cheap meat. Ask yourself the question: are we demanding cheap meat, thereby forcing cheap farming practices (battery chicken rearing, accelerated growth in pigs)? Or are the farmers choosing to create cheap meat, and as a result we are buying it? In either case, it has to stop, judging by the diseases and terrible maladies that

are gripping our meat-producing industry these days: BSE, foot and mouth, blue tongue and avian flu are just a few of the more significant examples.

I have checked my diet, and come to the realisation that vegetables need to play a large part in my consumption. Meat, very high-quality meat – which I can only afford every ten or twelve days – I will eat with my family, who are the ones that I care about the most. I wouldn't want my son and daughter to be consuming some of the chemicals that are being put into those intensively farmed animals. We all need to lower our intake of low-quality meat right now.

Organic

I could go on about the benefits of buying fresh, local and seasonal, but if the product has been sprayed with pesticides, then it may be fresh, but it isn't as good for you as something that hasn't been sprayed. And this is where organic becomes the issue (see page 62). If something has been grown organically, with the Soil Association mark of approval (in the UK), you can be reassured that it's not going to do you any harm.

However, organic food tends to be a little more expensive to buy than non-organic, primarily because it takes longer to produce without chemical aid. (Perhaps this will change as consumption of organic food rises, as surely it must.) Another criticism is that organic vegetables and fruit go off more quickly, for presumably the same reasons. The principles need a bit of looking at too. Fruits or vegetables from abroad may be labelled organic, but are practices there as stringent as those specified by the Soil Association — and what about those food miles? The organic movement has only just (late 2007) addressed the problem of foods travelling long distances: the Soil Association recently announced that foods would not be allowed to be sold as organic if they were air-freighted, unless they were Fairtrade (a small step in the right direction, perhaps). And I would always choose to buy the non-organic carrot picked that morning from a local allotment, in preference to an organic carrot that might have travelled 500 miles before it reached me. Freshness is more important.

'Free-range' is debatable too — does this mean one metre or three metres square in which an animal might roam? And I don't much like the idea of organics being involved in big business. Supermarkets are now offering sections of organic fruit and vegetables, which is wonderful (unless from South America), but it alarms me somewhat that supermarket buying pressure could be applied to organic producers — high yield, perfect condition (why?) and cheap prices — as it already has been to conventional farmers. Organic producers would have to compromise their principles quite considerably to accede to this sort of pressure: organic vegetables just don't conform to anyone's ideas of perfect looks, and organic animals just do take longer and cost more to produce.

I believe that we should all now be eating sustainable, ethical, organic food (maybe not all at the same time). I certainly believe that it is better for us, although current scientific research can't prove that plants grown organically are nutritionally superior. Organically-reared animals, however, because they are mainly grass fed, tend to have less saturated fat, which is definitely of benefit to us as consumers.

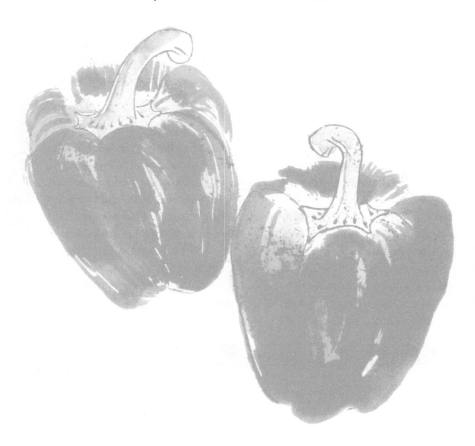

GENETIC MODIFICATION

The 'modification' of plants is nothing new. We have been doing it for centuries: grafting one type of citrus on to another, and changing the colour and shape of vegetables (the original wild carrot was white and spindly, and appeared as both red and black before it finally achieved its day-glo orange in the seventeenth century). But genetic modification, particularly of food, is something different.

Genetic modification (GM) is the transference of genes from one organism into another, sometimes totally unrelated: the most famous (apocryphal) story concerns transferring flounder genes into a tomato to make it frost-resistant! The multinational agrochemical companies who control the GM market claim GM is for mankind's benefit – to make crops grow better, to make them pest resistant, to make them more nutritious – but a principal motive is profit. It is possible that these huge companies could patent the seeds and processes they are marketing, and this might ultimately lead them to having control over everything we eat. In Third World countries, these GM seeds are being introduced because of drought and pestilence, but the seed has only got one year's life: the plant will not set seed for the following year. Therefore the farmer is at the mercy of the seed provider, and this could have terrible consequences for sustainable agriculture in the Third World.

Ecologically there are fears that growing GM crops might mean a return to the monocultures of intensive farming (if potentially without the chemicals), and escapes from GM crop fields could threaten indigenous plants and could certainly contaminate organic crops. Healthwise, no one seems to know what effect eating GM foods might have on us, so why on earth would we want them?

Fairtrade

The Fairtrade Foundation, set up in 1994, has many links with organics, but aims more towards good working conditions for producers of food, mainly in the Third World. Workers' safety is assured, there is no forced child labour, and fair wages and prices are paid. Many Fairtrade foods are still produced using chemicals, but there is a continuing movement towards organics, sustainability and protection of the environment. Food miles is an issue, obviously, but with something like bananas — which my family couldn't do without — at least I know that Fairtrade banana growers don't have to suffer financially if and when there are supermarket banana price wars in the UK. Fairtrade 'guarantees a better deal for Third World producers', and I think fair trade must be much more ethical than free trade or aid.

What Your Body Needs

I'm probably being a bit fanciful now, but I want to try and re-introduce a natural skill that has been lost. We know now that our bodies need vitamins, minerals, protein, carbohydrates and fibre. (I'm no nutritionist, so I'm not going to be specific.) But at one time we instinctively knew what our bodies needed. The human body was designed to know how to feed itself: it would have been a matter of trial and error at first for primitive man but, over millennia, the senses of sight, smell and taste would have identified, memorised and passed on the knowledge of foods that were good. And these foods would have been, by necessity, fresh, local, seasonal and organic. Early man had no choice.

When we stopped growing food for ourselves, perhaps two generations ago, was probably when we lost the ability to immediately identify the foods we needed. But that ability should still be there, and you only have to recognise it and allow it to resurface again. (Interestingly, I think children still naturally know what they need, perhaps we lose it as we age.) For instance, the way that I choose foods is based on where I go to shop, and I know there is no way my body is going to get the sustenance it needs from my local corner store. But if I go to the supermarket or farmers' market, where fresh and seasonal produce, preferably organic, is on display, I will find something I want to eat, and something my body needs. Fresh seasonal foods just look better: plump, juicy, firm to the touch, colourful, appealing and nutritious. (I'd like to experiment and take someone vegetable shopping with me who had no knowledge of food at all: I'd bet money that they would instinctively choose the freshest.) I think it works subconsciously sometimes, even with me. One day last autumn, I noticed some sunflowers in my son's school garden; that evening I served my roast pumpkin at the restaurant topped with toasted sunflower seeds. A perfect seasonal match, but not one I had written on the menu at the beginning of the week!

This, roughly speaking, is how I think, and it would be great if this book could empower people to think this way too. Right now is the ideal time to re-tune flagging senses, as we've never had so many good foods to choose from. And, a further benefit, honing your senses in this way actually forces you to look at foods that aren't packaged — not only are you choosing fresh and good foods, you are also instantly negating the need for packaging. Perfect...

WHERE AND HOW TO BUY

Where you buy depends to a great extent on where you live. If you are a city dweller, you won't have access on a regular basis to farm shops, but what you will have are local shops, supermarkets and, possibly, a weekly farmers' market. How you buy depends on the shopping time you have available: I have very little, so I order organic vegetable boxes weekly, and access other things online for home delivery. How you buy depends also on trust and common sense, as already outlined, as well as that gut feeling about what you are looking at — and, of course, on how much you have to spend.

Local Shops & Markets

This was once the way we all shopped and, ethically, it would still be the best, saving food miles, contributing to the local economy, offering fresh, seasonal food. But with the advent of supermarkets, some forty to fifty years ago, local shops began disappearing, and they still are, unable to afford high rents, and unable to compete with the supermarkets' cheap prices. Red and yellow lines in town centres didn't help either, making parking a problem for potential shoppers.

I would always choose to buy my limited amount of organic meat from my local butcher, fish from my trusted local fishmonger and, if I didn't get my vegetables and fruit from boxes, I would buy those locally as well. My nearest local shop in North London is actually Turkish, and the prices there can compete with if not beat those at the supermarket: bunches of squeakily fresh parsley for under £1, and watermelons like Zeppelins for £2. However, this has all been imported (probably by road rather than air), and if not the acme of ecological buying, it is still pretty good — and reveals how little the produce must be worth at source if the retailer is still making his margins here.

Interestingly, because traders were forced out of shops, many took to selling their wares from stalls on the streets, and we seem to be experiencing an upturn in the UK in that sort of market economy and street markets in general. (And this at a time when, on the Continent, they seem to be turning more to mass-market buying.) I think local food stalls and markets are great, and I like the idea of wandering down on foot, (ethical) shopping bags at the ready, and seeing what's on offer. Fish and meat, other than preserved, I would be wary of, but you can occasionally find some good produce.

Farmers' Markets

The essence of 'market' to me is fresh produce that comes from farmers, but, oddly, the concept of farmers' markets as we know them now was only introduced to the UK in 1997. The basic idea is that local producers/farmers sell direct to consumers: the produce must have been locally grown, caught or reared (or baked/preserved in the case of secondary produce) by the stallholder, and must be sold by the stallholder. Local usually means within 30–40 miles of the market, but in some cases, London for instance, the radius can stretch up to 100 miles. The produce is not necessarily organic.

Farmers' markets are fantastic, with an endless and colourful array of fresh seasonal fruit and vegetables. I visited Islington farmers' market in September, one of the best months of the year for food. There were wonderful potatoes, tomatoes, fresh borlotti beans, radishes, squashes (lots of patty pans), huge white courgettes, peppers (some of them purple), Swiss and ruby chard, and a sea of strawberries, blackberries and apples. Some stalls sold meat, bacon, sausages and black pudding (although one of the producers was from Dorset!), organic eggs, butter and yoghurt. Aron and I drank some fresh juices, tasted some cubes of English cheese, and we could have bought some char-grilled lamb or beef burgers. I was surprised at how many 'ready' meals there were – fishcakes, fish pies, dressed crabs on one stall, meat pies – but I was also exhilarated to see so much evidence of British artisan production: goat's cheeses and brilliant jams, piccalillis and chutneys. Altogether Aron and I had a good time, looking, touching, tasting and buying.

However, that good time came at a price, because farmers' markets seem to be giving themselves a rather expensive image. I went home with a limited amount of food – admittedly very good food – but I had spent far more money than I intended, and still had all the basics to buy. Why, I need to ask of those farmer and growers, is the produce so expensive when it is at the height of its season, when it should be at its cheapest? Despite being impressed, I left with an empty wallet, and a recognition that this high cost is perhaps why supermarkets tick so many boxes in people's minds when shopping.

One of the greatest benefits of a farmers' market is that there is little packaging other than a brown paper or thin plastic bag. And I can't think of a better way of stimulating a child's interest in food: a market is so colourful, so busy, so social – and there are plenty of opportunities for tasting something for free, which children (and many adults) relish.

Farm Shops & Pick-your-own

I am very much in favour of buying from farm shops, as this will directly support the farmer. Farm shops are the farmers' markets of the countryside, in a sense. They can literally be on a farm, or in a separate roadside building, sometimes individually run, sometimes cooperatively, and the produce will be a little cheaper than at farmers' markets because there is no travelling involved. The produce is fresh, good quality, seasonal, often organic and very local: you might see it growing in adjacent fields or under (unheated) poly tunnels. I dropped into a farm shop in Somerset one day to buy some cured ham: the ham, boiled in local cider, had literally travelled 500 yards from the field where pigs had gorged on windfall apples. I also bought some Cheddar cheese and some pickled onions made by a neighbour. I love that sort of shopping, and if you're local, it makes ecological sense.

Pick-your-own businesses represent buying directly from the grower as well, and you couldn't find anything more seasonal. It's mainly soft fruits such as strawberries and blackberries: I haven't heard of PYO onions or potatoes, which would be far too laborious for the majority of us. Kids love picking their own, and it's a great way of giving them an awareness of where food comes from and how it grows. We all went to a kid's birthday party last summer, which was held at a strawberry PYO farm. The children ran around scoffing all they picked, and had a great time — but came away feeling a bit sick...

Arthur's Notes

Farmers' markets are, for me, a great place to buy a niche product, something you wouldn't find elsewhere, the very special seasonal vegetable not stocked in the supermarket or local shop (or grown in your own garden).

For the more frugal of us, perhaps coming at the end of the market day would be the best idea: stallholders might be willing, rather than drag produce back home again, to part with what they have left at a knockdown price.

I was irritated by fresh carrots sold with yards of greenery on them. Retaining this may keep the carrots fresh, but what was I to do with it, sother than compost it? It seemed such a waste and I had to cart it home.

But I was delighted by one example of much more ecological thinking: one stallholder had a box of vegetable trimmings that he was offering as rabbit food (he should have got together with the carrot man).

Supermarkets

I'm not at all anti-supermarkets, I just think that, as consumers, we have to be very careful when shopping in them. It is only in supermarkets that you can begin to lose sight of the fresh, local and seasonal mantra. Supermarkets have so much stuff on display, at all times of the year, that unless you are very well informed, you could make some unintelligent choices. The produce will look fresh, but it may have come from the other side of the world. Those peas may be labelled 'English', but they could have been grown in Somerset, shipped to a holding depot in Newcastle, then transported for sale in London. Or they could be from Spain. I'm not against buying produce from Europe, but it's the food miles I worry about, and none of this comes under the heading of 'local'. There will always be seasonal produce, but you will have to look for it, and read the labels carefully. Supermarkets now have organic sections, which I applaud in some ways – they are recognising what their customers want – but I also regret in others. Organics and the supermarket ethos just do not go together: they want perfection and shelf life, which don't exist in organics. I would honestly prefer to buy sustainably or ethically, locally produced food than supermarket organic food.

Ethically, supermarkets make me frown. They are vast organisations, they are taking over our food buying and food choices, and have already seen off many of the local shops I would prefer to patronise, as well as the milkman, who in my view represented the most obviously ethical food delivery system. Supermarket supply involves a lot of travelling, both by the product, and by us, going by car for the weekly shop, so this mode of buying involves a lot of carbon emissions. Supermarkets are the villain of the piece as far as packaging is concerned: wrapping cherry tomatoes in hard plastic cartons, and encasing peaches in polystyrene (and ready meals by the yard in foil, cellophane and cardboard). They assume we want perfect produce, that we cannot handle an apple with a blemish, a tomato that is lop-sided, or a cabbage with a few caterpillar-eaten, outside leaves (which nobody eats anyway). In the pursuit of perfection and shelf life, they pressure-hose the mud (and flavour) off potatoes, fill bags of chlorine-washed salad leaves with modified gas (you could buy a whole lettuce for half the cost), and sell us a single variety of strawberry, a fairly tasteless one, because it stores and travels well.

Supermarkets are extremely wasteful in what they choose to buy, wrap and sell. A senior member of the Soil Association used to be an organic farmer, and once supplied organic carrots to an unnamed supermarket. Because organic produce diminishes in quality quite rapidly, by the time the original quantity of carrots had reached the holding depot halfway across Britain, there had been a 60 per cent deterioration. Of the 40 per cent accepted by the supermarket, a quarter was discarded because it didn't look good enough. So from the original 100 per cent, only 30 per cent made it to the supermarket shelves; if a third of that didn't sell, then only 20 per cent, a fifth, of the carrots from those carefully tended organic fields, would actually have been benefiting consumers. That's madness.

Furthermore, if they are only taking 40 per cent, the supermarket will probably only pay for 40 per cent, thereby possibly forcing the supplier, organic or not, to accept a price at less than cost. No wonder many farmers and growers are going out of business. But what horrifies me most is that a proportion of those discarded vegetables will go to landfill sites, where they will help to create methane, contributing to global warming rather than much-needed global feeding. Even organic supermarkets, I'm afraid, are guilty of a number of similar sins, particularly in the buying from abroad and packaging areas, and they are very much more expensive.

I recognise that supermarkets are trying to please their customers, but we have to remember that we as consumers have the power. As I say again and again, they should not be allowed to dictate to us, we have to tell them what we want; it's demand and supply rather than the reverse. We are the ones spending the money after all.

Online Shopping

Or perhaps the end is in sight for conventional supermarkets? Supermarkets have slowly been recognising that the consumer has options, which is why many of them are now offering online services. I think this is probably where the ethical future of food shopping lies, and could be the beginning of supermarkets that don't actually exist other than on the web. There will be giant warehouses only, perhaps powered by water or wind, literally just holding zones waiting to receive orders by e-mail, and from which electric or LPG vans will deliver direct to your home. This would immediately cut down on the needless and wasteful travelling of products across the country, would obviate the use of shoppers' cars (one van could deliver to twenty households, saving nineteen journeys), and cut down on quite a lot of packaging too. Vegetables'R'Us perhaps, and it seems to me that such a service — delivering food to your door — may not be too different from that offered by the good old-fashioned milkman...

You would have to be computer literate, of course. But it is very easy, you are guided along the way by the websites, and you are a finger's click away from fresh produce. You click on to the site, scroll down the lists of produce, which is all photographed, and the foods often have dietary information attached. I went online to Waitrose Ocado after I returned from the farmers' market, and went straight to the organic section. I clicked on what I wanted, and then I was reminded about what I bought last time. Did I not need butter this week? (I'd bought it at the farmers' market.) It even reminded me to buy chocolate, which is my weakness...

The chief advantage of online shopping is convenience. You do it all in the comfort of your own home, or when you are at work (don't let the boss see you), and you can do it at any time of day or night. They will deliver whenever you want, often working until late in the evening, which is great for those who work all day or who work shifts, like me. They will also deliver all those bulky household goods that are usually very awkward to carry home (loo paper for instance). Online shopping saves me time.

However, there are disadvantages. It's quite boring sitting in front of a computer screen, and you lose out completely on the instinctive reaction to foodstuffs. You can't touch, smell or see what you are buying, and have to trust that some faceless employee will choose well for you. And sometimes it goes wrong, as it did with me — my card wouldn't go through, I had to fill in endless details, and I got even more bored...

WILD FOOD

Wild foods tend to be romantic to me – grouse, wood pigeon, white truffles and scallops. They all seem to hold a potency that is not so prevalent in farmed food: a potency in the richness and depth of flavour, the character and texture. I buy all my wild foods from trusted sources (game dealer, fisherman and forager). As wild food is rare and rather expensive, I treat myself every now and again, rather than live off it. But wild foods tend to be the most seasonal foods and you can really identify where you are in the yearly cycle by what is available from the wild.

Box Schemes

Box schemes are thought to be fairly new, but I remember my family having an organic box delivered every Wednesday when I was little — twenty-five years ago. It sat in the hall, big, black and full of mysterious things: kohlrabi that looked as if it had come from Venus, mud and spiders galore. It was like a wilderness being delivered to Muswell Hill, and I was too frightened to go near it!

Nowadays organic and non-organic boxes of fruit and vegetables (and sometimes other goods) can be delivered direct from the farmer or farm shop or from a specialist middleman. It's rather like the farmers' market coming to you, instead of the reverse. The produce should be fresh (picked the day before), local and seasonal, but sometimes, when fresh is scarce in late winter, early spring, boxes can include imported, which I'm not too keen on. You can order by telephone, of course, or online, and you can have a standing weekly, fortnightly or monthly order. And some of them offer recipes...

It's convenient again, saves you time and travelling (and emissions), but once more you don't know what's going to be in the box, and in the winter, you can get very tired of swede and turnip, however fresh they are... Delivery times are not usually so flexible as the supermarket online deliveries, so a box might be delivered when you are not there. A box containing two chickens once sat on my doorstep for hours, after which those chickens had to be thrown out. The company involved lost my trust and my trade. However, in general terms box schemes are great, primarily because you are empowering people to deliver you products that they are growing. And the boxes are re-usable...

Barter

Bartering is swapping something for something else, whether a product or a skill, and this is ideally how I should like to do business. It's green, it's sustainable, it's sociable and it's ethical. On an informal basis, bartering, as a means of 'buying' food, is alive and well, particularly in the British countryside. For instance, a family I know have eighty bantam chickens that lay plenty of eggs. Some of those eggs are swapped for cheese from one neighbour, for some cider vinegar or jam from another. Growers on city allotments probably do quite a bit of bartering too: 'I'll give you some of my excess runners for some of your beetroots.' Skills have a value as well, and are able to be bartered. If I were a thatcher, say,

I could thatch the local farmhouse and perhaps get three pigs in return. I'd give one pig to the local butcher in return for his butchering and jointing the three, and so on.

On a more formal basis, there are several organised systems of barter. 'Community currencies' is the generic term for these schemes, which utilise alternative types of money. Local Exchange Trading Schemes (LETS) are local, community-based mutual aid networks: people earn LETS credits by providing a service, and can then spend the credits on whatever is offered by others on the scheme (transport, food, home repairs, babysitting). Many LETS schemes are backed by local councils who see the potential for local economic renewal and community building. LETS can also be green, and contribute to environmental sustainability: they encourage local food suppliers, therefore reducing food miles, they promote sharing (such as lifts in cars), and they recycle, as members 'buy' each other's unwanted goods.

Time banks are a system of barter as well, more of skill and time than goods: people build up credits by being rewarded for unpaid work in the community. Time banks can be green too, promoting recycling. A Dutch initiative, the NU-card, is designed to promote environmentally friendly consumer behaviour: people are rewarded when they separate their waste for recycling, use public transport, or buy locally, recycled or Fairtrade.

These community currencies are taking the basic idea of 'barter' way beyond a simple exchange of eggs for cheese, but they are wonderful. It seems to me that everyone can benefit from something like this: any one of these schemes would foster community spirit, and give individuals and groups a real sense of self-worth and engagement, and in so doing would benefit society as a whole, and the environment too. The bad news is that in Britain the government has deemed that LETS and time-bank earnings are treated like cash income for those who are on social security benefits, and reduce those pay-outs accordingly. And these are the people who would most benefit from such schemes...

AUTUMN

*An overabundance of fruit and
vegetables, all of which have
soaked up the sun
of summer...*

The autumn equinox is celebrated when, once again in the yearly cycle, day and night are of equal length, usually around the 21st September. Hereafter the days get shorter, the nights longer, and the weather becomes gradually colder. Nature starts to prepare for hibernation: the leaves on the trees change colour and fall, and all plant activity slows down.

But you wouldn't think there was any slowing down, judging by the produce available in September. This is the month of harvest across the whole of the northern hemisphere, and it is a month of plenty: in fact we want for very little right through from July to October. This last September, I harvested huge marrows, great squashes and courgettes, tomatoes to die for, curly parsley, nasturtium leaves, gold, red and yellow Swiss chard, the final swansong of the basil and fabulous yellow beans. I felt like royalty walking through those beans, hanging down from their vines like wind-chimes. The lush green pastures have been eaten all summer long by cattle and sheep, and the autumn meat is delicious – it is a good time to try some mutton. September is quite decadent but not as much as October...

October is one of my favourite months. I love Hallowe'en, I love going on my yearly walk with my father – just us and the dogs, sleeping rough, and feeling the true change in the seasons – and I love all the foods that are available. In fact I think of October as the BIG food month. What we have now are fruits and vegetables that have been maturing all summer, that have had loads of sun, so they are ripe and sweet, but with a unique autumn richness and intensity. This is a good time for shellfish as well, and there are delicious crabs, lobsters, oysters and scallops. Wines are being made now because of the grape harvest, as are olive oils all over the Mediterranean. Flours are being ground from the summer's harvest of wheat, as is polenta from corn, some ground fine, some with the coarser texture that I prefer.

The weather in October can be great, but on the whole it is getting damper, moister, foggier. It's not freezing cold yet, and the warmish days and damp nights create the ideal conditions and temperatures for one of the most exciting foodstuffs in the world – wild mushrooms!

The clocks go back around the end of October, and the bright colourful produce of earlier in the autumn begins to change as we move into November. But there are some wonderful tastes to be enjoyed: the bright orange pumpkins of September are still around, and so are the wild mushrooms of October, along with rainbow-coloured chards, red cabbages so dark they are almost blue, and the last of the autumn fruits. Root vegetables are sweet and prolific, and onions, potatoes and leeks will all help flavour and bulk up the meat and game stews and casseroles our bodies need right now. I may start fattening myself up for winter in October, but I carry on through November too...

Arthur's Autumn Growing Tips

October is all about apples. Even a small balcony could have one of the 'super column' fruit trees on it. At Acorn House, we grow the newest cutting-edge apple and pear varieties in containers, fan-trained against the walls – and I've got a little fanned fig for fun.

The apples might be ready now. To find out whether they are ready to pick, hold an individual fruit in your hand and lift gently. If it comes away, it is obviously ready; if it remains attached, it needs a little longer. Store apples, wrapped in paper, in a tray in a cool place to maximise their storage life.

I'm allowing all my courgette and pumpkin plants to rot back into the soil. I wasn't tempted to haul them out when they started to die, as they make good mulching and add nutrients to the soil.

October might be the best month in which to think about starting a compost heap, as there is so much material around to get you started. If you look after it, it will be ready in six months, just when you are doing your spring planting! Be careful with autumn leaves, though, as they might take a little longer, up to 18 months: perhaps put those into a separate heap, or in black bin-liners with a few holes punched in them.

I've waited nine months to plant my apple and pear trees, because now is the time to do it (not spring or summer).

Lay down a poly tunnel, which is a bit of plastic stretched over a hoop. You could even do this over the top of a window-box to protect it throught the winter. You'd be surprised how much protection they give.

What I buy in September

Vegetables
Artichokes (globe), aubergine, beans (borlotti, broad, French, runner), beetroot, broccoli (calabrese), cabbages (red, Savoy), cardoons, carrots, cauliflower, celery, chard, chicory, courgettes, cucumber, endive, fennel herb, Florence fennel, garlic, horseradish, kale, kohlrabi, lamb's lettuce, leeks, lettuce, marrows, onions, pak-choi, parsnips, peas, potatoes, pumpkins and squashes, radishes, rocket, salsify, sorrel, spinach, sweetcorn, Swiss chard, turnips, watercress

Fruit
Apples, blackberries, blackcurrants, blueberries, damsons, elderberries, figs, greengages, loganberries, melons, mulberries, peaches and nectarines, pears, peppers and chillies, plums, raspberries, strawberries, tomatoes, whitecurrants, wild strawberries, worcesterberries

Fish
Black bream, crayfish, eels, haddock, herrings, mackerel, river trout, skate, sprats, wild salmon

Shellfish
Crab (brown, hen, spider), cuttlefish, lobster, mussels, oysters (native), prawns, scallops (hand-dived only), squid

Game
Grouse, mallard, partridge, rabbit, wood pigeon

Flowers
Lavender

Fungi
Ceps (porcini), chicken of the wood, field mushrooms, giant puffballs, girolles, horse mushrooms, oyster mushrooms, parasol mushrooms, summer truffles

Nuts
Cobnuts, hazelnuts

How I eat in September

The summer has delivered so much goodness. In fact, there are so many vegetables that it's literally picking, boiling and dressing (and preserving – I had to do a lot of this with my glut of beans). The autumn fruit are starting too – apples, pears, plums, damsons, sloes and figs (see Box, page 149). And I just revel in the blackberries, for September is when Aron and I go blackberrying, and we come back with purple faces and hands, with fewer fruit than we have eaten. Supermarkets should be awash with wonderful produce from the UK in September, and if they're not, I ask why not.

Because my squashes were so good this year, I've chosen to write about them – they have so many flavours, are so versatile, and so good for us (lots of Vitamin A). I also couldn't resist a brief word about our own English apples, so freshly and crisply welcome at this time of year, and plums.

Autumn squashes, including marrows, acorn squash and spaghetti squash, are fully ripe in September and October, having revelled in the sun all summer long. Their thin soft skin provides little protection, though, and they should be eaten within a couple of months. Winter squashes, with their tough waxy skin – among them butternuts, hubbards and kabochas – and pumpkins (there is no clear botanical distinction), which can also be found now, can be stored for up to a year.

Next month, when you are carving out your Halloween pumpkin jack-o-lantern (which used to be made from turnips, very much harder to carve), keep the flesh and seeds. Use the flesh as described below, and wash, dry and bake the seeds. I put them in my salads. Waste not, want not.

To cook your pumpkin or squash, boil and mash with freshly grated nutmeg and grated cheese. Or you could mix this with a little ricotta, season, and use as a ravioli stuffing. Roast is best though, as gondolas or wedges sweeten and caramelise on the edges. Steam in large chunks, and serve sprinkled with garlic, extra virgin olive oil and some chilli flakes.

Roast pumpkin or squash can also be used as the basis for a pumpkin soup. Use a soffrito (see page 142), perhaps adding about 6 anchovies, which add a depth of flavour (not for vegetarians, though). Use some potatoes as well, and a good vegetable stock. I occasionally add some farro grains, and they contribute a nutty texture and flavour. Finish with a little double cream, crème fraîche or soured cream (if your guests like dairy, I always ask), and perhaps a garnish made from a little crostini with grated Gruyère on top. Sometimes I completely cover the bowl of soup with a piece of toasted cheese the same size, like a lid.

You could even make a pumpkin or squash salad, to serve at room temperature, for salads don't have to be cold. Mix roasted pieces of pumpkin with leaves (autumn lettuces, rocket, dandelion, purple basil) and pomegranate seeds, some roasted pumpkin seeds, and a few chunks of cheese...

Apples are starting to come through this month, as well as the other characteristically British autumnal fruit such as pears, plums, damsons, sloes and quinces. The first three, if ripe enough, can just be eaten in hand, but the other three need to be cooked to be palatable: damsons cooked as a preserve or cheese, sloes steeped in gin (of course), and quinces are great poached, perhaps baked in an apple pie, or made into a jelly. I make fresh apple juice in my juicer, purée cooking apples to accompany pork, and purée dessert apples for my daughter, Tuula. I poach wedges of apple to serve with roast pork belly, and I also accompany that with an apple and yellow bean chutney (made with raisins, vinegar and a bit of home-grown chilli). And my apple pie with clotted cream (see page 37) is the star of the season.

I love plums, but I could so easily have turned against them. When we lived in Muswell Hill, our ancient plum tree bore so much fruit one year that a huge branch cracked off the main trunk. I was cooking those plums down for days — to purées, jams, cheeses, chutneys — and we were eating them for even longer. I love poached plums for breakfast, apple and plum pie is a great combination, and a plum sauce or spiced poached plums would be fantastic with venison or with the beef that is coming in at its best now.

Ribollita

My favourite ribollita was one eaten in Tuscany, and it really surprised me. It had chunks of pasta, carrots, cabbage, bread and tomatoes mushed together by hand, and then fried in a frying pan. 'Ribollita' literally means 'reboiled', but in more general terms it means 'reheated'. It's an Italian bubble and squeak...

For 6

1 head celery, roughly cut into 1cm cubes
2 red onions, peeled and cut into 1cm cubes
4 carrots, peeled and cut into 1cm cubes
100ml light olive oil
1 bunch parsley, leaves and stalks separate, finely chopped
3 garlic cloves, peeled and crushed
8 medium ripe tomatoes, blanched, skinned and roughly chopped
500g ruby chard (curly kale or cavolo nero), washed, blanched until soft,
    roughly chopped (retain some water)
300g fresh borlotti beans, cooked (see page 106) and drained
extra virgin olive oil
1 loaf ciabatta bread
sea salt and freshly ground black pepper

Cook the soffrito (the celery, onions and carrots) in the light olive oil in a large pan until deep brown and caramelised, about 30-40 minutes. Don't rush this process.

Add the finely chopped parsley stalks and the garlic, then the tomatoes, and cook for a further 20 minutes.

Add the chard, borlotti beans and some of the chard water, along with plenty of extra virgin olive oil (about 150ml — glug, glug, glug!). Tear out the centre of the ciabatta loaf in long shreds and add this to the soup. Check the seasoning, and add more extra virgin to finish.

Butternut Squash Risotto with Baked Ewe's Milk Ricotta & Chilli

This is a smooth, buttery vegetarian dish that holds the spice really well. The colours are wonderful and the ricotta makes an interesting topping. The amaretti add a little crunchy sweetness to a very soft, silky and elegant dish. This is a dish I have been working on and I think it's nearly perfect.

For 2

about 1 litre vegetable stock (see page 267), hot
40g ewe's milk ricotta cheese
crushed red chillies, to taste
finely grated zest of ½ lemon
2 tbsp extra virgin olive oil
200g butter
100g white onion, peeled and finely diced
100g white of leek only, finely diced
100g celery, finely diced
150g carnaroli risotto rice
200ml dry white wine
20g Parmesan, freshly grated

Roast Butternut Squash
1 medium butternut squash
3 tsp fennel seeds
a pinch of crushed dried chilli
1 tsp black peppercorns
sea salt and freshly ground black pepper
juice of ½ lemon
4 tsp extra virgin olive oil

To serve
2 amaretti biscuits, crushed
4 sage leaves, fried in a little light olive oil until crisp (drain well)

Preheat the oven to 220°C/Fan 200°C/Gas 7.

For the butternut squash, peel, seed and dice the flesh of the butternut squash and place in a mixing bowl. Using a pestle and mortar, smash together the fennel seeds, dried chilli, black peppercorns and a pinch of sea salt. Drizzle in the lemon juice and extra virgin olive oil. Pour this mixture into the bowl with the squash and mix well. Put the squash in a roasting tray and roast in the preheated oven until just cooked and lightly browned, about 30 minutes. Reserve and allow the mixture to cool. Purée half the squash.

For the baked ricotta, crumble the ricotta into a small non-stick baking tin or ovenproof dish, dust with a pinch of chilli, and sprinkle the lemon zest on top. Season with sea salt and drizzle over 2 teaspoons of the olive oil. Bake in the hot oven for about 10 minutes.

For the risotto, in a thick-bottomed sauté pan, melt half the butter and the remaining olive oil. Add the onion, leek and celery and sweat down for 15 minutes without allowing it to colour. Pour in the risotto rice and cook over a medium heat until the rice is opaque, about 8 minutes.

Pour in the white wine and cook until it has evaporated. Then pour in a large ladle of hot vegetable stock. Stir until the stock has evaporated, then add more stock. Continue like this until the rice is just cooked, about 20 minutes.

Add the squash purée and a pinch of chilli and stir. Add the rest of the squash, the remaining butter, the Parmesan, and salt and pepper to taste.

Serve the risotto in warmed bowls with the ricotta, crushed amaretti and deep-fried sage leaves on top.

Yellow Bean, Tomato, Mozzarella & Basil Salad

These yellow beans are usually tougher than their thinner, more delicate French/green bean cousins, but I love them. They are just meatier, chunkier and do more on my palate.

For 6

600–800g yellow beans
6 medium soft ripe tomatoes, at room temperature (I always keep my
    tomatoes at room temperature!)
extra virgin olive oil
balsamic vinegar
sea salt and freshly ground black pepper
1 bunch basil, washed
3 × 200g balls fresh buffalo mozzarella

Prepare the beans by topping, tailing and washing them. Drop them into a pan of boiling filtered water and cook until just soft, about 8–10 minutes. Drain the beans and reserve at room temperature.

Cut the tomatoes into differing shapes and sizes and put into a bowl. Drizzle in a little olive oil and vinegar and salt and pepper and mix with your fingers. Drop in the beans and tear in half the basil leaves.

Arrange the beans and tomatoes on a serving dish. Tear each mozzarella ball in half, to show the natural grain, and put on the dish. Tear the rest of the basil on top. Drizzle over some more olive oil and vinegar and serve.

Sirloin Steak with Roast Aubergine, Tomato & Pumpkin Seed Salad

Cooking a steak is sometimes a little daunting, but here I would like to put some fears to rest. A sirloin steak, from well-reared, -killed, -hung, -stored and -butchered beef cattle will have a little fat running through the main eye of the meat in flecks (this is known as marbling), and the meat will have a deep red, almost purple, colour. There will be a 1cm cream-coloured piece of fat (yum, this is where a lot of the steak's flavour is!) running across the top of the steak. A decent steak weighs about 200g; if this is too much for you, then still get the meat this size and share it.

For 4

4 × 180–200g sirloin steaks
light olive oil

Roast Aubergine, Tomato and Pumpkin Seed Salad
2 large pale aubergines
sea salt and freshly ground black pepper
light olive oil
1 garlic clove, peeled and very thinly sliced
1 small dried chilli, crushed
2kg fresh plum tomatoes, skinned and chopped
½ tbsp picked marjoram leaves
50g pumpkin seeds, toasted
extra virgin olive oil

To cook a steak medium rare, which seems to be the nation's favourite (well, at Acorn House anyway), I take the steak out of the fridge and leave it on a plate for 1 hour before I cook it. Putting it straight in the pan will drive the cold into the centre of the meat and not allow for correct cooking, so try to bring a little room temperature to the meat before you start.

Meanwhile, to make the salad, cut the top and tail off the aubergines, and then cut in half lengthways. Score the cut surfaces with a small knife in a criss-cross design and lightly salt. Retain in a colander.

In a large and wide, thick-bottomed saucepan, heat some light olive oil, enough to cover the base of the pan. Add the garlic and crushed chilli, and fry gently until golden brown. Add the tomatoes, and cook gently for 40 minutes to create a tomoto paste.

Preheat the oven to 200°C/Fan 180°C/Gas 6.

Quickly wash the salt off the aubergines and pat dry, then arrange the halves on a baking tray. Drizzle with light olive oil and season. Sprinkle over the marjoram and roast in the preheated oven until golden brown, about 25–30 minutes. Remove and cool.

Now the steak. First of all I give myself up to 15 minutes (from room temperature) to cook any individual steak to any degree of cooking. I then season liberally with salt and pepper and place the steak into a very hot pan without any oil in. Otherwise, the oil will burn and you will create free radicals in your food (cancer-forming, but let's not go too far with that one). Cook for 4 minutes and turn over, then cook for a further 4 minutes. Take the steaks out of the pan, and keep on a plate somewhere warm. Leave to rest for about 3–4 minutes.

Spoon a little of the tomato paste over the top of the aubergine, and finish with the marjoram and toasted pumpkin seeds. Sprinkle with some extra virgin olive oil and serve, with the steak.

Stewed Apples with Vanilla Clotted Cream & Runny Honey

Of all the recipes in this book, this is one of my favourites. Maybe I'm just a big kid at heart. It reminds me of my granny...

For 6

6 Bramley cooking apples
1 cinnamon stick
2 cardamom pods, split
150g caster sugar
250g clotted cream
1 vanilla pod, split
runny honey, to taste

Peel, core and chop the cooking apples. Put into a suitable pan with the cinnamon, cardamom and about 100g of the sugar. (You can always add more sugar later if it is not sweet enough for, as Albert Roux said to me, 'Once it is in, it is in!') Cook gently until soft but not completely a purée, about 10 minutes.

Whip the clotted cream in a bowl with the remaining caster sugar and the vanilla seeds. Put the apple purée into a bowl and dollop some of the cream on top of it. Drizzle over the runny honey to taste, and serve.

We don't usually think of figs as being temperate, able to be grown in English gardens: they seem far too exotic, plants that revel in Mediterranean warmth. But fig trees can grow quite happily in sheltered spots in southern England (perhaps in a glasshouse further north). The town of Worthing in Sussex used to be surrounded by fig orchards from the mid-eighteenth to the early twentieth century, and many 'un-manicured' urban gardens, dating from Regency up to Victorian times, will still boast a fig tree (and perhaps a mulberry or quince as well). If you know of a local tree with edible figs, or would like to plant one (they're easy to care for), enjoy the fruits at this time of year – if you can beat the blackbirds to them!

Fresh figs are usually seen in the markets – black, green or purple-red, with a bloom – coming in from the Mediterranean. When they're in season, my house and my restaurant pay enormous homage to them, bowls in windows at the restaurant, a central bowl on the kitchen table at home. Eat them raw in the hand, or with prosciutto and balsamic for a fantastic starter (much better than melon, I think). Bake them with honey, and serve with cream. Figs are great dried, and I eat more dried figs than I do fresh.

What I buy in October

Vegetables
Artichokes (Jerusalem), aubergine, beans (borlotti, French, runner), beetroot, broccoli (calabrese, romanesco), Brussels sprouts, cabbages (autumn, Savoy, red, winter), cardoons, carrots, cauliflower, celeriac, celery, chard, chicory, endive, fennel, garlic, horseradish, kale, kohlrabi, leeks, nettles, onions, parsnips, potatoes, pumpkins and squashes, radicchio, radishes, rocket, salsify, scorzonera, spinach, swede, sweetcorn, trevise, turnips, watercress

Fruit
Apples, blackberries, damsons, elderberries, figs, grapes, pears, peppers, pomegranates, quinces, rosehips, sloes, tomatoes

Fish
Black bream, eel, mackerel, river trout, sprats

Shellfish
Crab (brown, hen, spider), cuttlefish, lobster, mussels, oysters (native, rock), prawns, scallops (hand-dived only), squid

Game
Goose, grouse, hare, mallard, partridge, pheasant, rabbit, snipe, wood pigeon

Fungi
Brown cap mushrooms (chestnut or Paris), ceps (porcini), field mushrooms, giant puffballs, girolles, horse mushrooms, oyster mushrooms, parasol mushrooms, pieds de mouton (hedgehog fungus), trompettes de mort (horn of plenty), truffles (summer, white)

Nuts
Cobnuts, hazelnuts, walnuts

How I eat in October

I like to eat in October as if I were fattening myself up for winter — which is, of course, what would have happened in centuries past. They would have to eat while there was plenty, to keep themselves going through the winter months, when fresh food was unavailable. I was tempted to make this month one of decadence, and talk about ingredients that are rich, rare and expensive, with a splash-out menu of white truffle and cannellini bean soup, ravioli of lobster, roast porcini...

It wasn't a bad idea. I have been quite temperate elsewhere, and I wanted to demonstrate that 'eco' doesn't necessarily have to mean thrift and lentils. But I have restrained myself and I've chosen to discuss wild mushrooms only. I agree they are rather rare and expensive, but something so very special, and so very British...

Clean your mushrooms carefully, using a soft brush, and perhaps a slightly damp cloth on the caps. Never, never immerse them in water. Refer to a good mushroom book for more detailed instructions about preparation. Look out for insect infestation in the stems, particularly of ceps or porcini. You don't want to pay £45 a kilo, and then have to throw half away. (And, as a restaurateur, I have seen some very tricky offerings: porcini heads held on to stems by toothpicks, which you don't see until you start prepping them...)

I love mushrooms on toast, a very English thing, but my version is slightly more Italian. I mix a selection of mushrooms together — any of the wild ones in the previous recipe, to your budget — and to bulk them out a little less expensively, you can add button mushrooms. Put the prepared and cleaned mushrooms in a pan and heat until they start to steam and lose a little of their moisture. Now add some oil, which will conduct more heat, and increase the water coming out of the mushrooms. Move them around a bit, then tip into a colander. Put the pan back on the heat and add some butter, chopped shallots and garlic, and thyme. Then add the wet mushrooms, still hot, and fry all the flavours together. Let the water coming out of the mushrooms this time evaporate in the pan, as this intensifies flavours. When nearly ready, add some chopped parsley and fresh lemon juice. Toast a slice of sourdough or other good bread for bruschetta, drizzle with good olive oil (some new pressed oil might be around already), and pile the mushrooms on top.

When you have that basic cooked wild mushroom mixture, you can do quite a few things with it. Serve a fried egg on top of the mushrooms on toast. Put some of the mushrooms into a French or Spanish omelette or an Italian frittata (or in a ramekin and bake an egg on top). You could serve it as a warm salad, adding a little wine vinegar at the end. The mushrooms would make a great accompanying vegetable, especially with game (grouse, partridge, etc). When I worked at Daphne's, I finished off the mushrooms with a little brandy, then double cream.

I think these mushrooms would also be great for breakfast (perhaps reheated leftovers), with some good pancetta or bacon, sausage and fried eggs. They would be good in lasagne, cannelloni or ravioli, and in pastry pies, or chopped into duxelles and used in beef Wellington. You could serve the mixture with fresh or grilled polenta, or with pasta as a sauce.

A delicious mushroom soup can be made from that basic mushroom mixture. Make your basic potato base (see below), put the mushrooms on top, purée half and then mix the two together. But see my favourite soup below in the actual recipe section.

You can make this mixture of wild mushrooms into a mushroom pickle. Cook as above, then pour some vinegar over. This will last only a couple of days, unless you do as the Italians do, and top the vinegar with a layer of olive oil; this will set in the fridge and keep the pickle going for a day or so longer. The Italians blanch their raw porcini and then cover with oil alone.

Porcini mushrooms, known in French as ceps and in English as penny buns, are my favourite. I've been wild mushroom hunting a few times, but I have only ever found one porcino, in Piedmont. That single find has satisfied my hunter's lust, but I will never tire of eating porcini. They are so good they can be eaten by themselves, and raw, great as a salad with extra virgin olive oil and shavings of Parmesan. They can be deep-fried in thick slices in batter (three-parts filtered water to two of flour and one of oil). You can bake them plain, whole or in slices, or you can do something slightly more fancy. Make a couple of cuts into the stem and interlace slices of pancetta, garlic and some thyme. Season, drizzle with light olive oil and bake.

At the River Cafe we used to cook sea bass in *cartoccio* (in paper), with butter, Pernod and thyme and some pre-roasted slices of porcini. So good.

Potato & Porcini Soup

This soup sings the praises of the most wonderful of mushrooms. It highlights the character of flavours present, and I highly recommend this dish to anyone. I opened Acorn House Restaurant on this soup, which I serve hot (but not like lava!).

For 6

2kg King Edward potatoes, peeled and cut in half
2 bay leaves
sea salt and freshly ground black pepper
500g fresh porcini or cep mushrooms, brushed clean and sliced into
    5mm pieces
400ml double cream
a little freshly grated nutmeg
extra virgin olive oil

Put the potatoes into a large pot and cover with filtered water by about 3cm. Bring to the boil with the bay leaves and 2 pinches of salt.

If any scum rises to the top, skim it off. The water is to be used as the liquid in the soup.

When the potatoes are soft, tip in the porcini and whisk this whole mixture together with a strong whisk. The porcini will break up a bit. Look for a chunky consistency.

Pour in the double cream. Grate in a touch of nutmeg and grind in some black pepper and check for salt. Drizzle with extra virgin olive oil and serve.

Wet Polenta with Prawns, Chervil & Chopped Green Chilli

The yellows, greens and pinks of this simple dish are wonderful. It will impress at any dinner party, either as a starter or main course. The polenta takes a long time, I warn you...

For 6

36 large raw (whole) prawns (see page 185), peeled and deveined, shells
    reserved for prawn stock (see page 268)
2 bunches chervil, most of it roughly chopped
2 green chillies, seeded and finely chopped
extra virgin olive oil
sea salt and freshly ground black pepper
juice of 1 lemon

Polenta
2 litres filtered water
2 tsp sea salt
400g bramata polenta (not the instant stuff)
150g butter
150g Parmesan, freshly grated

For the polenta, bring the water to a boil in a thick-bottomed pan, and season with the salt. Pour the polenta very slowly into the water, whisking all the time. It is important to both whisk and pour slowly. Too fast and there will be lumps and the possibility that the polenta thickens too far. I find that this recipe works well but there are moisture conditions to bear in mind. The damper it is, the moister the polenta flour will be. So keep an eye on the consistency as you pour, and you will end up with the smoothest, most perfectly textured polenta.

When the polenta has been used up and the texture is just right (like thick double cream), turn down the heat and continue to stir until the lava-like spluttering has stopped and there is a gentle release of steam. Then stir every 5–10 minutes, to prevent it sticking on the bottom, for 50 minutes. Then stir in the butter and Parmesan, and reserve in a bowl over hot water while you wait for the prawns.

In a separate pan large enough for the prawns, warm them slowly with enough prawn stock to half cover them. Add most of the roughly chopped chervil, half of the chillies, 4 tablespoons of olive oil and some seasoning. Allow the mixture to come to the boil, then immediately turn the heat down. The prawns will quickly overcook, so beware!

Spoon some polenta into the middle of each plate, as much or as little as you like. I love wet polenta, so for me it's loads. Spoon 6 of the prawns on to each plate with plenty of liquid, then top with the remaining chopped chervil and chilli. Squeeze over a little lemon juice and drizzle over some more olive oil. Pick the remaining unchopped chervil leaves over each plate, almost allowing them to become a little salad on top of the whole dish. Serve immediately.

Roast Trevise with Prosciutto & Balsamic Vinegar

This dish looks amazing, and the bitter-sweet flavours are a clear indication of the season. You could also roast chicory (white endive) and ordinary radicchio like this.

For 6

3 heads trevise (see box on page 165)
3 garlic cloves, peeled and finely sliced
3 large sprigs thyme
extra virgin olive oil
aged balsamic vinegar (5 years perhaps)
2 tbsp picked marjoram leaves
sea salt and freshly ground black pepper
18 thin slices prosciutto
100g fine rocket leaves

Preheat the oven to 190-200°C/Fan 170-180°C/Gas 5-6.

Slice into the thick base stems of the trevise four times as if making a star, and then tear the whole head into 8 pieces along these slices. Splice each piece of stem base with slices of garlic and small sprigs of thyme. Put the pieces on a roasting tray, bases outwards on the lip of the tray, and cover the leaves with foil, so that only the stem-base parts are exposed. Roast in the preheated oven for about 40 minutes until the stems are soft, then whip off the foil and roast for a few minutes more. Sprinkle with some olive oil, a tiny amount of balsamic vinegar, some marjoram, and salt and pepper.

Arrange the pieces of trevise and prosciutto on the serving plates as you see fit — I like to gently wrap the trevise with the prosciutto, and then sprinkle over the rocket leaves. Drizzle over some olive oil, and finish with some vinegar.

Roast Rib of Beef, with Cannellini Bean, Frisée & Marinated Anchovy Salad

Ask your butcher to prepare the rib of beef for you, oven-ready.

For 8

1 × 3kg forerib of beef, 3 bones if possible
duck fat or light olive oil
2 carrots, peeled and roughly chopped
2 celery stalks, roughly chopped
1 white onion, peeled and roughly chopped
sea salt and freshly ground black pepper
½ bottle good red wine
750ml chicken stock (see page 265)
2 tbsp plain flour

Cannellini Bean, Frisée and Marinated Anchovy Salad
12 salted anchovies, prepared (see page 91)
finely grated zest and juice of 1 thick-skinned lemon
extra virgin olive oil
3kg fresh cannellini beans, podded
1 bunch mint
2 tbsp Volpaia herb vinegar
2kg frisée lettuce or endive
2 garlic cloves, peeled and crushed
2 small dried chillies, crumbled
light olive oil

Preheat the oven to 190°C/Fan 170°C/Gas 5.

To roast the beef, allow 15 minutes per 450g, so if you have 3kg, you are talking about 1½ hours. Heat a roasting tin on the stove, with some duck fat or light olive oil, and seal the edges of the meat until golden brown. Pour away the excess fat, and put the carrots, celery and onion, and any beef bones you've begged from the butcher, in the centre of the tin, with the meat on top. Season very well with salt and pepper, and put into the preheated oven; you'll find where the meat sits naturally, on its ribs. Baste every 20 minutes or so, and after 45 minutes, turn it over. When ready, allow the meat to rest for at least 10 minutes.

Meanwhile, prepare the various elements of the salad. Place the rinsed, drained and boned anchovies on a plate, and sprinkle with black pepper, the lemon zest and juice. Pour over enough extra virgin olive oil to cover and leave to marinate for an hour.

Put the podded beans and mint into a pan of cold filtered water and cook for 30–40 minutes. Drain and while hot pour over some extra virgin olive oil and a tiny bit of vinegar. Cook the frisée in a pan of fresh boiling, salted filtered water for 2–3 minutes. Drain and cool. Fry the garlic and chillies in a little light olive oil in a separate pan and once brown, add the cooked frisée and braise for a few minutes.

Empty the frisée and juices on to a serving dish, sprinkle over the beans and their juices, and arrange the anchovies on top.

While the meat is resting, deglaze the juices in the roasting tin with the red wine. Add the chicken stock, and stir. Sift in the flour, and stir and reduce until thick. Serve this sauce/gravy with the carved beef and the salad.

Warm Autumn Fruit Salad with Vanilla Custard

I love quince, I love the romance and the argument that this could well have been the forbidden fruit. But just take a bite of it raw, and you'll know why it's forbidden! However, it's wonderful cooked in jams, in apple pies or simply poached, and it has a great texture.

For 6

3 quinces, washed
3 litres filtered water
250g caster sugar
1 vanilla pod
1 cinnamon stick
1 star anise
1 bay leaf
3 pears, peeled
6 prunes
250g each of blackberries and strawberries

To serve
1 recipe vanilla custard (see page 273)

Place the whole quinces, water, sugar, vanilla, cinnamon, star anise and bay leaf into a large pot and bring slowly to the boil. Turn down the heat to a simmer and cook for 20 minutes. Then add the peeled pears and cook for another 20 minutes. Add the prunes and cook for a further 15 minutes. All of the ingredients will now be just soft.

Lift out the quinces and peel off the skins, then halve and remove the stones. There is a rather woody centre to quince so make sure you trim any of this out. Reserve the flesh in a bowl. Lift out the pears and cut away the flesh from the core. Reserve with the quince. Halve and stone the prunes and place in the bowl, then add the berries. Add a little of the sugar syrup cooking liquid, and taste.

Meanwhile, make the custard, and serve warm with the warm salad. I like to eat custard by itself, so I serve it at the side, rather than poured over...

What I buy in November

Vegetables
Artichokes (Jerusalem), beans (borlotti), beetroot, broccoli (calabrese, romanesco), Brussels sprouts, Brussels tops, cabbages (green, red, white), cardoons, carrots, cavolo nero, celeriac, celery, chard, chicory, endive, horseradish, kale, kohlrabi, leeks, lettuce, nettles, onions, parsnips, potatoes, pumpkins and squashes, puntarelle, radishes, salsify, spinach, swede, sweetcorn, turnips

Fruit
Apples, clementines, pears, quinces, rosehips, sloes, tomatoes

Fish
Black bream, eels, mackerel, skate, sprats, whiting

Shellfish
Crab (brown, hen), cuttlefish, lobster, mussels, oysters (native, rock), prawns, scallops (hand-dived only), squid

Game
Goose, grouse, hare, mallard, partridge, pheasant, rabbit, snipe, venison, woodcock, wood pigeon

Fungi
Ceps (porcini), chanterelles, giant puffballs, horse mushrooms, oyster mushrooms, parasol mushrooms, pieds de mouton, white truffles

Nuts
Almonds, Brazil nuts, chestnuts, hazelnuts, walnuts

How I eat in November

The most wonderful thing about living in Britain is that, even nowadays, game birds and animals seem almost to walk or fly out of every wood, field hedgerow, pond, marsh and wetland at this time of year. I tend to eat a lot of game in November – I love it – and I put it on the restaurant menu only occasionally because, although game is very definitely part of our heritage, it is quite an acquired taste. Game might not be so easily available to everyone as red meat or pork, but supermarkets are now beginning to stock it – I have seen farmed venison, the odd dressed pheasant – which is a good step forward. If you live in the country, no problem: you can shoot game yourself, or you can buy from shoots or from local butchers, who will acquire the birds or meat from local farmers.

So game is very definitely an ingredient for me, fresh, local and as near as possible to organic as it can be (just watch out for any lead shot). It has been said that some of the surplus animals killed at shoots go to landfill, and this is complete madness: it's such a waste of a wonderful food, and the thought of animals dying needlessly to feed man's sporting pleasure reduces me to tears. (Check your karma, lads.)

And there are so many wonderful ingredients around seasonally that seem to have been designed to go with that game: chestnuts, wild mushrooms, and all the root vegetables.

I love venison, which is one of the most amazing meats: it's very lean, full of flavour and texture, and good for those looking after their health as it's low in fat and cholesterol. You can buy it from the wild – but from a trusted source please – or from a good organic farm. I particularly like sika deer, which are not indigenous, but are now roaming wild in Britain; they have a wonderful flavour (but it depends of course on what they have been eating). I roast saddles (see page 36) and haunches, fillets and neck, and eat them hot. If there is any left over, I eat it cold with chutneys, or shred the meat and make a sauce for pappardelle (traditionally made with hare in Italy). I make a venison fillet tartare, and you could make a carpaccio; I've also produced venison sausages, venison salami, jerky and prosciutto – but all those would be a bit difficult to explain here... The main thing to remember when cooking venison is that because it is so lean, it can be very dry.

Wild rabbits have had rather a bad press in the last 50 years here in Britain because of myxomatosis. This virus, deadly to rabbits only, was first discovered in 1896 in Uruguay. It was imported to Australia in 1951 to control its large rabbit population where, initially, it had the desired, devastating, effect. The disease was then illegally introduced to France in 1952, and reached Britain the following year. Over 90 per cent of British rabbits were killed off, and many still believe that this was done deliberately, a viral solution to a farmers' pest. Whether this is true or not, and despite the fact that the virus is still around, wild rabbit populations are now flourishing again, and the meat is wonderful to eat. The flavour is delicate, not strongly gamey, and the texture makes a good change from that of chicken. If you buy wild – and I strongly advise it, farmed is bland – try to buy the whole animal, skinned and gutted: if the liver and kidneys are still present, as they should be, and are glistening pink, healthy, firm, with no odour, then the rabbit will be good to eat. I have seen the old classic ferreting for rabbits with hemp nets in Wales. It is so sad to see all these wonderful skills being lost.

Like venison, rabbit is very lean, and doesn't require much cooking. My favourite rabbit dish is a braise. Get the butcher to cut the rabbit into haunch, back legs and saddle, and then fry the pieces briefly in a casserole with butter, slices of garlic, pine nuts, sage and thyme before adding white wine (even Marsala), some raisins and seasoning. Put on the lid and leave for 18 minutes maximum. This is fast food and good food, and rabbit is not very expensive to buy...

Hare is the other furred game and, unlike venison and rabbit, it is only ever found wild, therefore you will have to buy it from a specialist game butcher. The most familiar and traditional British dish has the animal stewed in its own blood, which is delicious, but I like the old-fashioned crown of hare: the ribs curled round with the loin into a crown shape, basted with bacon and butter, and roasted. Wonderful, particularly served with chestnuts.

Game birds are perhaps my favourites, and there are plenty to choose from. They have their seasons, which are strictly adhered to, and the most famous date in the game calendar must be the Glorious Twelfth of August. People pay fortunes for grouse flown down from Scotland on that day. But game demands to be hung, especially grouse, and I think what they are probably paying for in August is last year's bird out of the freezer.

Hanging game birds depends on too many elements to list here, but any game bird should be given a little time, for the flesh needs to become a bit gamey. If eaten too soon, a grouse, say, will be too bland. But I'm not of the school that thinks a pheasant should be hung until it's blue or crawling. Just until a tail feather pulls out easily is about right.

Roasting game birds is the most common way of cooking them, although those a bit older (you can tell by the look of their feet) could be stewed. Pheasant, partridge and grouse are best cooked this way, as are wood pigeon, and the wild ducks (mallard, teal, widgeon). You should put some herbs in the cavities, and cover the breasts with bacon or pancetta. You can roast them plain, or nestle them in a bed of root vegetables. I cook most game birds for an average of 20–25 minutes in a medium to hot oven, and judge the doneness by feel: if the flesh is really soft, you need to cook it a little longer, as it will be raw; if it's very firm, you've gone too far. 'Firm jelly' is the texture guide.

Woodcock and snipe are treated differently, both being roasted fresh, guts and all. The snipe feeds off wetlands, so its innards are a bit fishy, but this gives a wonderful juxtaposition of flavours: fishy and meaty at the same time.

Pan-frying is another way of treating quite a few game birds: you take the breasts off, and pan-fry them separately, while you make a quick stock/sauce with the flavourful bones (see below). Pheasants are always bought in braces for, they say, like swans, they mate for life… Although they are good roasted (stewed as well), the legs are often a bit tough and sinewy. So what I sometimes do is cut the breasts and legs off separately, and purée or shred the leg meat into a little pheasant burger to serve alongside the breast. Add some breadcrumbs, perhaps some finely chopped spring onion, a spice like cumin or coriander, and fry in light olive oil. Wood pigeons, another favourite, can be treated in the same way.

A game gravy can be made very quickly. Once you have cut the breasts and legs off, chop the carcasses up and put in a pot with a bay leaf, some thyme and double chicken stock (see page 266). Bring to the boil, perhaps with a little red wine, and then reduce to get the strong flavour out of the flesh and bones. Strain, season to taste, and you will have a good game stock/sauce within 10 minutes.

There are many possible and delicious game accompaniments. You could roast a bird on a piece of good toast, which soaks up all the gamey juices. A traditional bread sauce is wonderful: take some day-old crustless bread, soak it in milk and double chicken stock (see page 266) and simmer with a bay leaf and an onion studded with cloves. I'm fond of the Italian *mostarda di cremona* — a sweet, hot and delicious fruit preserve — with game, and redcurrant jelly is good too. I like roast root vegetables (see page 228), or roast or boiled carrots or carrot purée. Sweet potato is good with game, and Brussels tops, simply blanched then rolled in butter or oil and lots of freshly grated nutmeg, is delicious. (Nutmeg is wonderful with game.) Game chips are classic, and they are basically fresh crisps, but I find this a bit weird (see page 229).

My favourite game accompaniment, though, is chestnuts, which are in season now. Cut an X in the bottom of each chestnut with a sharp knife and then add to a pan of salted filtered water, bring to the boil and cook for 15 minutes. Drain, and when cool enough to handle, peel off the skins. Use them whole, roasted alongside the potatoes or root vegetables, perhaps, or mash them and mix with potatoes for a potato and chestnut mash — perfect with grouse, woodcock or pheasant. Or you can take it just that little step further, and make a potato, chestnut and porcini mash. For 4 people, use 8 large potatoes, peel, cut in half only (or they become too waterlogged for mash), and cook until tender. (I often add a bay leaf to boiling potatoes, it adds a haunting flavour and richness.) As you mash them, mash in 4 large, fresh, raw porcini and as many cooked chestnuts as you like. Add butter and double cream to taste. If you can only get hold of dried porcini, add these to the potatoes while cooking.

Finally, there is an old rule about game. You are not allowed to swerve in your car to hit a game animal or bird, and if you do hit one, you must leave it for the car behind to claim. This is why, in the old days, the servants always rode in the carriage or car ahead, so that their master could pick up the resultant booty!

TREVISE

We are all familiar with radicchio, the red and white-leaved ball from Italy, that you can use to add colour – and some flavour – to salads. It seems to have made its way into every bag of leaves you buy. But trevise, its more elongated cousin, is less common, and I love to use this. Trevise is so named because it was grown originally in Treviso, an area in the Veneto around Venice. The leaves are longer, sturdier, redder, with streaks of white, and they are very flavourful. You can eat it raw – it makes a great salad with pomegranate seeds and roast pheasant – but I like roasting it and serving as a room temperature salad with a few slices of prosciutto and a dressing of sweet sticky balsamic vinegar (see page 156).

French Onion Soup

Every time I make this soup, I forget how brilliant onions are when caramelised. This soup catches all the characteristics and flavours of these melted onions. You can use a beef stock if you like, but I find it a bit too rich for me.

For 6

20 white onions, peeled and halved through the root
200g butter
2 garlic cloves, peeled and crushed
2 litres chicken stock (see page 265), hot
200g plain flour
sea salt and freshly ground black pepper

Slice the onions from tip to root as thinly as you can. Melt the butter in a large thick-bottomed saucepan and tip in the onions. Cook until the onions are meltingly soft, about 25–30 minutes, then add the garlic and continue to cook. The trick with these onions is that you just let them catch, meaning that the golden-brown smudge on the bottom of the pan gets scraped off each time it 'catches'. I do this for an hour or more. Each time I remove the colour, it adds to the depth and flavour of the finished dish. If you find the bottom not lifting off, then use a little of the hot stock, which helps to release the stickiness. But do try to keep it dry for as long as possible before the liquid goes in: the trick to the golden-brown colour and meaty flavour.

Preheat the oven to 190°C/Fan 170°C/Gas 5. While the onions are cooking, toast the flour. Put a thin layer in a baking tray, and bake in the preheated oven until golden, minutes only. Watch carefully, flour can go from golden to black in seconds. (You can use this toasted flour to enrich and thicken stocks and sauces.)

Sift the flour into the onion pan, and stir through well. Then add the stock slowly, stirring, and it will start to thicken, just like a roux. Take it further, adding stock, until you get your own desired soupy consistency. Season to taste. You could put a cheesy croûton on top, but I prefer it just with French flute bread and cold unsalted butter.

Spaghetti with a Rich Tomato, Pancetta & Red Wine Sauce

This is probably the dish I cook most at home, but only at lunchtime, I never eat pasta at night.

For 6

900g fresh spaghetti
125g Parmesan, freshly grated

Tomato, Pancetta and Red Wine Sauce
2 red onions, peeled and finely chopped
light olive oil
2 bay leaves
2 tbsp picked thyme leaves
400g smoked pancetta, finely diced
500ml dry Tuscan red wine
2kg soft ripe tomatoes, chopped
sea salt and freshly ground black pepper
100g butter
125g Parmesan, freshly grated

For the sauce, fry the onion in 2 tablespoons of the olive oil in a pan until soft, about 7-8 minutes, then add the bay and thyme leaves. Cook for 5 minutes and then add the diced pancetta. Fry the pancetta until just beginning to crisp, then add the wine. Let the wine cook and evaporate, then add the tomatoes. Soften and crush the tomatoes down and cook for about 20 minutes. Check and adjust the seasoning. Finish the sauce with a few knobs of butter and the grated Parmesan.

Meanwhile, cook the spaghetti in a pan of plenty of boiling, salted filtered water until *al dente*. Drain and put back into the pot. Pour half the sauce into the pasta and stir. Serve on to individual plates and finish each dish with a spoon or two more of the sauce. Sprinkle with the Parmesan to finish.

Soft Fennel, Borlotti Bean, Oyster Mushroom & Spinach Salad

This is a great combination, and the flavours really blend well with each other.

For 6

3 heads fennel
4 garlic cloves, peeled
sea salt and freshly ground black pepper
2 tsp fennel seeds
1 small dried chilli, crushed
3 tbsp extra virgin olive oil
250g oyster mushrooms
3 banana shallots, peeled and sliced
25g butter
1.5kg fresh spinach
100ml oyster sauce
300g cooked borlotti beans (see page 106)

Trim the fennel, cut the heads in half and then into quarters, and boil with the garlic cloves in a pan of salted filtered water until soft, about 15 minutes. Drain well.

Toast the fennel seeds in a dry pan, then crush them using a pestle and mortar with the dried chilli and 2 teaspoons sea salt. Mix in the olive oil, and pour this over the fennel when it comes out of the pan.

Slice the mushrooms, and fry them in a pan with the shallots in the butter until soft, about 5 minutes. Keep on a high heat, then add the spinach. Stir vigorously for a few minutes until the spinach has completely broken down. Keep cooking until all the water has evaporated. Then pour in the oyster sauce.

Warm up the borlotti beans, and serve all the different elements of the salad separately, in piles beside each other.

Game Burger with Sauté Potatoes

Basically this is burger and chips, but a bit flasher! Get your butcher to prepare the game, and mince the flesh together for you. Keep the bones to make stock for soups and sauces.

For 6

a brace of pheasants, meat removed and minced
1 wood pigeon, meat removed and minced
1 rabbit, meat removed and minced
2 tbsp chopped mint
sea salt and freshly ground black pepper
light olive oil

Sauté Potatoes
200ml light olive oil
1kg small potatoes, peeled and halved
100g butter
2 tbsp chopped parsley

To serve

400g button mushrooms, finely sliced and cooked in butter

2 red onions, peeled and finely sliced

180g mild Cheddar, finely grated

6 sesame-seed-coated burger buns, warm

Mix all the minced game meat together, with the mint, and season well. Divide the meat mixture into 6 balls, and pat each one a little bit flat to burger shapes, but not too thin.

For the sauté potatoes, heat the olive oil in a large pan. Drop in the dry halved small potatoes, and cook for about 10-12 minutes until light golden. Then pour off that oil, add the butter to the pan, and fry the potatoes for a further 5 minutes. By now they should be a lovely golden colour. Drain, sprinkle with salt and while hot, mix in the chopped parsley.

Meanwhile, cook the burgers in a little light olive oil in a frying pan, 4 minutes on each side. Then top each burger with the cooked mushrooms, the raw onion, and grated cheese. This should lightly melt the cheese before you put the burgers into the warmed buns. As relish, for me it's always ketchup and mustard. Some people like pickles. The Kiwis like beetroot and fried egg...

Chestnut Chocolate Cake

Dark rich chocolate cakes really characterise the season, and with the addition of chestnuts, we are moving towards the richer flavours of autumn.

For 8-10

220g plain flour, plus extra for dusting
2 tsp baking powder
½ tsp bicarbonate of soda
a pinch of fine salt
70g chocolate (63% cocoa solids), broken into pieces, plus 100g for the top
220ml milk
140g butter, plus extra for greasing
265g light soft brown sugar
3 medium eggs
1 tbsp golden syrup
150g cooked peeled chestnuts, chopped to quite chunky (about 12ths)
1 vanilla pod, the whole of it, finely chopped

Preheat the oven to 190°C/Fan 170°C/Gas 5. Butter and flour a deep 25cm round cake tin.

Sift together all the dry ingredients. Place the 70g chocolate and the milk into a heatproof bowl set over a pan of warm heated water and allow to melt. Mix the butter and sugar together in a separate bowl until creamy. Beat the eggs and slowly pour into the creamed butter and sugar. Add 20g of the flour mixture now. Stir in the golden syrup and chopped chestnuts and vanilla, and mix well. Fold in the remaining flour mixture. Gradually add the chocolate mixture to form a thick batter.

Pour into the prepared cake tin, and bake in the preheated oven for 45 minutes. Turn out on to a wire cake rack, and grate some more plain chocolate over the top. This will melt and create a lovely topping. Now allow the cake to cool.

I serve this with crème fraîche and a light dusting of good cocoa powder.

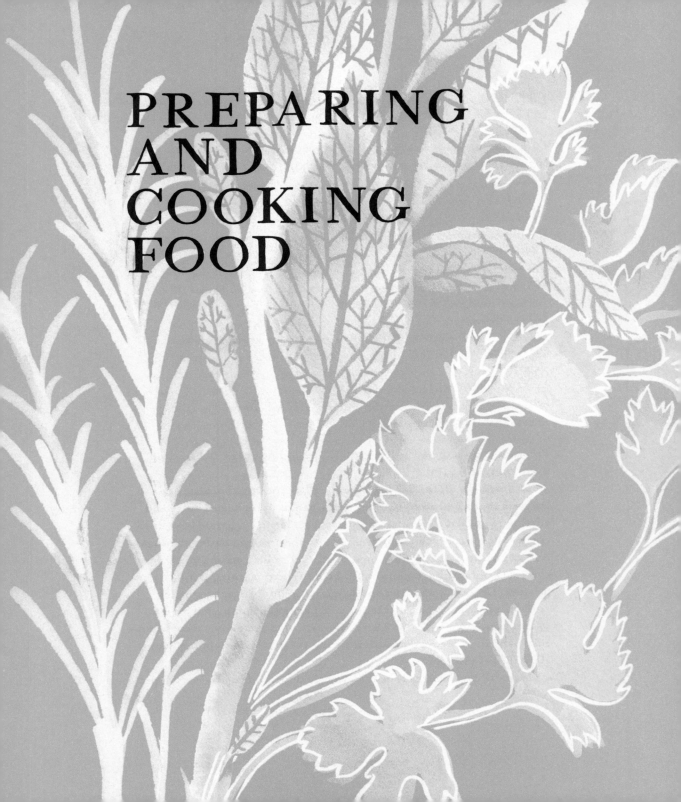

PREPARING AND COOKING FOOD

Food has been produced, in water or on land, I have gone out to choose and buy it, and now is when the food actually reaches my home, and I need to prepare, cook and eat it. As a result I will utilise quite a lot of energy in heating, lighting and cooking, and also in accessing the water that helps heat, clean and cook (and ultimately clean up again). The least I can do, if I can't individually solve every ecological issue, is try to reduce my personal impact on the world's supply of energy when I'm at home. I hope, in some way, this book will help you to become part of the growing environmental movement because, together, we can save the planet.

The primary sources of the energy we use at home for cooking (and lighting and heating) are electricity, gas, oil and coal. The last three are fossil-fuels, so are finite, and also produce carbon emissions. Electricity conventionally produced by utilising gas or coal is what I would call 'bad' electricity. 'Good' electricity comes from companies using alternative means, which are green, renewable and sustainable, such as wind, solar, hydro or biomass (see page 255). This must be the future, for the pinnacle of fossil-fuel use is about to be reached: gas and oil are also acquiring political significance as they diminish. And even if in the west we are cutting down on coal (the most carbon-emitting of all fossil sources of energy), India and China are now going through their Industrial Revolution, and at least one new coal-power generating station is built per week. In twenty years' time everyone needs to be psychologically ready to shift to electricity, whatever the generating power might be (we might even have found something new by then). Some electricity is produced by nuclear power. This worries me because, although it's green so far as lower emissions are concerned, there is the serious problem of highly toxic and environmentally damaging waste. Where do we store this? Interestingly, someone I respect, James Lovelock, the founder of the Gaia movement, has said that nuclear has to be considered as part of our energy future if we are to cut our carbon emissions.

MY ECO KITCHEN

One-third of all energy consumption is used at home: space heating uses about 60 per cent, water heating about 23 per cent, lighting and other appliances 13 per cent, and cooking nearly 3 per cent. So anything you can do at home to save energy will reduce the carbon footprint of your house and family. That means installing an efficient green boiler, lagging, insulating, wind-proofing, window-sealing, all the eco-friendly ways available to keep heat in once you have created it. It means turning off lights when you go out of a room, installing low-energy bulbs, not leaving televisions and music players on standby or mobile phones on charge. Our homes are full of appliances that eat energy.

The kitchen probably has the largest carbon footprint in the house. This is where the boiler is usually situated, and the fridge and cooker, all of which guzzle energy. At the end of 2007, I am in the process of fitting a new kitchen at home (well, second-hand). When a friend said he was replacing his old kitchen cupboards and appliances with new, I leapt at the chance. I shall strip ours out, recycling as I go, and see what I can fit in from the other kitchen. It's the ultimate re-use of materials, and I shall put as little as possible to recycling.

Cooker

I cook by gas, a fossil fuel, because I like the controllability of gas on the hob, but I am investigating whether good electricity might be better (because one day I won't be able to afford gas). My cooker is fairly basic, not brand-new but not old; it has four burners and an oven with a grill on top. I think the simpler the better, and I can cook the food I want to cook perfectly adequately on what I have already.

Agas or Rayburns are efficient cookers which, although they run mainly on fossil fuels, are very well insulated and provide heat as well as cooking food. (Their coolest ovens are perfect for making stock or drying tomatoes or strawberries...) I can't comment at all on microwaves, supposed to be the most energy efficient of all cookers, as I've never had one and never used one.

Arthur's Notes

If your oven is fan-assisted, it can heat up many times faster than an ordinary oven, thus negating all those recipe instructions of 'Preheat the oven for 20 minutes' (such a waste of energy). But you must remember that a fan-assisted oven temperature needs to be 20 degrees lower than a normal oven.

Clean your oven frequently (even if self-cleaning) as this keeps its efficiency up to scratch.

Check the seals around the oven door from time to time. It's here that heat can escape, wasting energy.

Fridge

I'm a chef, but the fridge I have at home is the smallest I've ever had, even though there are four adults and two children living in the house. I've done this deliberately, coming from two green angles. First of all, the fridge is A++ standard, which is the most energy efficient, and being small it uses less energy (which also costs less). Secondly, I only want to store enough food in mine for a few meals, with perhaps some basics. Typically my fridge holds rice milk, almond milk, whole organic cow's milk, a jar of tomato sauce, some Parmesan and yoghurt, with a head of cabbage or broccoli in the veg drawer, and only enough room left for a chicken or fish, the protein part of the meal. All other foods are stored elsewhere (see below). Because

I only like storing enough food for a few meals at a time, I don't freeze food, so I don't have a freezer. I know that freezers are vital for many people, particularly families: you can cook in batches and freeze some for later; you can freeze gluts of fruit or vegetables. They are useful for many, but just not for me. I'm not being necessarily eco or green (although it means one less energy-consuming appliance), it's just not my style of cooking or living.

Arthur's Notes

Old fridges use much more energy than new ones; if yours is over ten years old, it should probably be replaced. There is such a thing as a 'savaplug', which regulates the flow of energy to an old fridge (which is good in an eco sense).

Don't keep your fridge (or freezer) near the cooker or boiler, or dishwasher if you have one, or it will have to work harder, using more energy to keep cool.

Manufacturers say fridge condenser coils (at the back) need to be well ventilated, so you should leave at least 5cm between coils and wall – and dust them off every now and again.

A fridge should never be crammed full, which prevents the efficient circulation of cold air. Three-quarters full is about right.

Avoid leaving the fridge door open for any length of time. For each minute the door is open, the fridge will take 3 minutes of energy to cool down again.

New fridges (and freezers) run on ozone- and climate-friendly gases, but old ones still might contain CFCs and HFCs (unfriendly fluorocarbons, which will need to be disposed of professionally). Some supermarket fridges and freezers still contain these types of refrigerants...

Other Appliances

I have an eco kettle (which works out how much water you need and only boils that amount), a toaster and a juicer, that's all. The juicer is perhaps the most important for us, as it has the ability to deliver fresh juices whenever we like. Not only do we benefit in terms of vitamins and minerals, but there are no juice cartons coming into the house (negating waste yet again), and the worms in the wormery (see page 260) love the mush left over (particularly apple).

I could have a food processor, which would be great for Tuula's purées, but a potato masher or a mechanical *mouli-légumes* can do the job just as well, and they use elbow grease rather than electricity.

'Potts' & Pans

One of my friends has put his name to a range of non-stick pans, but I don't use non-stick at all. Research has suggested that the non-stick linings can release toxic vapours at quite a low temperature, and their manufacture involves environmental pollutants as well. Neither do I use aluminium, because it tends to taint acidic foods, particularly spinach, lemon and other citrus fruit, and vinegars. These acids and stirring with metal spoons can release particles of aluminium into your food and into your system (always use wooden spoons in metal pots). A cranio-sacral session once revealed how much metal there was in my body after twelve years of cooking in kitchens with aluminium pans: I was sick for ages afterwards.

What I use are good old-fashioned, thick-bottomed cast-iron or stainless-steel saucepans, frying and roasting pans, with tight-fitting lids. If these pans are well conditioned (see Box overleaf), they will not stick, and they should last you a lifetime. When people ask you what you would like for a birthday or Christmas present, get them to give you a good pan!

A well-conditioned pan is a really valuable commodity in any kitchen. Food sticks to many pans because they are slightly dirty. To condition or clean a cast-iron or stainless-steel pan, heat it on the hob with the inner base completely covered with table salt. The pores of the metal expand a little, allowing the salt in to clean them. Remove the pan from the heat, and rub the salt in and around the pan with a clean tea-towel (watch you don't burn yourself). Allow the pan to cool down, then pour the salt away. To finish the job off, brush the inner base of the pan with a little vegetable oil.

Storage & the Storecupboard

If you wondered where the rest of the food went, when I talked about how small my fridge was, well, it goes on top of the fridge. There I have a huge basket which, in season, is full of fresh vegetables and fruit — apples, bananas (organic Fairtrade, a mainstay for the children and me), broccoli, tomatoes, garlic, onions, potatoes, carrots. Many people would automatically put some of these in the fridge, but I find they can happily live at room temperature for up to four days. However, I'll use them up long before then. I think fewer foodstuffs really need to be chilled than we think (except perhaps butter for baking). Eggs are a prime example: who ever asks for cold eggs? I buy organic, and keep them at room temperature for the few days before they're eaten. (They're there to be eaten, not to be kept for three weeks.)

Some of the fresh produce keeps slightly better if encased in brown paper bags (which I save from shopping trips, or I buy separately). I use clingfilm very rarely. It requires quite a lot of energy to produce (fossil fuel-based), and it's only ever used once. There are fears that plastic particles can pass to the food it encases as well. And I'm not keen on aluminium foil, although it is now recyclable. I use lidded Tupperware boxes for leftovers (not that there are many), and put them in the fridge.

I buy very few cans and jars, primarily because I don't like using ready-prepared foods, but also, obviously, because I then have to get rid of them in some way. I do buy organic tomato ketchup in glass jars (which are best, they can be re-used at home, or recycled), and I do occasionally buy organic baked beans in cans. Organic cans aren't, but many cans of food are lined with resins containing a chemical, bisphenol-A, which allows the food in the cans to be heated to kill off bacteria without the metal in the can contaminating the contents of the can. Bisphenol-A is believed to be an endocrine disruptor, which has the potential to interfere with our hormone systems. Although the fears have never been confirmed, it's too much of a risk, and I shall stick to organic.

Sugar is a basic of most people's storecupboards, although not of mine. Sugarcane growing involves large amounts of fertilisers, plenty of water (so wetlands have been taken over by the crop), and chemical run-off from sugarcane production in Australia, for instance, has contributed to damage of the Great Barrier Reef. Sugar from sugar-beet, which is produced in Europe, requires considerable fertilisation as well, and all this for an 'empty' calorie. If you must buy sugar, try to get organic or Fairtrade, or do as I do, and substitute healthier alternatives such as honey and maple syrup.

Perhaps the most surprising — and certainly space-consuming — storage element of my eco kitchen is the way I deal with waste. I have three bins, which sit alongside each other near the sink: one, the smallest is for compostable waste (which I empty a minimum of twice a week); the second, slightly larger bin is for general waste (it's never full at the end of the week), and the largest is for recyclable waste (which I sometimes have to empty twice a week). If nothing else, the comparative size of the bins is very revealing! And this in an eco kitchen, where I try to reject as much unnecessary packaging as possible before I get the products home...

PREPARING
FOOD

Most of what I say here will be a lesson in the obvious. But less
obvious is the fact that you can use your instincts about food at
this time, as well as your three, highly-tuned, food senses of sight,
smell and taste. You should be able to see caterpillars (although not
bacteria) and black eyes in your potatoes to cut out. You should be
able to smell whether something is on the turn or off — and if you
put it to your tongue and it's fizzy or sour, then spit it out and
throw it out. Another sense, that of touch, is important when
preparing food.

Vegetables

Washing is the first step. When vegetables come to the doorstep, whether
at home or in the restaurant, they need to be washed, as soil can actually
carry some pretty nasty bugs and bacteria. If the vegetables are not
organic, they carry pesticide residues as well.

Depending on the vegetable, put it into a bowl of cold filtered water. If
potatoes are heavily covered in dirt (quite rare these days, but they are the
best), leave them in the water for a while to get the mud really wet, after which
it will slide off. Then they'll need a rinse in fresh cold water. New potatoes
you hardly need to touch: put in water, and simply roll around a little. I don't
usually scrape them. Broccoli and cauliflower I put whole head down and run
cold water from the tap over them, which comes out like a shower-head! Shake
it, and it's ready for preparation. I wash tomatoes, as they could have been
sprayed, but I don't soak them. Leeks are a bit different. Remove the outer
leaves, the tough green tops and the stringy root. Cut along the length of the

stalk, halfway through, and put into a bowl of water; swill around a bit so that any particles of dirt will be washed out of the leafy layers.

Fresh spinach leaves must be washed incredibly well, because as a chef — or indeed a domestic cook — your reputation can depend on it. Gritty spinach is not appreciated. What you have to do is have several bowls of water in which you can swish the leaves around; the first one first, then the second, then the first one again with clean water, then the second one again with clean water as well. In a professional kitchen we would be doing this with two whole sinks, but this isn't generally an option at home. Once you can't see any dust, dirt or sand in the bottom of the bowl, it is probably clean — but I would swish it through once more (and then this water clinging to the leaves you can cook it in)! And try not to buy spinach after it has been raining hard; it is a ground-hugging plant, and can get very splashed with soil and mud.

It is vitally important to wash any whole lettuces, especially those that have been organically grown or are from the farmers' market. Because they are in such close contact with the ground, the leaves can contain soil particles, and therefore the very nasty bug, *E. coli*. Put the separated lettuce leaves in a bowl of water, swill around and lift out into another bowl of water (rather like washing spinach, see above). A salad spinner is useful now. I'd do cabbage-type leaves in the same way, and although I am very thorough, I'm ashamed to say that a customer once found a (dead) caterpillar in a plate of cavolo nero. I apologised profusely of course, but at the same time, I thought it proved (although not in an ideal way) that the vegetable had been grown properly, without having been sprayed, debugged, deloused, hospital disinfected…

As for preparation prior to cooking, I tend to do as little as possible, and it's fairly obvious again: trim off anything inedible, but not more, and cut out any blemishes or bruises. If vegetables like carrots are of really good quality, they might just need a scrub with a good scrubbing brush rather than peeling. I cut the green leaves off young carrots (but that they are there at all at the point of sale annoys me). But you can save turnip or beetroot leaves, they're good to eat (prepare and cook like spinach). Never take anything off a beetroot, apart from those leaves (about 5cm from the bulb), or the colour will leach out of the vegetable while it is cooking. To prepare larger spinach leaves, grab hold of the stalk 'tail' in one hand and both sides of the leaf in the other. Pull the leaf down until it naturally peels away from the stalk.

And don't throw away the stalks of calabrese broccoli when you are cutting it into florets. If you strip off the outer layer of the stalk — think peeling a banana — the inside is deliciously crisp, rather like kohlrabi. You can cook this — good in a stir-fry — but I like to eat it raw as I would a carrot, and I serve batons on a crudités plate at the restaurant.

Some chefs like to trim out the core of a tomato — where the fruit meets the stalk of the plant — but I rarely bother, especially with the small and sweet cherry tomatoes. I don't skin tomatoes either — if you want to, slit the skin in a cross and immerse in boiling filtered water for 30 seconds — and I don't usually get rid of cores and seeds. I find these tougher bits, even after chopping, add another texture dimension to a sauce or vegetable stew, or a salad. If there are large bits of skin visible in a sauce, I'll pick them out with tongs or a fork. And I never purée a tomato sauce, as I like it chunky, but for kids I'd put it through a mouli (which gets rid of the skins anyway).

Fruit

Fruit are mostly grown off the ground (apart from strawberries), so you don't need to wash them to get rid of soil. They might have been sprayed, though, so a good wash is advisable. Compounds such as waxes and oil are used on some fruits — among them apples, pears, the plum family and citrus fruit — and these are water insoluble. You can easily remove the skin from citrus, but you may not want to peel an apple or pear, as most of the goodness and fibre is contained in or near the skin. New products (Vegiwash and Salad Spa are two names, see Directory) contain biological enzymes that strip away any such compounds and agricultural chemicals, and you can use them on a wide variety of fruit (and vegetables). I would always peel fruit for children, though, unless you know it's been grown organically. Every piece of fruit I bring into the house, before I put it in the fruit bowl, I immerse in a bowl of cold filtered water with a bit of Vegiwash or a touch of vinegar — and a little salt in the briefest of rinses for strawberries or raspberries.

Meat & Poultry

When I am in a butcher's shop, I must admit I quite often end up behind the butcher's block, explaining exactly what I need to a butcher who is not quite up to speed with restaurant meat techniques. But that said, there shouldn't be too much preparation of meat and poultry needed at home. Your good local butcher has been butchering, cutting, jointing, rolling and tying meat and poultry all his life. All you have to do is order or choose it, take it home, wipe it at most, and store it in the fridge if you're not cooking it straightaway.

For home cooking, you only really need smallish jointed pieces of meat, such as a couple of ribs of beef, a rolled piece of pork, chops, steaks, spare ribs. I buy organic chickens whole, and joint them myself if needed. You could obviously buy larger meat joints, but will they go in your oven? I once foolishly bought a leg of lamb that didn't fit into my roasting tray or oven: I didn't have a saw handy, so I held the knuckle-bone over the edge of the table and took a hammer to it. (One bonus of this do-it-yourself butchery was the marrow!) Your butcher will remove the knuckle-bone from a leg in a much more professional way, and he should be willing also to bone a leg or shoulder or similar. At a farmers' market recently, I saw a sign excitedly proclaiming: 'Learn how to bone and roll a shoulder of pork!' Did anyone potentially buying realise how large that joint would be — and why would anyone not in the profession need to know?

Once you get your meat or poultry home, don't ever attempt to wash it. Water and oxygen are the two worst accelerators of decomposition. Keep it dry, possibly in the butcher's waxed paper, and store immediately in the fridge. Before cooking meat or poultry, take it out of the fridge a couple of hours in advance, so that it can come to room temperature. Cover it with a clean cloth or one of those old-fashioned food covers. If you were to put it cold into the oven, it would take longer to cook, and it would become dry, as it takes a lot more heat to force the cold out.

Fish & Shellfish

I would always buy my fish and shellfish from a trusted fish supplier or fishmonger. Staff behind the fish counter at a supermarket are only there to weigh and pay, usually nothing else. I tend to buy fish whole and gut and prepare it myself (fishmongery was part of my training). In fact, I usually cook my fish whole, as you retain many vitamins and minerals. But if you're buying whole from the fishmonger, the general rule is that you get them to pull the gills and guts out. Even sardines and anchovies need to be gutted before cooking (but not perhaps sprats…).

When you get your whole fish home, gutted and gilled, wash it inside and out thoroughly. Dabble with your fingers to get rid of the bloodline along the spine: if not removed, the blood will spread during cooking and taint the flesh. I tend to take fish eyes out too. All of these are particularly important when making a fish stock with (white) fish heads. I hear people say 'My stock was grey' (probably the eyes), 'My stock was bitter and brown' (probably blood), and 'My stock was gritty and dark' (probably guts).

Do not wash your fish though, if it has already been filleted, which would not only wash away flavour but, as with meat, speed up the decomposition time. I usually leave the scales on a fish, particularly if I'm going to cook it whole, as this protects the tender flesh from drying out and also retains flavour. After cooking, you just pull off the skin, and you have the lovely flesh exposed. Too many people cut too much off whole fish — the scales, heads, fins, tails — and then complain that the flesh is dry. And so it would inevitably be with so many exit points for the precious juices. If you have to cut the head off a fish because it is too big for your oven, cover the exposed bit with foil (perhaps the only time I use it) to stop it drying out.

I rinse all my raw shellfish in cold filtered water. Pulling off mussel beards, and checking for open mussels or clams is about all you can do. And just remember to pull out the black vein from the back of the raw prawn before cooking, as it can sometimes be gritty.

COOKING FOOD

I'm not into cheffy food despite all my years of training, and the primary ethos of Acorn House is to bring home cooking into the restaurant arena rather than the other way round. In fact it was my family that actually provided inspiration for the restaurant menu: I wanted to cook and offer things that they could happily eat if they came in — so no foie gras or caviar, but asparagus, pea and broad bean soup, pumpkin risotto or a warm salad of new potatoes, green beans and tomato…

My Style of Eating

At the risk of repeating myself (I am, I know, but it's worth it), I cook foods that are fresh, local and seasonal, preferably organic. I cook them simply and basically, with recourse to few of the complicated techniques, sauces and garnishes of haute cuisine. I've been there, though, and done that — and still love to eat that way occasionally — but my preferences and instincts now tend rather more towards the Italian way of eating: good basic ingredients, simple cooking methods, judicious and delicious combinations, and uncluttered and clean flavours. That doesn't of course preclude the use of influences from elsewhere: my mackerel fillet marinated in soy and ginger is decidedly eastern, and my duck confit is classically French. When asked to define the Acorn House style of cooking after we had opened, I called it 'modern London'. And I think it is just that, reflecting the diversity of the city, and all its converging food influences.

We don't eat much animal protein at home: we might have an organic steak once a fortnight, a roast chicken at the weekend. We eat vegetables primarily, by themselves or as soups, with eggs, cheese, pasta, rice, pulses and grains, and non-GM tofu. This attitude is reflected in the restaurant menu, where the main thrust is vegetable salad-based, with cold or hot main courses, some for meat and fish eaters, some for vegetarians; these mains almost serve as an accompaniment to the salads, rather than the other way round. Diners can also choose how much food they want, which is a very home-based idea — two to four salads by themselves, or two or three salads with their main — and this does away with restaurant portioning (always a matter for debate with some customers), and combats wastage, a topic very close to my heart. I've seen what is thrown away from customers' plates in restaurants — for there is nothing in this world so wasteful as a restaurant — but I think the Acorn House food waste bin is the smallest I've ever encountered! (Anything that is left over, of course, goes to the desiccator, the wormery or the compost heap, see pages 256–263.)

A diet based mainly on plant foods is a healthier one anyway, I believe, especially if those plants were grown organically. I don't think we really need much animal protein in fact (although I am far from vegetarian), but what we do eat at home should be the best quality possible. At one point, I wouldn't buy any meat unless it came from an animal with a name, perhaps the ultimate in traceability. Billy, a huge bullock of about 750kg, took us nearly a month to cook and eat at the restaurant — but we knew where he had come from, what pastures he'd been grazing...

Cooking and eating are about giving and experiencing pleasure: it's friendly. I share a house with three other adults and two children. There is always something going on in the kitchen: someone having a late breakfast, or an early lunch, Aron clamouring for something to eat on coming home from kindergarten, then one of us cooking an evening meal for all to share. It is very much the hub of the house, as most kitchens should be: warm, inviting, easy, casual. We've managed to recreate this homely ethos at Acorn House: customers come in from the building above or from elsewhere, order their breakfast coffee or mushrooms on toast to take away — and while waiting, cut and make their own hot buttered (and jammed) toast. People can breakfast all day if they choose, but we also have takeaway on offer, so that lunchtime diners can have boxes of salads, with some freshly sliced prosciutto or salami from the selection on offer — I call this 'dining al desko'. Acorn House is the canteen for nearby workers, but it's not dissimilar to a home kitchen, very much my style of cooking at home.

Eco Cooking

I'm as ecological about cooking at home as I am in the restaurant. The produce is fresh, local and seasonal, we're dedicated to healthy eating, all our meat and fish are from sustainable sources, not the product of intensive farming, and we never use produce that has been air-freighted. Both buildings are run on green, 'good' electricity, we drink filtered tap water (purified at home and in the restaurant). We compost and recycle, and in every way we are committed to responsibility for the environment. If only all homes and restaurants could be, what a difference that would make...

Green cooking involves all these elements, but it also perhaps requires a slight change in your actual approach to cooking, particularly where saving and retaining energy is concerned. Although I don't cook all that much Chinese-style food, I think that my general approach to cooking is quite Chinese in essence. In a densely forested Britain, we had plenty of wood to burn, so an oven roasting and baking culture was able to develop. In China, wood fuel was limited, so the food culture became one of speedy dishes, trying to make the most of as little energy as possible. In more northerly parts of China, they might have one-pot stews, but the principal national mode of cooking must be the quick stir-fry, which is very green!

I cook similarly, trying always to use as little energy as I can, both to save it, and because I don't think some things need all that much cooking. For instance, I don't light the gas under a pan until the food, some spinach or mussels, say, is actually in it, and I don't preheat the oven for 20 minutes as some recipes suggest, I just bung my food in (although the heat for baking has to be much more precise). I sometimes just pour boiling filtered water over finely chopped vegetables – and spinach leaves – and leave them for a few minutes; often that is enough cooking. Occasionally I might cook some vegetables for a proportion of their cooking time, then turn off the heat source, leaving them to continue cooking in the hot water alone. We don't need to cook things at high all the time; light boiling or gentle frying should be enough to cook most things adequately and deliciously...

I would never dream of having all four burners on the stove blazing away at the same time. If I had four vegetables to cook for a salad, I'd blanch them all in the same filtered water, putting the hardest ones, the ones that would take longest to cook, in first, followed by the others at the relevant times. I don't steam much, but a pot with several layers, potatoes in the water in the bottom, with beans and/or carrots, and/or fish on top, is a very green way of cooking. I'd always save the water I'd blanched, cooked or steamed in, to make the sauce or a stock for soup the next day; if it was too strong in flavour, I'd cool it down and use it to water my plants or the garden (it will have lots of vegetable goodness in it).

Or you could take the idea one step further, and cook everything in one heatproof and ovenproof pot, a stew or casserole for instance. By frying/ searing first in the same pot, and then adding the liquid and the lid, you are capturing all the flavours and textures of the frying, and retaining all the fragrance of the steam as the food cooks slowly on the hob or in the oven. If you present the cooking dish at the table, you are saving on washing up as well!

If I turn the oven on, I'll utilise it to the full, cooking a whole meal in it – the meat, vegetables, potatoes (sometimes all together in the same tray) – and I often try and cook something else, perhaps for the next day, at the same time. I always try to use the heat of the oven after I've finished cooking, as an oven takes really quite a long time to cool down. I'll pop in some halved tomatoes or strawberries to dry (or you could do very thinly sliced apples, pineapple, whatever), or I'll put chicken bones in to brown a little for stock to use in my one-pot wonder the next day. You could dry out breadcrumbs for coating foods, or make 'breadsticks': I cut up pitta bread and dry it in the turned-off oven for Aron to dip into hummus or aubergine purée.

These thoughts may seem obvious, but by cooking in one pot, rather than baking a potato, frying a pork chop and boiling some greens, you are saving quite a lot of energy. It's a small change in your attitude to cooking, but it could contribute to a large saving in energy.

Arthur's Notes

Always have pans with good and tightly fitting lids, so that energy is retained. The pots will boil quicker, and the food will cook faster. You also use a quarter less energy.

Although I usually like to cook things fresh, you could occasionally cook in advance. For instance, if boiling potatoes for supper, do a few extra and take them out after about 10 minutes; then you will have par-boiled potatoes ready to roast for next day's lunch.

If cooking on an electric oven, turn the heat off 10 minutes before your dish is to be ready. There will still be enough heat to finish the dish.

Don't open the oven too often when baking or roasting, as this can reduce the temperature by as much as 25 degrees.

Don't put a small pot on a large burner, you don't want all that heat to be wasted. And flames licking up the sides of a pot is heat you don't need.

I don't know how to use a pressure-cooker, but that's possibly the most eco of all cooking methods: all in one pot, one source of energy, and quick cooking.

Think laterally. Sometimes I cook hard-boiled eggs in the same pan I am cooking vegetables or pasta in...

And, a tip I learned from Albert Roux, when cooking vegetables, bring those from underground to the boil in cold water, those from above the ground plunge into boiling water.

Cooking for Children

As I've said, my family were to a large extent the inspiration for how I've chosen to cook at Acorn House. I think customers realise that too, as we have quite a few children eating with their parents and grandparents. If Aron comes in, he could immediately have many of the dishes on offer, any day of the week: the broccoli, the pumpkin, or the sweet potato or bean soups. If he wanted a bit of animal protein, he could have a thinly sliced piece of lamb, some mackerel or sea bream. One of my pet hates is the children's menu in restaurants, which usually offers fatty, processed foods: sausages or deep-fried nuggets of some unidentifiable meat, with deep-fried chips and canned baked beans. But children, if they are introduced to good food from an early age and aren't exposed to too much relentless TV advertising and peer pressure at school, can eat a much more varied and healthier range of foods than we think. And I believe that they can naturally veer towards foods that are good for them: they haven't quite lost that instinctive feeling about food.

At the time of writing, my son Aron is three and a half, and my daughter Tuula is nine months. Because she is so young, she is vegetarian. We are following all the obvious stages of weaning, as we did with Aron: no potential allergens, such as cow's milk (we use goat's instead), berries or nuts, and no salt and sugar. We are trying out one type of food at a time: mashed banana one week, then mashed sweet potato or broccoli. *Al dente* is not the culinary watchword here: all her foods have to be cooked very well in order to purée successfully, and in order for them to be properly digestible (I see the end result in her nappies, after all!).

When I cook food for Aron, he doesn't have much animal protein, perhaps a chicken leg or a bit of fish every couple of weeks at a weekend lunchtime. His protein needs the rest of the time are adequately supplied by organic cheeses and yoghurts, nuts and seeds, and he has an occasional beanburger or a GM-free soy sausage, both served with organic baked beans and a green vegetable. I sometimes cook him mashed potatoes with French beans sticking out like a hedgehog, or some home-made fish fingers. I cut sustainable white fish, pollack perhaps, not necessarily cod, into fingers, then breadcrumb them and deep-fry them with some chips. Deep-frying is not a bad way of cooking, so long as the oil is hot enough, and the food is drained really well. (And the oil is out after two uses, to go through my Bokashi system, see page 261.) He has good lunches at school, and drinks filtered water, rice and almond milks.

Aron always has a sustaining breakfast: some muesli, porridge or organic Weetabix with rice milk and honey, or pieces of toast or oatcakes with butter and something on top (peanut butter — he loves peanuts — pear spread or organic jam or honey). Sometimes he eats a tortilla wrap with jam and peanut butter together (I like that too). I tried once to include mashed banana, but he wouldn't have it.

Children love holding their food, much better fun than using a spoon (a knife and fork later). So Aron is very keen on crudités and dips: fingers of cucumber, carrot or pepper, perhaps dried pitta strips or breadsticks, with organic or home-made hummus or aubergine purée. He also loves fruit to eat in the hand: his favourites are bananas, grapes, apples and pears, and he goes mad for strawberries. He's passionate about those packs of raisins that are too small for me to get my finger into!

Food should be exciting and enticing for children, never something just to eat because Mum and Dad said so. Children should also know about food and where it comes from, and we take our two regularly to zoos, farm parks and pick-your-own fields where they can see cows being milked, people pulling potatoes out of the ground, and can actually pick (and probably eat) a strawberry or raspberry themselves. Another way of involving them is letting them help in the kitchen. Aron and Paloma make bread together regularly, and often I am greeted when I get home with a (roughly) whale-shaped biscuit he's baked that afternoon. I try and include the two children when I'm cooking at home too: both of them get their hands in the mixing bowl when I'm baking, and Aron is ace at flouring cake tins and rolling pizza bases. If I'm grating carrots or cheese, he's there alongside me, and eating most of it when I'm not looking.

I'm not too upset about this sort of snacking, as I think he takes in more nourishment through his snacks than he sometimes does at his main meals. The three-meals-a-day, full-tummy concept — for both children and adults — is very much a western thing, and children should probably graze rather than sit down at specified times. I keep bowls of food on the kitchen table — fruits like grapes, or a mixture of peanuts and raisins — and often when I am playing with Aron in his room, he'll disappear for a minute and come back munching. He was hungry, and those nuts fulfilled his immediate need. It may not be long until supper, but no matter. Aron will eat when he is hungry, and so long as what he eats is good for him, I'm not going to discourage him.

As an adult, you have the opportunity always to check what you are putting into your body, but children have to rely heavily on those around them to feed them healthily. Therefore, as parents and guardians, we must be doubly aware of, and hold ourselves responsible for, what our children consume. My brother was very hyperactive as a child, and so my mother, in all her wisdom, started to look at what was being fed to him at school and at home. She found the hyperactivity diminished when she cut refined sugars and the dreaded E numbers out of his diet.

For instance, E122, which is a red food colouring, is in many processed foods that children might have, like jellies, sweets, marzipan, brown sauce, etc; it creates asthma and hyperactivity, and is carcinogenic to animals. E951, aspartame, is an artificial sweetener, so if trying to cut back on your child's consumption of sugar, avoid this like the plague. It is in soft drinks, chewing gum, diet drinks, anything which claims it is sugar-free, and, most horrifically, it is in children's medication. It can cause depression, anxiety, asthma, fatigue, hyperactivity, aggression, migraines, insomnia, irritability...

The following is a list of E numbers, which my mother drew up after my brother's problems were recognised, and stuck on the fridge door for us to be aware of and memorise (this 25-year-old list is off the top of my head!): E102, E104, E110, E122, E123, E124, E127, E128, E129, E131, E132, E133, E142. These potentially harmful additives are a classic example of the human diet echoing the grander scale of the planet: toxins, chemicals and general pollutants being consumed either through ignorance of or disregard for the outcome.

NOT COOKING

Before man discovered fire, all foods would have been raw, so to a certain extent our bodies have been designed to eat raw foods. Once we learned how to cook, many more foods would have become accessible: what had previously been indigestible and unpalatable — primarily the grains — could become part of the diet, and indeed the grains are now permanent staples in cuisines all over the world.

Some people choose to eat a diet that is entirely raw. Although I am a great advocate of raw food, I like cooking as well, and would think that about 75 per cent of our diet could (perhaps should) be raw. In one sense, raw food is optimum food: it still possesses its undiluted energy, and as soon as you cook it, you are taking away a lot of its potential. Raw vegetables and fruits are packed full of vitamins and minerals, many of which are destroyed by cooking, or at least diminished. At the same time, of course, many raw foods are so fibrous that they would be indigestible to many eaters. I give Tuula, my baby daughter, a raw piece of carrot to suck, but she can only actually eat that carrot cooked. My grandparents might have a problem with too much raw food in their diet as well, and their vegetables might have to be cooked, perhaps even more than *al dente*.

Fruits are the obvious raw foods, and we should all eat as many as we can, perhaps for breakfast: an apple and a banana, or strawberries and blueberries, with some oats would be perfect. You could add some organic honey, some toasted nuts and seeds, some organic cow's milk (or rice or almond milk), and that breakfast would happily carry you through to the midday meal. You could serve the fruit with some yoghurt, or purée them together to make a smoothie.

Many more vegetables than tomatoes (actually a fruit) can be eaten raw. I serve crudités at the restaurant, vegetable sticks to dip into (cooked) purées of chickpeas or aubergine. That would make a good start to a meal, even if cooked food were to follow. Small broccoli or cauliflower florets can be used in salads (or with dips as well), as can grated carrot, zucchini (courgettes) or beetroot. Raw zucchini are actually delicious in a salad; I do one with raw, thinly sliced button mushrooms. I love to have a fresh vegetable juice every week, perhaps the best way to get raw goodness into your body. And it's easier — you don't have to chew your way through a raw beetroot and six carrots. Put chunks through the juicer and you get instant vitality. However, raw vegetables, particularly beetroot, can be very powerful. I once had a beetroot, apple and carrot juice when I was hot and thirsty after cycling. My body and my kidneys reacted straightaway, and I nearly fainted. That taught me a lesson... Too much beetroot!

Raw foods fulfil most of my eco principles about ingredients. They have to be fresh, seasonal and locally sourced — preferably the beansprouts from your sprouter (see below), or the carrot plucked from your allotment or window-box. The best raw food is undeniably the one you have grown yourself. In fact, when I'm picking a vegetable from the garden, at work or at home, I tend to eat quite a lot of it then and there.

If you haven't grown it yourself, then you have to be even more meticulous about knowing how and where a raw food was grown. Thorough washing might get rid of some agrochemicals, but not all, so if you want to eat raw, you really have to buy organic. This is particularly important when feeding children. Those bags of raw cut carrots in the supermarket worry me: the carrots were probably grown in nitrate- and phosphate-enhanced soil, they were then industrially washed and cut, and packed in gas-filled bags to keep them looking fresh. Raw they may be, but fresh and good they may not be.

Fish and meat can be eaten raw too. When I was at Cecconi's, I put steak tartare on the menu, an old recipe from the 1960s. The ladies that lunched were particularly keen, perhaps because it was good in a reducing diet sense (as are most raw foods). Carpaccio of beef would be similarly nutritious and slimming. The meat has to be top quality though, as does the fish for something like sushi. I love sushi: I like the fact that the raw fish is good for me, and that the rice base fills me up! Other shellfish can be eaten raw too, and when in New Zealand, I once prepared an eleven-course food fest of sashimi, where everything was raw from lobster and salmon, to oysters and scallops.

I have had people come into the restaurant and say that, as an environmentally-friendly restaurant, we should be serving only raw and vegetarian food. I always say that although I can prepare them anything they like, part of the Acorn House ethos is not to tell people what they can't eat, but to show them the most responsible way to eat what they want.

Sprouting

The ultimate in grow-your-own at home is sprouted pulses, grains and seeds, and sprouts are among the healthiest of foods, containing a huge number of nutrients. Enzyme activity is said to be highest in seeds, grains and pulses just after they have sprouted – this is the beginning of the adult plant, after all – and it is believed this can directly benefit the human body's own enzyme system.

Sprouts can be eaten as a snack – a handful instead of a biscuit would be healthy and dietary – added raw to salads (or different types mixed in a salad), used as a garnish, or included at the last minute as the raw crunch on top of a stir-fry. You can buy commercial sprouters, which are efficient and inexpensive, but it's much simpler to re-use empty glass coffee jars or similar. Try and involve the children, they would enjoy watching the sprouts grow and then, I hope, enjoy eating them!

The timing and size of sprout depends on the type of seed used. Mung beans produce the familiar and large Chinese beansprouts, and the tiny mustard and cress sprouts are already familiar to us, often appearing in shops ready-sprouted, in small plastic trays. Sprouts have different flavours as well as textures: fenugreek seeds are used ground in Indian curry mixtures as a spice, and their sprouts are spicy as well, great on top of an Asian type salad.

Buy your pulses, grains and seeds from a good supplier, with a fast turnover, to ensure freshness. Put your chosen pulse or seed into a wide-necked glass jar, enough to cover the base in a thick layer when you turn the jar on its side. Cover with cold filtered tap water, and leave overnight in a warm place, then strain. Rinse again with cold water and strain again, then cover the top of the jar with a piece of cheesecloth held on by an elastic band. Put into a cool dark place, on its side, with the seeds or pulses evenly spread, and leave for 12 hours. Repeat this rinsing and draining — doing so through the cheesecloth lid — twice a day for up to 3 days, when the sprouts should have appeared. Allow a little light and air for a day, and the sprouts should be ready to eat. Try to eat the husks as well as the sprouts, as these are good sources of fibre.

Pulses
Aduki beans, Blackeye peas
Chickpeas, Lentils, Mung beans
Soya beans

Grains
Barley, Buckwheat, Maize, Millet
Oats, Rye, Wheat

Seeds
Alfalfa, Fenugreek, Garden cress
Pumpkin, Radish, Sesame
Sunflower, White mustard

WINTER

*Cold days, nights by the fire,
warming comfort foods, and
the promise of spring
to come...*

The ancients celebrated the winter solstice of December, naming it Yule. This was when the new year's cycle began, and the sun child was reborn, an image of the return of all new life. One can begin to understand why Christmas and our own New Year came to be celebrated at this time.

The weather is cold in December, yes, although not so cold as in January and February, and the light is inert and dull — perhaps why we have made the principal celebrations of the month so 'sparkling' and 'merry', the antithesis of grey. Regarding fresh ingredients, December is fairly lean, but as a food and cooking month, it is perhaps the most hectic of the whole year. Everyone wants to be fed, to be warm, to have a good time, and as a person who supplies all those things, I am at my busiest. And I find myself slowing my own consumption down, ready for the mother of all blowouts as Christmas fast approaches.

As with the cut grass in March, the characteristic smell of December to me is that of clementines. Imported they may be, but they are very definitely part of our celebrations. I buy three boxes for our huge family get-together, and they're never enough. We put the peel on the open fires, which wafts a wonderful aroma throughout the house, and because of all the children, we are still finding half-eaten fruits hidden under sofas in February. And, as for Christmas leftovers, I find I'm cooking those for about four days afterwards.

In January we are in the middle of winter, when produce is at its very leanest, and the weather is usually unpleasant. Warming, deep, rich and hearty stews, broths, one-pot wonders, even one-pot roasts are the order of the day. January is probably the quietest month of the year for me, after the New Year excitement has died down. I actually look forward to it, to cooking and eating simply, for there's no way I could continue to consume as I did in the last two weeks of December. Potentially, January is a time for reflection, looking back on the year past, on the successes of the garden, and looking forward to what I will grow, cook and eat in the coming new year. It's a preparatory month for the rest of the year.

February is the most miserable month for most of us in Britain. It's usually dark, rainy and windy, and fresh food is scarce. It's the back end of winter. However, hope is in the air. The nights are getting gradually lighter, daffodils are beginning to appear, and the sap is rising. This is when the trees and plants begin to reverse their cycle after the cold of the winter: the energy rises up from the roots, buried deep in the soil, and back into the branches; and buds begin to emerge. In many ways, February is actually the beginning of the natural year's cycle, and although there is very little fresh produce ready, nature begins to reawaken.

Historically, in preparation for the year ahead, the body makes use of this period of scarcity to cleanse itself. It is no accident that this is the beginning of the Lenten fast. Many of the foods available now have an important role to play in the body's cleansing process, such as the bitter leaves of dandelion, endive and chicory. February is definitely the 'detox' month (although don't forget the comforting pancakes on Shrove Tuesday).

Another resource that we once would have been about to turn to at this time of year is the remainder of the winter larder. In February, all the hard work put in at the end of the summer to build up supplies for winter — curing meats, drying mushrooms and preserving fruits and vegetables — is going to be most appreciated. If the larder was well stocked, there should still be things left like dried beans and fruit, nuts, bacon, ham and sausages (salami), dried mushrooms, pickles, jams, preserves and cheeses. That familiar pub staple, the ploughman's lunch, is an historic example of this: it consists of cheese and pickles, foods that would have been left over after the winter, and eaten when the ploughman was out preparing the land for the spring sowing — and the whole cycle starting again.

Arthur's Winter Growing Tips

In my garden at home, throughout the year, there is a phenomenon that I call the transmigration of slugs and snails. Because of my beliefs, I cannot kill them, so if I spot them on my sage, they tend to fly, ever so gently, over the hedge into my neighbours' gardens. I'm not at all certain that they don't do the same to me, and I suspect there is a constant to and fro movement of these particular pests in North London. If one day I was hit on the head, my theory would be proven...

Any vegetable beds that become vacant now should be dug over and manured or composted. In milder parts of the country, it might not be too late to plant a green manure of alfalfa, clover or tares, which can be dug in before the spring planting. (Don't let the green manure plants set seeds, though!)

You could leave a few runner bean pods on the plants until they turn brown; use the beans inside for next year's crop. Cut the plants down and compost them, but leave the roots in the soil; like broad beans and peas, the roots of runner beans contain nitrogen, which contributes to soil health and fertility.

Put seed potatoes in the holes in cardboard egg boxes, with their 'eyes' (from which the sprouts will grow) uppermost. Place in a cool room or greenhouse, and give them plenty of light. A north-facing window in a garage or shed would be ideal. Then plant them in soil in March/early to late April, depending on variety.

You can keep seedlings and small plants warm in the soil during winter, even if you haven't got a greenhouse. Cut 2-litre plastic bottles in half lengthways, and place them over the plants as mini cloches.

Try using cardboard egg boxes as indoor seed trays. Fill the little containers with seeding compost, and plant herb or vegetable seeds. Water as normal, and when the seedlings are big enough, plant out in the garden, egg box and all. Plastic egg boxes can be used too (although they can't be 'planted'), and when closed, their translucent tops act almost as a built-in propagator.

If your garden is overlooked or windswept, you could plant a line of Jerusalem artichoke plants now to act as a screen or windbreak in the summer months. They grow quickly – up to 2–3 metres high – and then you can harvest the vegetables from October. Two for the price of one! In the meantime, put up a wind-break made from bamboo or something similar.

In our potato barrel we grow a few unusual blue-fleshed Salad Blue potatoes for fun. Why not grow one potato plant inside a black bin bag filled with soil, with the bin bag tied loosely round the stem of the potato. You'd get back more than you'd planted.

What I buy in December

Vegetables
Artichokes (Jerusalem), beetroot, broccoli (purple sprouting), Brussels sprouts, Brussels tops, cabbages (green, red, white), carrots, celeriac, celery, chard, chicory, endive, horseradish, kale, leeks, lettuce, nettles, onions, parsnips, potatoes, pumpkins, salsify, spinach, swede, turnips

Fruit
Apples, pears, rhubarb (forced), rosehips, sloes

Fish
Eels, haddock, mackerel, sprats, whiting

Shellfish
Cockles, crab (brown, cock, hen), mussels, oysters (rock)

Game
Hare, partridge, pheasant, snipe, venison (doe), woodcock

Fungi
White truffles

Nuts
Almonds, Brazil nuts, chestnuts, hazelnuts, walnuts

How I eat in December

Just like squirrels, my family could partially exist at this time of year on nuts, seeds and dried fruit. At one time this would have been early man's subsistence diet, for fresh foods would have been rare, and animals, birds and man would have competed for what was still available on plant, tree or bush. The Romans introduced many of the fruit and nut trees that we now take for granted in northern Europe, among them the temperate pears, apples, plums and cherries, as well as those which can only grow in sheltered positions, such as grapes, figs, peaches and apricots. Crusaders returning to England from the east in medieval times introduced dried fruits and nuts such as sultanas, raisins, dates and almonds, and it must have been at this time that these foods became part of our British culinary consciousness: how else would our traditions of plum pudding, Christmas pudding and mince pies still be so strong?

If these expensive imported dried fruits and nuts were once used in celebratory foods, I now use them primarily as snacks. Nuts and seeds are the 'eggs' of the vegetable world, so are packed full of oily nutrients (all produce oils); fruit's goodness and flavours are intensified by the drying process, so I think you can eat your fill! They are wonderful substances, really good for the whole family — apart from babies, of course, and the very few unfortunates who are allergic to nuts. Do tell anyone you are cooking for if you are including nuts. A nut allergy is incredibly dangerous…

Nuts are fantastic. They are oily, tasty, full of nutrients, and they are so versatile. If you are vegetarian, vegan, meat-free or dairy-free, nuts are almost essential. Aron loves nuts to eat in the hand, particularly peanuts in the shell and cashew nuts. I try and buy cashews plain, when they haven't got that heavy, greasy, salty texture. At this time of year I have a bowl of nuts on the kitchen table full of almonds, hazelnuts, walnuts and Brazil nuts; the nutcracker is nearby. I love pistachios (which I grind up to use in a sweet soufflé), sweet chestnuts and macadamia nuts, and my favourites, which I buy too many of (in their brief season), are cobnuts. Culinary nut oils, particularly hazelnut and walnut, are delicious, strong, instantly recognisable, and very expensive to buy. Add them to your house dressing for a distinctly different and delicious flavour. I use mainly sunflower oil in my frying, which is made from sunflower seeds. Peanut oil is widely used as well, as is sesame seed oil in Asian cooking. I use sesame oil over my salads, with a touch of wine vinegar.

A combination of nuts and dried fruit as a snack is full of power — and calories. Sometimes I make a mistake before lunch or dinner and grab a handful from the bowl, and then I don't have any room left for the meal. Whenever I go out walking I take a packet of nuts and raisins, much more powerful and sustaining than a Mars bar; they would be good on a long flight too, better than the in-flight food, and would be really good for the jet-lagged digestion.

Nut salads are brilliant, and you can play around with different flavours and textures. There's the classic Waldorf, in which walnuts play a major role (with apple, celery and lettuce); nuts would go happily with blue cheese in a salad, and with avocado (although that's for a different season). You can toast the nuts slightly, either whole or roughly chopped, and add to a well-dressed salad as a crunchy and tasty topping. I do a great winter leaf salad — crunchy celery, some celeriac, organic iceberg lettuce (from a poly tunnel), and some dandelion leaves if I can get them; I serve some warm nuts on top (cashews are great). What would be even better is to toss the warm nuts with some salt, pepper and paprika before adding to the salad. That would make a lunch in itself.

Nut butters are something I eat quite often. Peanut butter is the most familiar: as a young teenager, I used to take a tub of organic peanut butter and a pint of milk to help me through my homework... Aron and I both enjoy it as a spread with bread and butter, and I do a satay-style chicken dish with it. There are other nut butters: try almond, macadamia or cashew nut. Cashew butter spread on good bread with lovely strawberry jam on top is delicious, and very sustaining. Almonds ground down and mixed with icing sugar and egg whites, makes one of the most familiar of sweetmeats, marzipan.

I've mentioned nut milk before, it's what I have regularly in my small fridge at home instead of cow's milk. You can buy it in the shops, or you can make it at home. Purée the nuts and add water, then drip through a piece of muslin. It has a lovely rich texture, and you can make almond milk blancmange, almond milk pannacotta, etc.

I make nut sauces too. I blanch walnuts in milk, then pull the outside skin off. You crush down this white nut in the mortar (brushed first with a tiny hint of garlic), along with white bread, wine vinegar, salt, pepper and extra virgin olive oil. This makes a white pesto or salsa bianca, which is great with pasta. You can do this with other nuts as well, almonds for instance. To make a green pesto, instead of the traditional pine nuts, you could use walnuts, almonds or peanuts (along with garlic, extra virgin olive oil, basil and Parmesan).

Cooked nuts are good too. I use nuts (and seeds and dried fruit) in stuffings for birds, and simply roasting some nuts, then salting and/or spicing them when out of the oven, makes a great canapé. They can be baked into breads, or ground and used as flour.

We eat a lot of seeds at home, and throughout the year we have a bowl on the kitchen table with pumpkin seeds, sunflower seeds and raisins, sultanas or currants, sometimes sesame seeds. We snaffle some as we pass, even Aron, and don't hanker after chocolate biscuits (often). You can eat them raw, or toast them for extra flavour. I serve toasted seeds on top of cereal, porridge, yoghurt or mixed fruit for breakfast, sometimes with honey, sometimes with some dried fruit. Sesame seeds are used in the glorious tahini, which I use in sauces (but I don't make my own, the bought organic is delicious). And pine nuts (actually a kernel or seed rather than a nut) can be used in pestos, or toasted and sprinkled on top of salads and other dishes. (Try to buy Italian, they are much more creamy than Chinese.) But seeds can be baked into biscuits and breads, both savoury and sweet, and they can be baked and spiced for a canapé, or sprinkled on top of salads, where they add incredible texture. I try to dry-roast the saved seeds from when I cook pumpkins and squashes, and eat them the way the Spanish do, but it must be an eating habit they acquire in childhood. I've been trying for years, but I always end up with a mouth full of dross!

Dried fruits are magic at this time of year. We have the fresh citrus coming in from abroad, but I love the intense flavours and interesting textures of dried dates (always Medjool), dried mango, apricots, pineapple, prunes, figs, bananas and apples, not forgetting our own currants, and the more luscious raisins and sultanas. Most of these are coming in already dried, but be careful to buy organic or Fairtrade: some non-organic dried fruit uses sulphur as a preservative, and some fruits have too much added sugar for my taste. I don't dry much fruit myself, apart from tomatoes and strawberries, and those usually only when the oven has just been switched off from cooking something else. But you could try it at home, at a very low oven temperature (110-120°C/Fan 90–100°C/Gas ¼-½): thin slices of apple or pineapple could work well.

What's great about dried fruit is that you can eat it as it is, or you can rehydrate it. I make a winter salad of rehydrated dried fruits, including prunes and dates, which I serve with crème fraîche. When I am cooking an apple purée for Tuula, I will sometimes include a slice of dried pineapple: this plumps up, and adds an extra flavour and texture. I bake prunes with rhubarb and apple in a crumble. When I am cooking lentils, I often include a couple of dried apricots, which melt in, adding sweetness and unctuousness — and with a spot of ground cumin, the flavour is unbeatable.

DABD (Day After Boxing Day) Soup

This is the sort of hearty soup my father makes, with leftovers, which the family tuck into after Christmas. This is really a rough guide to show you how thrift can be delicious, and good for you, and it might deliver some respite from the fatty, high cholesterol diet of the past few days. Everyone will love it.

For 6–8

1.5kg pork bones (leftover from Christmas Day), roasted
3 carrots
1 head celery
2 onions, peeled
200g pearl barley
100g red lentils
6 garlic cloves, peeled
3 bay leaves
½ bunch thyme
2 tbsp Volpaia herb vinegar
1 tsp ground allspice
1 dried red chilli
leftover cooked vegetables (potatoes, Brussels sprouts, parsnips), chopped
extra virgin olive oil
sea salt and freshly ground black pepper

Put the pork bones in a pot large enough to accommodate all the ingredients. Cover with 5 litres cold filtered water. With nothing else in the pot, bring to the boil and then skim off any foam rising to the top. Then add all the remaining ingredients except for the cooked vegetables and oil, and bring back to the boil. Skim once more, then turn down and simmer for 2 hours. Add the cooked vegetables, and some olive oil. Check the seasoning, and pull out the bones if you like — but I take the soup to the table, bones and all.

Scrambled Eggs on Toast with Smoked Salmon & White Truffle

This is my favourite Christmas breakfast, and one that I have every 2 years. So please excuse the slight expense. It really is worth it, and I serve it with very cold rosé champagne. My father Chris adores this, and it is great to see his face every time he eats it. Nice one!

For 6

18 large eggs
sea salt and freshly ground black pepper
200ml double cream
1 large white bloomer loaf, sliced for toasting
100g butter
300g smoked salmon
100g white truffle, finely grated

For the best scrambled eggs, break all the eggs into a metal bowl, and lightly season with salt and pepper. Place this bowl over a pan of boiling water and whisk slowly, allowing the eggs to catch slightly. Whisking too vigorously will create a rather fine type of scramble, which I don't really like. I want some texture to the eggs. As the mixture comes up to heat, watch that it does not overcook. Now here is the trick: pour in the double cream to take the immediate heat out, and stir. This will allow you a little time to toast the bread now and pour the champagne. Scrambled eggs for me should always be hot so don't hang around here.

Drop in a knob of butter for richness and check the seasoning. On each plate, place a piece of buttered toast and a good dollop of the eggs. Lay 50g of the salmon next to the eggs and top the whole dish off with about 15g of extremely finely grated white truffle. Eat it fast.

Potato, Cheddar, Bobby Bean & Pickled Onion Salad

I play football on Boxing Day with my 4 brothers, and with the addition of our 8 children, the team is getting bigger! Getting back for lunch, with nothing on the table, this is quick and easy, and goes down a treat with a little local cider.

For 1

120g cooked potatoes, in large chunks
80g cooked large French beans
60g Cheddar, broken into thumbnail-sized pieces
4 medium pickled onions
2 sprigs curly parsley
2 tsp extra virgin olive oil
sea salt and freshly ground black pepper

Arrange the ingredients on a plate. Drizzle over the olive oil and lightly season with salt and pepper.

Slow-roasted Pork, with Spinach, Orach & Potato Salad

Unless for some reason you know how to skin and bone a pork shoulder, asking your butcher to do it is no problem. I always ask for the bones to be kept and cracked in half. Use these in your DABD soup (see page 208). This is an old Italian recipe, for pork cooked in milk; the milk coagulates the protein of the pork, and you get these wonderful creamy blobs of milky protein...

For 12

1 shoulder of pork, skinned and boned
3 heads garlic, cut in half horizontally
1 big bunch sage
4 lemons, peeled (without pith), peel finely chopped
15 juniper berries
at least 1kg small porcini or button mushrooms (I can't believe I've just said that!)
250g butter
4-5 litres milk, warmed
1 cinnamon stick
freshly grated nutmeg, to taste

Spinach, Orach and Potato Salad
at least 700g baby leaf spinach
350g young tender red orach leaves (or another red leaf)
2kg Ratte or Roseval potatoes (even Purple Congo), cooked, and halved or
    quartered, depending on size
4 slices white bread
extra virgin olive oil
balsamic vinegar
lemon juice (from above)
sea salt and freshly ground black pepper

Season the shoulder's fatty side and place fat-side down into a large, cold, flameproof casserole dish. This should be bigger rather than smaller, as it is the surface area that is important in the cooking. Turn on the heat to medium and allow the temperature to rise. I find this is the best way to render the fat off the shoulder; continue on medium for 25 minutes to really start to melt the fat. Increase the heat to allow the golden colour of this dish to start to show. Another 10 minutes and this side should start to look golden and already smell delicious. Turn the meat over and on a high heat keep colouring until deep golden brown, about 15 minutes. When you can't colour it any more, take the meat out of the pan and pour away all of the melted fat (keep this), you will be surprised how much there is! There should be some lovely flavours in the pan right now and we must try to keep them.

Put the garlic, sage, lemon peel, juniper berries and mushrooms into the pan with the butter and fry them all until golden too. There are some wonderful deep rich flavours in this dish because of all our hard work at this time. Tip out these ingredients into a colander, just keep the solids, and let the fat pour away (keep of course for recycling). Separate out the mushrooms, and keep for later.

Put the meat back in the pan over a medium heat and begin to ladle in the warm milk, and add the cinnamon, nutmeg and all of the fried ingredients. Put the lid on, but leaving a little space; you want a steamy, humid atmosphere for the pork. Continue to add the milk as the rest evaporates. This dish will take at least 2½ hours, but is so worth it (mind you, a turkey takes 4). Add the reserved mushrooms about 5 minutes before serving, just to warm through.

To start the salad, wash and dry the spinach and orach leaves, and put on to a serving dish with the potatoes. Toast the bread until crisp, then break into croûtons over the top of the salad. Dress the salad to taste with olive oil, balsamic vinegar and lemon juice. Check and adjust the seasoning.

You know the pork is ready when you can cut through the centre of the meat with a spoon. Check the seasoning and serve on a large serving platter, with the mushrooms, and the salad on a separate dish.

Brandy Pannacotta with Mincemeat Sauce

If you want, you could do this whole recipe in one big dish, rather than in six individual moulds. Or put the pannacotta mix in a big jelly mould — it is actually what you could call a cooked cream jelly.

For 6

1.2 litres double cream
1 vanilla pod, split
finely grated zest of 2 lemons
3 gelatine leaves
140ml milk
160g icing sugar
brandy, to taste

To serve
home-made mincemeat, brandy and double cream

Put 900ml of the cream, the vanilla and lemon zest into a large pot and boil to reduce down to 600ml. Pass through a fine sieve into a bowl, making sure you get all the vanilla seeds into the cream.

Soak the gelatine in the milk for 10 minutes, and then warm up the milk in a pan until the gelatine disappears. Pass that through the same sieve into the cream in the bowl, so you really wash out all the flavours. Place the bowl on top of another bowl full of ice, and stir to take the heat out of it.

Whip the rest of the cream with the icing sugar in a separate bowl to form soft peaks, and here's the trick to a perfect pannacotta: fold the whipped cream into the gelatine mixture, and pour in as much brandy as you can handle (start with 2 tablespoons, and remember who is going to be eating the pud). Keep stirring that mixture until it begins to set.

This allows for all of the vanilla seeds to be evenly spread through the pannacotta.

Pour into six ramekins or small metal bowls or moulds, and refrigerate until set, up to 4 hours. To turn them out, plunge them bottom-down in a bowl of boiling water for 1 second, then flip them over and out on to a serving plate.

I always have a jar of good local organic vegetarian mincemeat in the fridge at this time of year. Take a few tablespoons and let them down with brandy and double cream to taste. Warm up a little, then serve as a sauce, over the top and around the edges of the turned-out pannacottas.

What I buy in January

Vegetables
Artichokes (Jerusalem), beetroot (stored), broccoli (purple sprouting), Brussels sprouts, Brussels tops, cabbages (green, red, Savoy, white), carrots, celeriac, celery, chard, chicory, cima di rapa (brassica family), endive, horseradish, kale, kohlrabi, leeks, lettuce, nettles, onions, parsnips, potatoes, pumpkins and squash, salsify, spinach, swede, turnips

Fruit
Apples, oranges (blood, Seville), pears, rhubarb (forced), rosehips, sloes

Fish
Haddock, mackerel, scallops (hand-dived only), whiting

Shellfish
Cockles, crab (brown, cock, hen), mussels, oysters (rock)

Game
Hare, partridge, pheasant, snipe, woodcock

Nuts
Almonds, Brazil nuts, chestnuts, walnuts

If I had cooked a large bird, I would strip the carcass of leftover meat, boil the carcass down for a stock either for soup in which to use the meat (with lots of vegetables) or a risotto, which would also use the meat. Leftover pasta is great in a salad or a pasta bake, or can be used as a last-minute ingredient in a soup.

With such a large family, we always tend to cook too much spaghetti – and the chickens go mad for it, they must think it is worms!

I plan ahead. Whenever pot-roasting or slow-roasting meat or poultry, I shred and dice whatever is left over, perhaps run some chopped parsley through it, and place into a suitable container that will allow me to turn it out on to a plate as if it were a terrine. And usually something like a pork shoulder, with its fatty content, will allow for thin slices to be cut and served with a salad, quite refreshing.

On Boxing Day, I always purposefully cook too many potatoes, as turning on the oven uses up a lot of energy. But I can mash them up the next day, cold, and mix with leftover cooked veg, fry in a frying pan as bubble and squeak, and serve a fried egg on top for a great breakfast.

In my kitchen, one of the most effective ways in which to watch out for food waste and costs is by using everything up throughout the whole year.

Particularly at Christmas time, my kitchen seems to fill up with leftovers from both snacks and large meals, and rather than waste all this great food, I tend to store it all up. Then I deliver a delicious lunch the next day without anyone noticing that it consists of leftovers, and no one becomes jaded by the fact that they've eaten Brussels sprouts for 3 days. On the one hand it saves money, but on the other, environmentally, I am using every last bit of food.

How I eat in January

Arrgh! Cabbages were something of a horror in my childhood. The smell from the kitchen was often enough for all of us to play hide and seek with my mum when she called us for dinner. But oh, how far I have come since then! I now happily eat anything and everything, and the variety of the cabbage family never ceases to amaze me. There are kales, red, white and green cabbages, miniature cabbages (Brussels), cavolo nero, cauliflower and broccoli, and many others. Their colours, shapes and sizes all differ, as do their flavours, and this has helped to inspire me to use them in many different ways. And cabbages are really important in our diets, as they are packed full of vitamins and minerals. The humble cabbage has carried us through the centuries — it is one of the oldest known vegetables — being hardy and trustworthy, honest and workmanlike. It is also with us throughout the seasons of the year in its differing guises. You can do a lot worse than relying on the cabbage family for sustenance.

The cabbage family began with a plant that was leggy and loose-leaved, rather like kale (a close and possibly even older relative), then it was persuaded to form a head or heart. One cultivar formed a head of loose or tight leaves, giving us the blue-green, crinkly- and fairly loose-leaved Savoy cabbage and the tight-headed white and green cabbages (as well as the loose-leaved curly kale, and spring greens). Another cultivar of the headed cabbage was made to change colour, thus we have red cabbages. Yet another was persuaded to grow numerous small budding heads on long stalks (in Belgium), and Brussels sprouts were created. Cabbages which were encouraged to flower developed into cauliflower and broccoli and their close relatives.

An old staple of the British Isles was pottage, a thick soup made with things like barley and cabbage, and often without the scarce meat. It is a great and hearty dish, and one I find myself connecting with every time I eat it, as it is something my ancestors would have eaten and been thankful for.

In my early days with the Roux brothers, I blanched and stuffed cabbage leaves to create parcels of succulent minced game. These I gently steamed and served with a wonderfully rich veal jus.

Red cabbage is delicious eaten raw. When it is cooked, the colouring pigment can turn from that appetising red to a distinctly unappetising lilac-green. To prevent this, add some vinegar when cooking. When I worked in France, I made the most wonderfully rich casserole of shredded red cabbage, to which I added raisins, brown sugar, star anise, bay leaves, red wine, butter and that all-important red wine vinegar. I casseroled this in a low oven (150°C/Fan 130°C/Gas 2) for about 2½ hours, stirring occasionally. This is good with game, or sausages, or anything...

In Italy, I have shredded and cooked Savoy cabbage on the stove for 2 hours with peeled apples, sultanas, Marsala wine, thyme and honey. This was to accompany a roast loin of pork.

At the River Cafe, I cooked cavolo nero (black cabbage) and garlic cloves until soft in a pan of boiling filtered water, then puréed it all to a fine paste and mixed into soft wet polenta as a garnish for wood pigeon. One of my favourites is boiled cavolo nero on bruschetta with the first of the new season's extra virgin olive oil drizzled over the top. It's so simple and really is the taste of winter.

Many cabbages don't require long or complicated cooking. Some can be shredded and simply stir-fried with garlic and other flavourings. Curly green kale I eat at this time of year at home, simply stir-fried with light olive oil and some soy sauce sprinkled over the top. You could also add shreds to soups like ribollita, or a more Scottish way, mixed with potatoes and grain. You could use leaves in bubble and squeak. (Did you know that kale was once known as 'cole' or 'colewort' in England, which become 'collards' in the US?) Spring greens (see page 18) can be used in the same way.

Many cabbages don't need cooking at all. In New Zealand, I made a wonderful coleslaw salad with red and white cabbage, home-made mayonnaise and toasted cumin seeds ground up and sprinkled in.

At Kensington Place Restaurant, I cooked Brussels sprouts in butter until a very dark caramel colour, and then I deglazed them with chicken stock and used them as a garnish for grouse. Otherwise, boil them in a pan of plenty of salted filtered water, uncovered, until just tender. They can be eaten with melted butter, or coated with a cheese sauce. Chestnuts and Brussels sprouts is a combination popular in Belgium and in the UK, particularly at Christmas. Cooked sprouts can be shredded and used with potatoes instead of cabbage in bubble and squeak. Raw sprouts can be grated and eaten raw in salads, or stir-fried. They make a good vegetable purée and soup.

Savoy Cabbage Soup & Ricotta Toast

It's a good simple skill to have, making a good chicken stock. A lot of the Jewish friends I have swear that chicken soup cures all their ills — and I have to agree. If you're tired or run-down, or generally unwell, just the chicken stock alone will help you to recover.

For 6

1 Savoy cabbage
1.5 litres nice and rich double chicken stock (see page 266)
sea salt and freshly ground black pepper
6 slices ciabatta bread
2 garlic cloves, peeled
150g ricotta cheese
75g Parmesan, freshly grated
extra virgin olive oil

Remove and discard the tough outer leaves and core of the cabbage. Slice and wash the remainder thoroughly. Bring the stock to the boil in a large pan, add the cabbage and cook until very tender, about 10-12 minutes, then season to taste.

Toast the ciabatta and rub with the garlic. Place a piece of toast in each soup bowl, spoon over the cabbage then ladle over the hot stock. Finish with the ricotta, then sprinkle with Parmesan and olive oil.

Squash Lasagne

This is a real winter warmer. I always feel I should work harder after this lasagne. It's a really powerful dish. Have it with a chilled glass of white wine and you will be set for the afternoon.

For 6 as a starter or 4 as a main course

1.5kg butternut squash, halved, seeded and cut into large chunks
sea salt and freshly ground black pepper
600g fresh pasta dough (see page 269), rolled into lasagne sheets
1 medium onion, peeled and chopped
2 celery stalks, chopped
50g butter
2 tbsp light olive oil
200ml sweet white wine
400ml béchamel sauce (see page270)
250g York ham, chopped
freshly grated nutmeg, to taste
lots of freshly grated Parmesan

Cook the squash in a pan of boiling, salted filtered water for about 20 minutes. Check that it's cooked, then drain. Cook the lasagne sheets in a separate pan of boiling, salted filtered water for a few minutes, just until they rise to the surface. Drain and leave on a cloth to dry.

Preheat the oven to 200°C/Fan 180°C/Gas 6.

Fry the onion and celery in half the butter and the olive oil in a pan for 10 minutes, then add the wine, and continue to cook for another 3 minutes to cook out the alcohol.

Remove the skin from the squash and put the flesh back into the warm saucepan. Whisk it to eliminate the lumps, adding a bit of the cooking liquor if needed. Mix in the béchamel, the onion and celery mixture and the ham, then season and grate in some nutmeg.

Cover the bottom of a medium baking dish with the pasta sheets, then spoon over some of the squash mixture. Repeat until all the ingredients have been used, but make sure you finish with a layer of pasta. Grate lots of Parmesan over the top, and put on a few small knobs of butter. Colour the top in the preheated oven for 20 minutes. Serve hot.

Chickpea, Medjool Date, Quinoa, Feta Cheese & Parsley Salad

I came across quinoa (pronounced 'keenwa') 5 years ago and thought nothing much of it. But everywhere I look for nutrition and vitamins, it keeps showing up. So now I am eating quite a lot of it. It's really good for you, and my daughter Tuula loves it. You can find it in good delicatessens or health-food shops, or you can use brown rice instead. Chickpeas are really good for you too! Perhaps I should rename this 'the good salad'...

For 6

200g cooked quinoa (cooked according to instructions on packet)
400g baby leaf spinach
6 Medjool dates, cut in half and stoned
300g feta cheese
1 bunch chervil, picked
100ml house dressing (see page 270)
6 tbsp finely chopped flat-leaf parsley
sea salt and freshly ground black pepper

Chickpeas
300g dried chickpeas, soaked for 24 hours
1 small potato, peeled
1 fresh red chilli
2 garlic cloves, peeled

For the chickpeas, drain the old water off the chickpeas and rinse well. Tip into a pan, cover by at least 5cm with fresh filtered water. Add the potato, which seems to soften the skins on the chickpeas (don't ask me how, just a trick I learned!), the chilli and garlic. Bring to the boil and skim off the scum, turn the heat down to a simmer and cook for 1½ hours. Make sure the water does not evaporate too much, and keep it topped up if the chickpeas become exposed.

When cooked, pull out the potato, chilli and garlic, and reserve the chickpeas in the water until needed. Don't throw the water away or the chickpeas will dry out! (Incidentally, when I make my own hummus, I use that potato and the soft garlic with some of the chickpea water, lemon juice and bought organic tahini — which makes it so creamy.)

For the salad, put the drained quinoa in a large bowl. Wash and dry the spinach well, and add to the bowl. Mix in the chickpeas, dates, feta, chervil, house dressing and chopped parsley. Season lightly and place on the table. Wait for the empty bowl.

Fillet Steak with Oxtail & Mashed Potatoes

This is a real treat for the darkest days, one to have with a great glass of red wine. Try it on your friends, and surprise the hell out of 'em!

For 4

4 × 175g fillet steaks, trimmed
25g unsalted butter
500g mashed potatoes (cooked until soft, then mashed with butter and milk to taste)
2 spring onions, trimmed and sliced into fine rings

Braised Oxtail
500g oxtail
sea salt and freshly ground black pepper
25g unsalted butter
50g shallots, peeled and finely chopped
25g carrots, finely chopped
25g celery, finely chopped
50g button mushrooms, thickly sliced
750ml red wine
500ml chicken stock (see page 265)
1 fresh bouquet garni (bay, parsley, thyme and 1 celery stalk, tied together)

Preheat the oven to 180°C/Fan 160°C/Gas 4.

For the oxtail, trim the oxtail of all sinew and fat. Cut into segments and season with salt and pepper. Colour the oxtail in the butter in an ovenproof braising pan. Add the shallots, carrots, celery and mushrooms, and fry to colour lightly. Then add the red wine and boil to reduce by half. Add the stock and bouquet garni, and bring back to the boil.

Skim off the scum. Cover and braise in the preheated oven for 2 hours. Remove the oxtail and flake the meat. Set aside in a warm place.

Skim the sauce and pass through a fine sieve, pushing a little. Keep hot.

Fry the steaks in the butter in a pan to your preferred state of doneness, and rest for several minutes.

To assemble, place the mashed potato in the centre of the plates, lay the steaks on top, and then the flaked oxtail. Add a sprinkling of the spring onions and spoon the seasoned sauce around the mashed potatoes.

Tiramisu

A delicious dessert for all the family. Some recipes ask for alcohol, and you can add that if you like, but this is one for the kids. It's the simplest of recipes: play with it if you like, and add white chocolate, vanilla seeds or orange-flower water. Hey, you make the calls after all!

For 6

2 medium egg whites and 4 medium egg yolks
150g icing sugar
420g mascarpone cheese
200g sponge fingers
180ml fresh strong coffee, cooled
180g plain chocolate, grated
good cocoa powder, for dusting

Stiffly whisk the egg whites in a clean bowl. Beat the egg yolks with the sugar in a separate bowl until pale and thick. Fold in the mascarpone gently, then fold in the egg whites.

Make a layer of sponge fingers on the base of a deep, rectangular dish and brush with the coffee. Spread over some of the mascarpone mixture to cover the fingers and sprinkle with some of the grated chocolate. Continue this way until the ingredients are all used up, making sure you end with a layer of mascarpone. Dust with the cocoa and some more grated chocolate and refrigerate for 4 hours before serving.

What I buy in February

Vegetables
Alexanders, artichokes (Jerusalem), bay leaves, beetroot, broccoli (purple sprouting), Brussels sprouts, Brussels tops, cabbages (green, white), cauliflower, celeriac, celery, chard, chicory, dandelion, endive, horseradish, kale, leeks, lettuce, nettles, onions, parsnips, potatoes, pumpkins and squashes, salsify, scorzonera, shallots, spinach, swede, turnips

Fruit
Apples (stored), oranges (blood, Seville), rhubarb (forced)

Fish
Mackerel, skate, whiting

Shellfish
Cockles, crab (brown, cock, hen), mussels, oysters (rock)

Game
Hare, rabbit, venison

How I eat in February

February is a testing month for the seasonal chef. But while it may not be the most exciting month in the kitchen, we can try to appreciate it, and not simply bemoan its scarcities. Although there is almost nothing new coming through in February, there are still sweet root vegetables around, which I am concentrating on here, as well as the bitter leaves — and that old English favourite, rhubarb, starts to make its annual appearance.

The root vegetables have been in the ground all winter (or in storage) — the beetroots, parsnips, turnips, swedes, celeriac and carrots — and during that time they have grown in size and their sugars have matured. This is the time for sugar-beet too, and I don't really know why we moved away from enjoying it as food (probably because the entire crop is now used in the sugar and biofuel industries): they are delicious boiled and mashed with butter and black pepper.

I usually peel root vegetables in February, but if parsnips and carrots are really good quality, you can scrub them clean instead, which helps to retain the nutritive qualities near the skin. But something like celeriac has to be peeled, as its skin is so thick and coarse. Scrub or peel your root vegetable, and then...

For the simplest of mashes and smashes, put diced celeriac (or parsnip, carrot, turnip, swede, beetroot) into a pan, cover with lightly salted filtered water, and boil until tender. Drain, add a knob of butter, then mash with a potato masher, or put through a *mouli-légumes*. I would add some thyme to celeriac, some wine vinegar to beetroot (with a bay leaf in the boiling water), and honey to parsnips. Swede just needs black pepper, as much as you can handle.

You could smash your root vegetable instead of mashing it, so that it still has some texture (aka lumps!). One of my favourites is smashed swede, with lots of salted English butter and cracked black pepper. I don't think you could beat that with a pan-fried pork chop on the side, especially if you deglaze the pan with some sweet cider, thin slices of garlic and a few herb leaves (parsley or rosemary). Cook this down almost to a syrup, and serve with the chop. The swede is almost like an apple sauce in texture, and you won't need anything else, apart perhaps from a simple green.

You could have a mixture of roots together as a mash or smash — try parsnip and carrot, or swede and sweet potato. For a different taste, put your diced root vegetable(s) into a pan with butter and light olive oil and sweat and fry with some sliced garlic and thyme until it softens and just begins to catch on the bottom. Add a little white wine or vegetable stock and cook on until the vegetable is soft and slightly smashed looking. The liquid will have been absorbed, and the flavour will be intensely sweet. The vegetable will still have some lumps in it, but it will all be very soft. A perfect accompaniment for meat, poultry or game, or you could use it as a pie filling, under pastry or mashed potato.

Take a spoonful of the root veg mix taken to the smashed stage, and put it into a Spanish omelette. Sprinkle some goat's cheese on the top, then finish in a hot oven (220°C/Fan 200°C/Gas 7). You could serve this as a main course, or cut into wedges as a snack/canapé. You could put the same root veg mixture into the bottom of a ramekin, break in an egg and bake in a medium oven (190°C/Fan 170°C/Gas 5) until set.

Root vegetables make marvellous root soups, most of them with a potato base (see the soup on page 153). You can make a soup with one vegetable alone, but you can also mix them. For a healthy and satisfying February rooty soup, dice five different root vegetables, and add to a large pan with a little butter and a couple of garlic cloves. Stir through for a minute, then add flavourings — thyme, a bay leaf, some dried chilli — and carry on stirring for about 15 minutes. Add some vegetable stock (see page 267) and/or filtered water, cover and bring to the boil. Skim, then simmer until the vegetables are tender. Season to taste with salt and pepper, and you might like to add a touch of wine vinegar. Serve chunky or smooth, thick (like the Italians prefer) or thinner with more liquid, it's up to you. Finish with chopped parsley.

To vary this soup, you could flavour it up with some bacon lardons added at the initial stages, or you could drop some clams or mussels in for the last few minutes of cooking. You could add some diced yellow or white beetroot towards the end of cooking for another texture, but if you add purple, be prepared to end up with a purple soup!

If you keep the soup chunky and fairly thick, it can be used as the vegetable basis for a piece of protein, such as a grilled chicken breast or pan-fried mackerel fillet.

Another way of utilising that thicker, chunkier soup is to put it in an ovenproof dish, then arrange slices of good dried or day-old bread on top. My choice would be grilled or toasted sourdough bread — I don't think Mighty White would hack it… Grate over some good strong Cheddar or Gruyère, and bake in a medium oven (190°C/Fan 170°C/Gas 5) until the cheese has melted and coloured. The bread will absorb the vegetable juices, and you will have a crisp, soft, meaty and hearty dish without any meat. Your body won't crave anything else.

Roasted roots are wonderful. You can cut them into medium slices or discs, mix with fresh herbs, garlic, butter, salt and pepper, and roast until soft and golden. My favourite way is to take a mixture of roots, which I have peeled and cut into rough chunks — carrots, parsnips, beetroots, celeriac, swede, turnips, even potatoes — and put them into a large roasting dish. Add some good olive oil, some whole garlic cloves, thyme and chilli flakes. Sieve in some organic bouillon powder (Marigold), and perhaps add a little balsamic vinegar for its sweetness. Put into a hot oven (230°C/Fan 210°C/Gas 8) and roast for about 50 minutes, turning once. The top bits caramelise, and the underneath is soft and soggy. Great with almost anything — lamb, beef, pork, even mackerel — or with organic vegetable sausages.

You could put the above vegetables raw into a roasting dish, with your chosen flavourings, and put a whole chicken or some chicken joints on top. Drizzle with oil and bake in a moderately hot oven (200°C/Fan

180°C/Gas 6) for an hour. This mode of cooking is very close to my eco heart, all done in one dish, and all in the oven!

You can make salads with some root vegetables. Boil 3 or 4 large beetroots in filtered water with a touch of wine vinegar and salt (or use unpeeled carrots or turnips). Once tender, squeeze the skins off, and you will be left with glistening, tender flesh which your knife will just slip through. Dress the slices with house dressing (see page 270), warm or cold, and serve as a salad by itself, or accompany with some smoked eel, gammon or ham. It would be good with some flakes of smoked mackerel over the top. To turn this into more of a main course, add some chopped chicory, cicoria bitter leaf or endive on the top, perhaps some freshly grated horseradish, and lots of crusty bread.

An unashamedly purple beetroot risotto would be spectacular. Add some beetroot cubes to the soffrito (see page 142). To finish, add dollops of crème fraîche, and sprinkle with freshly chopped fennel herb.

I love grilled celeriac. I take a whole root, peel it and cut it into discs, which I then blanch until there is just some bite left. Without oiling it, I then char-grill it — or use a cast-iron griddle — until it is caramelised, dark brown and striped.

You could also deep-fry root vegetables for game chips to go with game such as venison, partridge or pheasant, or crisps for grown-up or children's parties (my son Aron loves them). Peel and thinly slice raw beetroots, sweet potatoes, parsnips, celeriac, and deep-fry in clean vegetable oil until cooked and crisp. Drain and dry on kitchen paper, sprinkle with salt and serve.

Cockle Soup

Cockles have rather a bad reputation in Britain, because of those vinegared paper cupfuls we used to eat at the seaside (which I loved). But now I have discovered how great they can be, particularly in this soup, and in a sauce for pasta.

For 6

2kg cockles, washed and soaked in clean filtered water
125ml dry white wine
100ml light olive oil
2 celery stalks, chopped
1 red onion, peeled and chopped
1 carrot, chopped
4 tomatoes, skinned, seeded and chopped
200g potatoes, peeled and diced
1 tbsp chervil leaves
1 sprig rosemary
sea salt and freshly ground black pepper
6 slices country bread

Throw away any broken cockles or open cockles that won't close when gently tapped. Put the cockles in a large frying pan, add the wine and put over a high heat for 5 minutes or until the shells open. Drain and reserve the liquid. Remove the cockles from their shells (and reserve) and strain the liquid through a fine sieve.

Heat the olive oil in a pan and add the celery, onion and carrot, and cook over a low heat for 10 minutes until light brown. Add the tomatoes and potatoes, the cooking liquid and 1 litre filtered water, and bring to the boil. Add the chervil and rosemary, lower the heat and simmer for 1 hour. Add the cockles, taste, and then season. Take out the rosemary. Put a slice of bread into each bowl, and ladle over the soup.

Baked Penne with Chicken, Porcini & Parmesan

This is a bit of an Italian classic. It's something we played around with at Fifteen, and I think Jamie liked it!

For 6

80g dried porcini mushrooms
light olive oil
6 chicken thighs, boned, skinned and cut into bite-sized pieces
sea salt and freshly ground black pepper
3 garlic cloves, peeled and finely sliced
550g mixed fresh mushrooms, cleaned and cut into bite-sized pieces
400ml white wine
650g dried penne
500ml double cream
200g Parmesan, freshly grated
1 bunch basil, leaves picked

Preheat the oven to 200°C/Fan 180°C/Gas 6.

Put the porcini mushrooms in a bowl and pour over just enough boiling filtered water to cover them (approx. 200ml). Put to one side and soak for a few minutes.

Heat a saucepan big enough to hold all the ingredients, and pour in a splash of olive oil. Season the chicken pieces with salt and pepper and brown them gently in the oil. Strain the porcini, reserving the soaking water, and add them to the pan with the garlic and fresh mushrooms. Add the wine, with the strained porcini soaking water, and turn the heat down. Simmer gently until the chicken pieces are cooked through and the wine has reduced a little, about 5 minutes.

Meanwhile, cook the penne in plenty of boiling, salted filtered water until *al dente*, then drain well.

Add the cream to the pan of chicken, then bring to the boil and turn the heat off. Season well with salt and pepper, then add the drained penne to the creamy chicken sauce and mix. Add three-quarters of the Parmesan and all of the basil and stir well. Transfer to an ovenproof baking dish or non-stick pan, sprinkle with half the remaining cheese and bake in the preheated oven until golden brown, bubbling and crisp, about 10 minutes.

Divide between your plates, and sprinkle with the rest of the cheese.

Lentil, Bitter Leaf, Sweet Potato & Miso Salad

Lentils are an important part of a healthy diet, and provide important nutrients, particularly to vegetarians and vegans. I've chosen European lentils, a staple for millennia, but a thoroughly modern ingredient.

For 6

300g Castellucio or Puy lentils
2 garlic cloves, peeled
2 tsp pale miso
1 fresh red chilli, seeded and finely chopped
3 tsp chopped mint leaves
6 tbsp extra virgin olive oil
sea salt and freshly ground black pepper
300g sweet potato, washed
200g each of dandelion, bitter cicoria or chicory and radicchio leaves
2 tsp Volpaia herb vinegar

For the lentils, quickly rinse them and tip into a suitable pan. Cover with 5cm filtered water and add the garlic and miso. Bring to the boil and simmer for 30-40 minutes. Check the texture, some people like them a little nutty, but I prefer mine well-cooked, I think they are easier to digest.

When cooked, pour the lentils into a colander and then into a bowl. Add half the chilli and half the mint, and drizzle in 2 tablespoons of the olive oil. Check and adjust the seasoning.

Meanwhile, for the sweet potato, wash and cut it into 2cm cubes, and slowly bring to the boil. I don't boil my sweet potato too vigorously, as I find it tends to fall apart slightly. Strain when cooked, season with salt and pepper and reserve at room temperature.

Wash and dry the salad leaves thoroughly. Arrange the sweet potato and leaves on a serving plate and then spoon over the lentils, and sprinkle with the rest of the mint and chilli. Drizzle over the remaining olive oil and the vinegar, and season the whole dish with a little more salt and pepper.

Duck Confit with Green Curly Kale, Red Chilli, Vinegar & Ginger Salad

The kale is a wonderful partner to duck, and the vinegar just cuts the fat nicely. This is one dish I have had on the menu for ages, well, the duck confit anyway! Make this wonderful dish a day in advance.

For 4

4 large duck legs
4 juniper berries
100g rock salt
2 tsp thyme leaves
50g caster sugar
900g duck fat

Green Curly Kale, Red Chilli, Vinegar and Ginger Salad
1kg curly green kale, washed and trimmed
2 fresh red chillies, finely chopped (with seeds if you like that extra bite)
50g fresh root ginger, peeled and finely diced
4 tsp Volpaia herb vinegar
extra virgin olive oil
sea salt and freshly ground black pepper

For the duck confit, put one duck leg in the bottom of a deep bowl. In a mortar, crush the juniper into the salt and put the thyme leaves and sugar in. Sprinkle a little of this salt mixture over the duck leg, turn it over, and sprinkle with more salt mixture. Add another duck leg, and sprinkle in the same way. Continue until you have seasoned all four legs. Cover and leave in the fridge for 6 hours, turning the legs over halfway through. Don't leave them too long, as the salt will start to leach out the liquid from the meat, which will also become too salty.

Preheat the oven to 140-150°C/Fan 120–130°C/Gas 1-2.

Wash the salt off the duck legs and pat them dry with kitchen towels. Bring the duck fat to a soft simmer in a flameproof baking dish in which the duck legs will just fit. Add the legs, making sure they are under the fat, cover and place into the preheated oven. Cook for 1½ hours, and then remove from the oven. Leave to cool in the fat. Chill for at least 24 hours.

For the salad, put the kale in a pan of boiling, salted filtered water, and cook until just soft. This can take 10-12 minutes, because kale is very sturdy and hardy. I also like to cook it a little further as it is easier to digest, and still very good for you. Drain and leave the kale to cool on a tray. Sprinkle over the chopped chilli, chopped ginger, the vinegar and olive oil to taste. Season with salt and pepper.

Pull the whole duck legs out of the fat, being careful not to pull the bones off. (Save the fat, delicious for roast potatoes.) Put the duck legs in a tray and heat through in a (preheated) top temperature oven (240°C/ Fan 200°C/Gas 9) for 5 minutes, just to crisp up the skin. Serve hot with the salad.

Arthur's Vanilla & Lemon Birthday Cake

This is the kind of cake I cook for birthdays, and would like to have for my own (which is this month). Lemon and vanilla are a wicked combination. I was shown this by an American friend, and I love the way they use buttermilk.

For 8–10

420g unsalted butter, slightly softened, plus extra for greasing
330g plain or pastry flour, plus extra for dusting
220g caster sugar
2 vanilla pods, split and finely chopped
finely grated zest and juice of 4 lemons
4 extra large eggs, at room temperature
½ tsp baking powder
½ tsp bicarbonate of soda
a pinch of fine salt
180ml buttermilk, at room temperature

Lemon Icing
275g icing sugar
1 vanilla pod, split and seeded
20g caster sugar
20g salted butter, at room temperature
4 tsp fresh lemon juice (see above)
4 tsp hot milk

Preheat the oven to 180°C/Fan 160°C/Gas 4. Butter and flour a 25 x 14cm cake tin. Line the tin with baking parchment and butter that as well.

For the cake, combine the butter and sugar in the bowl of an electric mixer fitted with the paddle attachment. Beat until creamy and white. Add the finely chopped vanilla pods and seeds. Stir in the lemon zest. Beat in the eggs, one at a time.

Sift the flour, baking powder, bicarbonate of soda and salt into a separate bowl. Combine 4 tablespoons of the lemon juice with the buttermilk in another bowl. Add the dry ingredients alternately with the liquid ingredients to the butter mixture. Remove the bowl from the mixer and use a spatula to give a couple of last folds from the bottom of the bowl.

Pour the batter into the prepared cake tin and tap lightly to level the surface. Bake in the preheated oven for 50-55 minutes, until a skewer comes out clean when inserted into the middle of the cake. Cool for 10 minutes, and then turn the cake out on to a wire cake rack and leave to go completely cold.

For the icing, put the icing sugar in a bowl. Pound the vanilla seeds and caster sugar together in a mortar to release all the vanilla fragrance, then add, along with the butter, to the icing sugar. Pour the lemon juice and hot milk over them and whisk until smoothly blended. Spoon the icing over the cake and spread down the sides. Leave to set.

CLEANING AND DISPOSING

Most kitchens I go into these days, whether domestic or professional, scare me to bits. Chefs at all levels toss everything they consider waste into a large black bin bag, from cans to fish guts, from vegetable peelings to glass bottles and cigarette ends. Then the bags are put out on the street and the next day they're gone. Where to? Do we know? Do we care? And the same thing happens in homes, although the quantities are obviously very different. There is nothing quite so wasteful as the average restaurant.

But if we want to protect our planet, we all have to become accountable for our waste. We have to realise that the Earth, just like our bodies, will get sicker the more rubbish we pile into it. Although waste may be an inevitable by-product of cooking, we must do everything we can to minimise the amount we throw in the bin. We need to deal with it by refusing, reducing, re-using, recycling and composting – or better still, not creating it in the first place.

We must also be more careful about the way we clean up in the kitchen and the eco house in general. Water, essential to cleaning, is the life-blood of the Earth, and there is a limited supply of it left…

CLEANING UP

The penultimate act in the producing, buying, preparing and cooking food cycle is the cleaning up. And this is an area that is worrying in an ecological sense. Cleaning up involves water (which is in short supply) and products which are polluting and damaging to natural ecosystems. The answer, although it's far from simple, is to try to use less water, and to try and use products, if necessary, which will have less of an impact on the environment.

Water availability is an essential component of human welfare and productivity. At the rate we are currently stripping the world of water, we are in effect surviving by taking from our future, and the future for our children could well be waterless as a result. And if there is no water, there is no food... Water is said to be a renewable resource because of the water cycle (in brief, evaporation, condensation, precipitation), but as the Earth's population increases, as demand for water from agriculture and industry increases, and as global warming takes effect, everyone on Earth — humans and animals — will be competing for a rapidly diminishing supply.

Each of us uses about 150 litres of drinking water per day in the UK, but only 13 per cent of that is consumed. The rest is used for washing — dishes, clothes and ourselves — with a small proportion used for the garden and washing the car. We use double the amount of water today that we did in the 1950s, and water is drying up all over the world. If we were to remember this every time we turned on a tap, we could be doing something to avert a potential future catastrophe. Every little helps...

For instance, I only wash dishes once a day. I don't have a dishwasher, although these can be energy and water efficient, so I use the kitchen sink. I perhaps rinse breakfast dishes, to prevent cereal sticking. Then I run a large bowl full of hot water in the evening, put in my ecological dishwashing liquid, and wash everything in hot soapy water: glasses first, then cutlery, plates, bowls, colander, sieves and lastly the pots, which I fill with the water from the bowl and put to one side. Then I fill the bowl again with hot water to rinse everything. The pots get scrubbed then rinsed. Those two bowlfuls will do pretty much all of my dishes for the day, considerably less than the 45 litres used by most modern dishwashers (and considerably less in energy as well).

Arthur's Notes

A water boiler that gives you hot water on demand is less costly in energy terms than one that heats a whole tankful of water you might not use.

Fix inexpensive spray devices on taps, which are more economical in water usage.

Don't let taps drip, which can mean huge water loss. Replacing worn washers will save water and money.

Do your vegetable preparation and dish-washing in bowls rather than sinks of water. If the water isn't too greasy or soapy, it can be re-used to water plants inside or outside.

Use environmentally sensitive washing-up liquids, and other household cleaning products (Bio-d and Ecover are two good names, see Directory). They may cost a little more, but some of the incredibly strong products available are hazardous to both human and animal health, and literally do cost the Earth.

Try some more natural solutions to soaps, etc: lemon juice is a good cleanser and steriliser, salt can go to work on spills in the oven (and pans, see page 178). Baking soda and/or vinegar can work on other problems such as a blocked sink. The liquid from a Bokashi system (see page 261) is very good, diluted slightly, for blocked sinks or drains.

Only run your dishwasher when full, which is more cost-effective. You could stop the cycle at the drying stage, which saves energy; open the door, and there should be enough residual heat to dry the dishes adequately.

Use environmentally-friendly shampoos and soaps, and recycled loo paper. My new restaurant, The Water House, has toilets that don't use paper at all: the toilets use air and water, which clean and flush at the same time.

Why don't you get a meter for your water? Research has shown that people use significantly less water once they see what they are using, and realise they have to pay for it.

Do you really need to wash your pans? For example, if you keep one pan purely for cooking pasta, it may not need more than a rinse between uses.

GETTING RID
OF WASTE

Humans and nature produce waste. But there is a difference. Natural waste is essential waste: leaves fall from the trees and rot down to enrich the soil, which in turn enhances the following year's growth; animal carcasses and droppings also feed the soil. Even oxygen, the gas that is vital for our survival, is essentially 'waste', a by-product of photosynthesis, when plants utilise carbon dioxide, sunlight and water to produce energy (and the oxygen without which human life would not be possible). What I try to do — and something we should all be trying to do — is to be as natural in dealing with waste as possible.

Waste is based on consumption. It may sound crude, but you can tell a lot about your body by the waste that comes out of it — revealing whether it is healthy or suffering from a rubbish diet, whether it is experiencing over- or under-consumption, or whether it is dehydrated. It's the same with your house: you can tell a lot about your buying and consumption by the amount of waste you have to deal with daily: whether you buy and consume sensibly, in an eco-friendly way, whether frugally or extravagantly.

And to take the metaphor even further, our planet too is beginning to show the effects of the waste generated by its inhabitants, not least in the increased levels of carbon dioxide (produced mainly by our burning of fossil fuels), which is contributing to planet warming. Some of that waste is incinerated (when toxic chemicals, including more carbon dioxide, can be released into the atmosphere), but most gets carted off to be buried in the earth, in huge landfill sites, to fester for decades. Each of these landfill sites — and they are now close to running out of places for them, in both Europe and America — produces large amounts of methane, a strong greenhouse gas many times more potent than carbon dioxide. Our planet, its soil and its atmosphere are becoming sicker, the more waste we pile into them.

There are many different types of waste in terms of the home and kitchen, but in essence they fall into two major categories: unnecessary and unavoidable. You have to learn to recognise the former when you buy: can I use that bag again, will I find that box handy at home, or do I just not need that extra piece of packaging? And unavoidable waste, such as vegetable trimmings, we can use in a positive way, in composting (see page 256). We all have to learn to be responsible for the amount of waste we take into our homes, and ideally learn how to eliminate it: otherwise you should be able to reduce, refuse or re-use it ('recycling' is another matter, see page 250). In fact, I think children should be given lessons in school on how to lessen or eliminate their waste.

And this of course doesn't include the other types of 'waste' that exist — waste of space, waste of energy and waste of time. Waste of every type needs to be harnessed. If it is unavoidable, then I shall use it in some way. As an ethical consumer — trying to buy organically where possible, sustainably, fairly, encouraging the companies who are operating and manufacturing in an ethical way — I consider myself responsible for that waste, and therefore I am responsible for disposing of it.

Reducing & Refusing

Unnecessary waste is what we primarily need to reduce, and most of this comes in the form of packaging. Once upon a time, people would go shopping every day, perhaps on foot, and bring home fresh foods loose or in paper bags, with the occasional can of beans or fruit. Nowadays, with the advent of supermarkets, the growth of ready meals, and the increased use of cars, the patterns of shopping have completely changed. Shoppers now stock up once or twice a week instead of daily, and the food they buy is protectively wrapped within an inch of its life, in bottles, jars, cans, cartons and packages consisting of polystyrene or hard and soft plastics (sometimes all three). Items other than food come excessively wrapped too — televisions, computers and all sorts of electrical appliances among them. We have to reduce the amount of waste we accept, which should hopefully reduce the amount produced at source.

'Refusing' is another, if slightly confrontational, way of negating waste. In Germany and Austria, shoppers actually tear excessive food packaging off in store, or post it back to the store. Packaging in these countries has now been very much reduced — and recycling quotas are high. Come on Britain, there's an environmental war being fought here. Isn't reducing our packaging the least we can do?

Arthur's Notes: Unnecessary Waste

Quite a lot of unnecessary food waste comes from over-buying – and then forgetting about it and leaving it in the fridge to go off. Before you go out shopping, take a look at what you have already in the fridge and storecupboard. Try to make a shopping list based on what you need, which will immediately cut down on your consuming and spending!

Choose to buy loose fruit and vegetables rather than those wrapped in cellophane, styrofoam or plastic. Put them in the bags or boxes you have brought with you from home. (You'll discover you can fit very much more in your bags without all that unnecessary packaging there usually is, thereby eliminating the need for more bags.)

Stick a note on the back of your front door to remind you to take bags (etc) with you when going shopping, so that you don't bring home yet more.

I find boxes more eco-friendly than plastic bags, and I can always find a way to re-use them at home, whether cardboard or ply (extra storage in cellar or attic).

Buying in bulk, even if it takes up space, is much more eco-friendly – and economical. You probably would do it only once a month, and it will save on petrol and packaging. Perhaps you could even share bulk buys with family or neighbours, which would reduce wastage even more.

Take your own packed lunch to work with you (in a washable container, which will cut down on the packaging inevitably encasing a bought sandwich or salad. And indeed store food in washable containers rather than foil or clingfilm.

Arthur's Notes: Unavoidable Waste

Any leftover organic material – veg trimmings, eggshells, fruit skins, even occasionally cooked veg, rice and pasta – can be composted in some way to provide food and fuel for your vegetable garden (see page 256).

We all unconsciously or unthinkingly waste energy. Collecting the children from school in the car may be unavoidable, but shop for your supper at the same time, to avoid another journey. Even turning the heating down a fraction saves some energy: what's wrong with putting on an extra jumper? And if we all went to bed and turned the lights off an hour earlier than usual, quite a lot of energy would be saved. Some wastage is completely

unavoidable, though: if I didn't leave the bathroom light on at night, my son wouldn't be able to find his way there when he woke up...

Think about your method of cooking. If you need the oven on for one aspect of the meal, try to cook everything in the oven. A roast joint with roast vegetables is delicious, and it will have minimised energy wastage.

Don't throw away the wood ash from your indoor fire or bonfire. Scatter it around plants that are susceptible to slug and snail damage: for some reason, they don't like it and will stay away. (It would also be useful on your compost heap.)

Re-using

Re-using reduces waste. We are living in a throwaway society, where nothing is built to last. But if something still works, can be fixed or worn, then it should be re-used because, in most cases, this will consume far less energy than recycling it.

We should all buy sensibly for a start, whether it be furniture, clothes, pots and pans, ovens, fridges or cars. All of these items should be made to last, both at source and when it becomes part of you and your life. Don't rush to buy a new table when the old one begins to wobble: mend it. When the fridge breaks down, get the engineer in rather than buy new. In the developing world, for instance, they re-use everything (and here it is out of necessity): when a car tyre bursts they cut it up and use the rubber as sandals, for instance. As far as footwear is concerned, I have used up all my own shoes over the last few years until they can't possibly be mended any more. I now have four pairs only – and I studiously avoid going into trainer shops because I am going to wear my current pair until they rot off my feet! The same with my car: I'd like a new, preferably electric car, but they are too expensive and probably too small for my family, so I shall continue driving my grandfather's car – which is at least 25 years old (although I have the engine tuned regularly) – until it finally gives up the ghost.

I suppose the concept of re-using is a return to a slightly older way of living, to a form of thrift, which is no bad thing. But even if you can't re-use or repair something yourself, there will probably be someone who can: charity shops and schemes are always looking for goods to sell or to send abroad to the developing world, and many local councils have community schemes whereby furniture and electrical goods such as fridges, can be given to those in need. As a last resort, many broken items can be stripped down to components which can be used again.

What I should really like, though, is that manufacturers start to make goods that we, as ethical consumers, really want to buy, something that lasts. We are dictated to at the moment by producers, but it ought to be the other way around. We should be saying, 'I want something that I can use again and again, so produce it for me.' It's demand and supply rather than the reverse.

As for the future, there is potential in a couple of areas. There is talk about us being one molecule away from producing a plastic that is stronger than steel, a plastic that is so advanced that recycling and re-using it would not be an issue. Steel itself takes so much energy to produce and re-use, that it will probably become obsolete, and this new plastic could easily take its place. And they are thinking similarly in other areas, in planned re-use: a major car company is in the throes of designing a car that will be made up from reusable components — 98 per cent of that can then be broken down and used in refrigerators; three or so years later 80 per cent of those fridges will be used to make kettles. This is the ultimate re-using, and it represents a huge advance in technology.

So we may become more biological, and eco-friendly, but we have to achieve such a lot very quickly. We need to pioneer a consciousness of waste, and an awareness of how to refuse it, re-use it, recycle it, eliminate it, and we need to do so now. We might have a fantastic car that we can turn into a fridge in three years, but if we can't drink our water, and our land is infertile...

Arthur's Notes

When you go shopping, take some paper or plastic bags, bowls, Tupperware boxes or ziplock bags with you. A good idea is to have separate boxes or ziplock bags for meat and fish. They can be washed between uses.

Keep old plastic bottles, the bigger the better, to store your deep-frying oil once its useful life is over. Then you can take it to be recycled.

Always re-use leftover food. Don't throw anything away until you have thought carefully about what to do with it. Cooked pasta from the night before can be re-used in a soup or a salad for lunch the next day; pieces of cooked veg can be mixed with other ingredients in a stir-fry. Use your imagination.

Don't throw away clothes or other fabrics without thinking about how you could re-use them. Tee-shirts make good dusters, tougher fabrics could become floor scrubbers, bath towels which have begun to fray at the edges can be cut down to make kitchen towels. Some looser-weaved fabrics can be turned into the equivalent of muslin or cheesecloth, for use in straining (a fruit jelly, for instance).

Buy re-used articles. Scour charity shops and car-boot sales for items you can happily take into your life. That old metal *mouli-légumes* that someone didn't want any more will purée your vegetables just as well, if not better, than the newest electrical food processor.

Recycling

The first lesson in consumption is not to bring any unnecessary item or packaging into your home, and recycling is the last resort when dealing with. Recycling in its truest sense would be using a product over and over again ad infinitum. But at the moment every recycled product seems to have a limited lifeline and, however many times it reappears, ultimately I feel *everything* ends up in landfill.

The core of the problem lies in the fact that the recycling process, whether of paper, glass, metal or oil, uses a lot of energy. I'm not anti recycling per se, but I can't become as excited about it as everyone else seems to be. Recycling will come into its own at some stage, I'm sure, but it's not yet living up to its potential. The concept has accelerated too quickly, and ardent recyclers haven't thought it through properly. It needs more time to grow up.

However, people are trying very hard, and so am I. I will always recycle rather than be responsible for sending something to landfill. The very fact that individuals, local authorities and governments are now aware of the problems of waste and its disposal is heartening enough. And it is undeniable that most people who recycle say they feel good about it, and feel they are doing good. We just need to do better. Mother Nature has got recycling down to a fine art — check out the water cycle, recycling at its finest — and we should take a few lessons from her book.

To be positive, recycling may create emissions, but on a lesser scale. Virgin materials that would otherwise be used in producing things new — such as wood and aluminium ore — are conserved, as is the energy that would be expended in the gathering of them.

At home, if you haven't been able to avoid or refuse, many things can be sent for recycling: glass, paper, plastic (although this is the most debatable), metals, foil, cardboard and textiles. Many local authorities will do this for free, and often there are centres to which you can take materials not collected from the doorstep. (Seeing the queues of cars, exhausts billowing carbon monoxide, at some of these recycling centre's, makes me wonder what the point is.) Restaurants and other catering establishments have to pay for collection of food waste and glass, for instance, which is why many of them are put off recycling (and why so much glass from the catering industry ends up in landfill).

The traceability of recycling is something we should be totally aware of. No longer can we, as responsible human beings, not be accountable for what we throw away. There is no point in separating out your glass for the council to collect, if what they do is put it straight into landfill. You have to be aware; you have to become involved. According to the Environment Agency, for instance, about half of the recycled bin material thrown out each year in the UK ends up overseas. Old clothes would serve a useful purpose, if clothing those who would otherwise have nothing, even including the 'miles' involved, but sending plastics to China to be recycled is madness.

One kitchen product that can successfully be recycled is cooking oil, and this recycling is infinitely preferable to the oil being thrown away and polluting land or water. At Acorn House we donate our used cooking oil, saving it in empty drums and containers, to a company which transforms it into biofuel – and the taxis which service the restaurant run on biodiesel. I like the circularity of that idea, that people might be run home by a cab run on the same oil that cooked their meal!

Current regulations in Britain say that biofuels should compose 5 per cent of the transport fuel mix by 2010. The EU in turn has said that by 2020 all cars must run on 20 per cent biofuel. Cars running on biodiesel may reduce carbon dioxide emissions by nearly 80 per cent compared with petroleum diesel, but the whole question of biofuels still worries me. Ethanol and biodiesel, the two primary biofuels, are now produced from the USA to India, from Europe to Brazil, from sugarcane, corn, sugar-beet, wheat, barley (ethanol), and the oils from rape, soya and palm (biodiesel). A tropical weed called jatropha, with a seed which is 40 per cent oil, is now being cultivated for biodiesel.

Biofuels may be carbon neutral, and they may be cutting down on our extraction and use of fossil fuels, but their cultivation is reaching massive proportions. It is farmers, many in Third World countries, who are now producing fuel, often at the expense of food (fuel is, ironically, much more cash-rewarding). Not only do monocultural plains of fuel-producing plants threaten the world's biodiversity, but they can also threaten the world's farm economy which is already struggling to feed billions of hungry people. In parts of the world reliant on subsistence farming, biofuel production could force out food crops, bringing with it the risk of food shortages and famine.

And recent research by a group of international scientists in the journal *Atmospheric Chemistry and Physics*, suggested that rapeseed and maize biodiesels were calculated to produce up to 70 per cent and 50 per cent more greenhouse gases respectively than fossil fuels (mainly in the form of nitrous oxide, which is 296 times more powerful as a greenhouse gas than carbon dioxide... Arggh, what do we do?

Arthur's Notes: Recycling Glass

I've said this already, but I am all for the return of the milkman, who represents the ultimate in re-use of glass. We got our milk in glass bottles, then we emptied, washed and returned them. He then delivered us some more milk in more glass bottles. (Apparently milk bottles are re-used about twelve times.)

Make trips to the bottle-bank at the same time as you are going shopping or driving the kids to school, which keeps the environmental impact of the journey to a minimum.

Re-use glass jars with lids for storing foodstuffs from packets (seeds, nuts, rice, etc), or for nails and tacks if you are a DIY person. Or why not take to making your own jams and preserves at home, a good way of re-using those jars?

Recycle all glass containers, not just food jars and bottles. Those glass bottles of aspirin or cough mixture are all recyclable. Give glass containers for recycling a quick rinse when doing the washing up.

Arthur's Tips: Recycling Plastic

I've said it before, and I shall say it again, take your own bags with you when you go out shopping. Refuse to accept plastic bags in shops.

Don't buy wrapped foods that don't need wrapping – apples, melons and grapefruit already have adequate wrapping naturally.

If it does not already do so, try to persuade your local authority to start a plastics collection scheme.

Try to buy recycled plastic: bin-liner bags are an obvious example, but you could also find recycled plastic water butts, composters and seed trays.

Arthur's Notes: Recycling Paper

Recycling is not just about collecting materials and taking them to the recycling bank, it is about 'closing the loop' and buying recycled products in turn. Paper mills cannot produce recycled paper if there is no demand for it...

Buy recycled paper – you should easily be able to find recycled stationery and toilet paper. In Britain, it is estimated we use the equivalent of a quarter of a million trees annually for our Christmas cards and wrapping paper, so do try to find recycled cards and paper. And don't forget to send them to be recycled after the festivities.

Councils are good these days about recycling paper, so always send your newspapers and any other scrap paper (once it has been used on both sides) for recycling.

I give old pieces of paper that are blank on one side to my children for drawing on. Sometimes I use the blank sides, cut into smaller squares and fastened together in some way, as a pad by the telephone.

Buy and use fabric cloths for cleaning up in the kitchen rather than paper towels.

Use fabric handkerchiefs instead of the paper equivalent.

Biomass is a very ecological way of producing energy, and I suppose you could say it's a cross between composting and recycling. Biomass consists of organic matter, and for energy generation, the materials used can be animal or vegetable – waste wood, municipal waste (methane from landfill is used for energy), straw, cow dung, poultry litter, perennial grasses and coppiced fast-growing trees such as willow and poplar.

Biomass is said to be 'carbon neutral'. If you burn coal, you release carbon trapped billions of years ago, which means extra carbon in the atmosphere. Biomass materials, on the other hand, take already existing carbon out of the atmosphere while they are growing and return it as they are burned, therefore they are not contributing any extra carbon. If coppiced wood, for instance, is managed sustainably, as a constantly replenished crop, when carbon is released by burning tree biomass, it is reabsorbed by the new trees growing. Many green power stations are now using biomass, and individual biomass stoves or boilers can be bought. (A wood-burning stove isn't too different in concept...) I think biomass has huge potential, because of its low carbon cost, because it gets rid of waste, and because it cultivates trees, the latter contributing to the environment and to biodiversity.

COMPOSTING
WASTE

One of the world's most valuable resources is soil. One of man's least attractive attributes is the waste he produces. But much of this waste, particularly organic waste, has a value in that it can be processed naturally into a material, humus or compost, that will enrich and amplify that soil. We must do everything we can to create a balance, to give back to the Earth, and composting is one of the best, easiest, cheapest and greenest ways in which to make a real difference. (And if we all did it as communities, think how effective that would be, see page 76.)

Composting organic waste means that it won't be going to landfill (where it creates methane and pollutes the water table), and you will be trapping the energy of that waste (it's full of vitamins and minerals after all). You could go the non-green route, and just add commercial fertilisers to the soil to speed growth of plants. This will only provide food, though; adding humus or compost gives the soil good structure as well as nutrients, which is much more useful and practical. Your vegetables and fruits will be all the healthier and happier for it. Good compost is like a multivitamin for the soil.

Composting is not an exact science, although it is a very complex one. It is more like good cooking, relying on common sense, a feel for your ingredients, and a certain amount of experience.

The Compost Bin

Making compost is easy and doesn't take too much time or energy.
Compost bins can be bought from garden centres and DIY shops (often
made from recycled plastic), or you could make your own, preferably
from re-used or sustainable wood or from wire netting (there are plenty
of books and websites which will give you fuller details). Many councils
sell home composters to residents, often at a reduced cost. You could
simply make a compost heap in a corner of the garden, but that won't be
so unobtrusive, might smell, and it won't work quite so efficiently.

What happens in the compost bin is a microcosm of what happens in
nature; the bin is simply an environment in which the natural process
can be speeded up. Basic soil, after all, is composed largely of organic
material – waste or dead animal and plant matter – which is worked on
by microorganisms, bacteria, fungi, millipedes, worms etc, who eat it,
excrete it, aerate it and turn it into healthy humus which will nourish
soil. So to feed and encourage these organisms and encourage them
to multiply, you should create favourable conditions: they need air (to
supply oxygen); they need moisture (but not too much: if the bin is
uncovered, rain will soak in and leach the nutrients away); and they need
warmth (both within and without the bin). They also need nitrogen, and
the correct balance between carbon and nitrogen must be maintained.
Many older plants contain a lot of carbon, and the microorganisms need
nitrogen to break it down. This can be added in the form of activators
such as animal manure (horse, cow, poultry), bone, fish meal or seaweed
products or, perhaps the simplest of all, layers of nettle or comfrey
leaves. A closely compressed bin without air, with too much or too little
water, or with too little warmth or nitrogen, will not rot because the
microorganisms cannot live.

You will probably have to turn your compost every now and again, water
it if conditions are too dry, and aerate it, but in general it is not too
demanding of attention. Depending on the ingredients, the season and

the weather, you could have good compost within twelve weeks to six months: materials will rot down faster in spring and summer than in winter. Once the humus is dark brown, softish and smells like good soil (even thought it might have recognisable pieces of eggshell remaining), it will be ready. Dig into the soil or use as a top dressing.

Arthur's Notes

The basic composting ingredients are a mix of 'greens' and 'browns'. Greens consist of waste from the kitchen and garden: grass clippings, soft prunings, fruit and vegetable trimmings and peelings, crushed egg shells, tea bags, coffee grounds, etc. Browns consist of scrunched-up or shredded cardboard and egg boxes, and a proportion of leaves.

You should not add dog or cat faeces, or fatty or cooked foods such as meat, fish or cheese (which might encourage vermin).

Try to avoid tough hedge clippings, woody prunings or too many autumn leaves, as these would take too long to rot down.

Newspaper, although it can be shredded and composted, is probably better sent to be recycled into more paper.

Canals played an enormous part in the UK's industrial growth, and they are still commercially important in other parts of Europe. Although ours are mostly used now for leisure pursuits, they could be substantially re-used and returned to a creative and sustainable working role. For instance, I am using the Regent's Canal in London to cool and heat our new restaurant, The Water House, and British Waterways are actively helping us. This idea could be adopted elsewhere, and we would be saving enormously in energy as a result. I am also trying to put a barge outside our new restaurant into which I shall put all the compostable waste from the restaurant. This will make soil for growing my fresh vegetables, which I shall water with grey water from the restaurant. This idea could be adopted in a community sense elsewhere on the canals: city estates, street's and country villages could compost in barges, and grow their own vegetables. You could fill the canals of London with these barges full of nutrition!

For an alternate method of fresh food delivery, you could take barges of good soil out into the countryside, plant them and then deliver into the city barges of food, of carrots, courgettes, potatoes, which will be as fresh as could be. Although a barge may take two days to go thirty miles, the vegetables are still growing, and they can be watered from the canal...

Wormeries

If space is at a premium or you haven't got a garden in which to site a compost bin, you could acquire a wormery, which is usually small enough to fit in a kitchen (and it won't smell). This in turn is a sort of microcosm of the compost bin, a box of soil, organic waste, and some very special worms. Wormeries are easy to find, in garden centres or online (see Directory), and they are not expensive. Don't attempt to make your own wormery with garden worms, as these (usually the much larger lob worms) would not survive in the cramped space of a wormery box.

The special worms used in wormeries are fast and efficient natural composters. Each worm eats and digests up to half its own body weight of waste every day; although that 'food' is then excreted, the waste rapidly reduces in volume. The worms excrete a high-quality humus known to gardeners as 'black gold', and also create a liquid, which is a fantastic garden fertiliser (when diluted with water). One of the most important tasks of the wormery operator is to remember to draw off this water regularly through a little tap; I forgot to do this when I first started with worms, and drowned the lot.

Wormery boxes are generally three-tiered, with glass on the front, through which, in theory, you can watch your worms at work — but really it is like watching paint dry... You start by putting your kitchen waste — small pieces of fruit and vegetable peelings and trimmings, tea leaves, coffee grounds, stale bread, hoover dust, etc — in the bottom tier with the worms. When that bottom tray is filled, you fill the middle tray, then the top one. The worms will move up this 'tower' and, by the time the top tray is full of waste, the bottom tray should be filled with compost. You remove this and use the compost on your plants, then replace on the top, and start filling with fresh waste. This is almost like a biodynamic cycle: you put the waste vegetable in the wormery, and then put the worm-processed result on the garden to grow the same vegetable next year. You could also make a worm 'tea': soak the worm compost, or vermicompost, in water for a natural and organic liquid fertiliser.

Worms don't like everything: they might baulk at citrus fruits and skins, onions and garlic, fat, vinegar and meat. You need to get the balance between 'browns' and 'greens' right, just as with your compost heap. They also like an ambient temperature, not too cold and not too hot. I urge everyone to buy a load of worms!

Bokashi

The Bokashi composting system is a Japanese invention, and it consists of a pair of recycled plastic containers with airtight lids, and taps at the bottom where excess liquid can be drained off. You put your kitchen waste into one of the containers, and sprinkle a proprietary bran mixture, which contains bacteria, fungi and yeasts, in between layers. These organisms then start to work on the waste, eating and digesting it, until after about a week or so, you leave that first container to ferment, and start adding waste and bran to the second bin. A bin will take about two weeks to ferment fully, by which time it will look like a pickle rather than compost: this can be dug into the garden soil, or put on to the compost heap, where it will break down fairly rapidly, or you can add it to the wormery, where the worms will convert it very quickly to compost and liquid feed.

The Bokashi system doesn't take up too much space, and it doesn't smell. Its main advantage to me at home is that it eats up my cooking oil, which is quite difficult to get rid of in other ways. I soak paper with the oil, sprinkle Bokashi bran on top, and the system breaks the oil down to a carbon sludge, which I can compost, and water, which I put on the garden.

Large-scale Composting

I have talked about the composting we can do at home — a bin in the garden, a wormery in the kitchen — but there is scope for larger-scale composting, not least the community-based ideas I discussed on page 76. However, on an even larger scale still, processes are available that can cope with, and render into compost materials, the organic waste that comes from municipal waste collections, the waste from restaurants and similar catering outlets, the waste from farms (slurry), etc.

Businesses which produce waste, such as mine, should have desiccators on site, but mine at Acorn House is the only one in the western world. It is in the same room as I compost my waste, and in which I keep my wormeries. I put in my waste, turn the machine on, and seven hours later, I have a friable dust, and quite a lot of liquid. Both are capable of being used as soil additives, although in a very dilute form: I added some of the desiccated dust to one of my wormeries and, because it was so dry, it sucked the moisture out of the whole wormery, and the worms died. However, used intelligently, a desiccator would solve quite a lot of problems in the municipal and restaurant waste arena: it makes the waste smaller, by separating liquid and desiccable material, it saves the waste going to landfill, and, if the quality of the original material was good enough, the end-product can be used to enhance soil. I am experimenting with the desiccator's use of energy at the moment, as I am finding it to be quite high.

With strong public opposition from local communities to landfill alternatives such as incineration, anaerobic digestion (AD) has been mooted as a possibility, and indeed is already used in this country and abroad, mainly in the area of sewage treatment, both municipally and agriculturally (although, sadly, quite a lot of this sewage still finds its way into our rivers and into the sea). AD is a biological waste-management system, and basically it is performing the same role as composting, but on a much larger scale. In Denmark, for instance, there are close to twenty AD plants which treat animal manure, crop residues, abattoir wastes, industrial wastes, sewage sludge and source-separated household organic waste.

'Anaerobic' means without air, and so the waste is processed in a closed container, and is digested down by microbes which can survive in an airless environment. There are by-products, and these include biogas (which can be burned to generate heat and/or electricity, or upgraded to a biofuel), and fertilisers and soil improvers (if the original materials were appropriate). AD also offers a major environmental aid, in that processing wastes in AD digesters makes the resultant residue more stable (and compacts it); even if these processed wastes were then taken to landfill, the degradation process thereafter would be much less damaging to the environment (and wouldn't take up so much space). For instance, AD takes under 35 days to stabilise waste, whereas in landfill, unprocessed biological waste might emit methane and other hazards for over 35 years. However, once again, AD digesters guzzle a lot of energy, but I think it is probably worth it.

It is appropriate to finish this chapter, and a seasonal book, talking about using food waste for compost. For composting is perhaps the most important way in which we can all do something for our planet: produce a material to help feed and replenish the soil. And in that soil the food for next year can flourish and grow, a complete circle... In the end is the beginning...

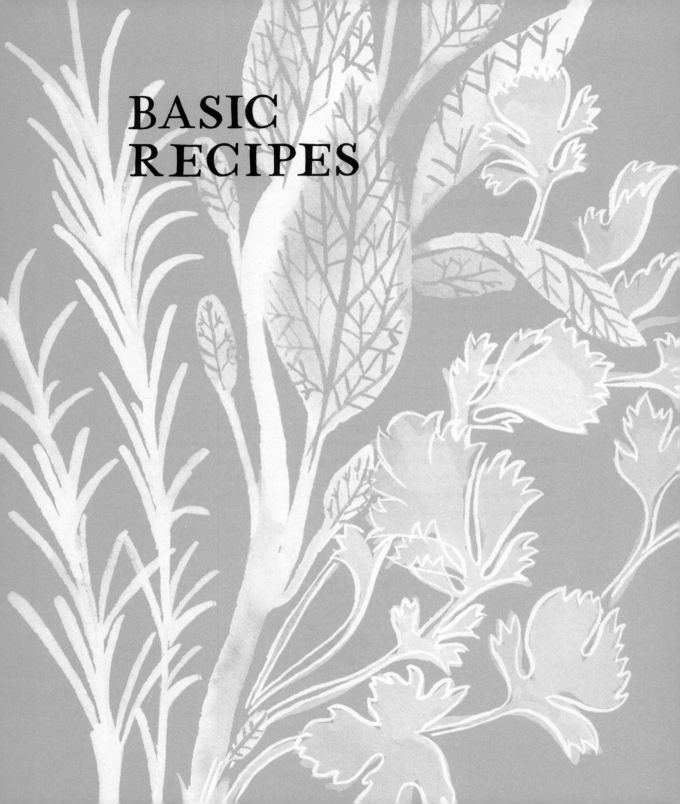

BASIC
RECIPES

Chicken Stock

This is a basic chicken stock, which you can use for soups, sauces and risottos.

Makes about 2 litres

1 large chicken for boiling
2 white onions, peeled and roughly chopped
2 large carrots, peeled and roughly chopped
2 celery sticks, roughly chopped
1 leek, cleaned and roughly chopped
1 bulb garlic
2 bay leaves
2 sprigs thyme
1 tbsp white peppercorns
1 small dried red chilli
a pinch or two of fine salt

Place the chicken, vegetables and flavourings (except the salt) into a large pot, cover with cold filtered water, and bring to the boil. Skim off any scum from the top and add an additional 3 litres cold filtered water. Bring back to the boil, and then reduce to a simmer. After 2 hours of simmering, strain all the liquid through a fine strainer. Add a touch of salt and allow to cool. Chill in the fridge for a couple of days, or you can freeze it for up to 3 months.

Double Chicken Stock

This is a chicken stock made with chicken stock, and the flavour is much more intense. I use it for simple soups, in which the taste of the stock is paramount.

Makes about 2 litres

1 large chicken for boiling
1 white onion, peeled and roughly chopped
1 large carrot, peeled and roughly chopped
1 celery stick, roughly chopped
1 tbsp white peppercorns
1 small dried red chilli
chicken stock (see recipe above)
a pinch or two of fine salt

Place the chicken, vegetables and flavourings (except the salt) into a large pot, cover with chicken stock, and bring to the boil. Skim off any scum from the top and add 3 litres cold filtered water. Bring back to the boil, and then reduce to a simmer. After 1½ hours of simmering, strain all the liquid through a fine strainer. Add a touch of salt and allow to cool. Chill in the fridge for a couple of days, or you can freeze it for up to 3 months.

Vegetable Stock

As with all stocks, this can be used in soups, sauces and risottos. It's obviously the one to use when cooking for vegetarians.

Makes about 2.5 litres

2 onions, peeled and roughly chopped
2 carrots, roughly chopped
1 bulb garlic
2 leeks, cleaned and roughly chopped
1 head celery, roughly chopped
a handful of parsley stalks
3 sprigs thyme
1 tbsp white peppercorns
1 dried red chilli
a pinch of fine salt

Place all the ingredients in a large pot and cover with about 3 litres cold filtered water. Bring up to the boil. Skim off any scum from the top and reduce the heat to a simmer. Cook for 20 minutes, then turn the heat off. Pass the liquid through a fine sieve when slightly cooled. Chill in the fridge for a couple of days, or you can freeze it for up to 3 months.

Prawn Stock

Use this for the prawn caramelle and polenta recipes on pages 99 and 154, but I also use it for soup, and it's delicious as the base of a prawn risotto. Never throw away prawn shells, as you can save them up in the freezer until you have enough to make a stock. You could do the same with lobster or crab shells.

Makes about 1 litre

500g prawn shells, heads and all
2 carrots
2 celery stalks
2 large shallots, peeled
1 star anise
trimmings from 1 fresh red chilli
200ml vermouth
1 bay leaf
2 litres cold filtered water

Put all the ingredients in a large pot, and as it comes to the boil, skim off the scum. Turn down to a simmer, and cook for 40 minutes. Strain through a sieve and then boil to reduce by half. Use as required, chill in the fridge for a couple of days, or you can freeze it for up to 2 months.

Acorn House's Fresh Pasta Dough

This recipe makes quite a lot, but the mixture works best with these proportions. If too much for immediate use, give some to your friends!

You can colour your pasta. For green, you could use cooked and very well dried spinach or parsley purée, but I find nettles the best (see page 19). Use a handful of purée instead of one of the egg yolks. For red pasta, use a handful of cooked and very well dried beetroot purée in the same way.

Makes about 1.5kg

1kg type '00' fine milled pasta flour
9 egg yolks
6 whole eggs

Tip your flour into a dome shape on a large, dry work surface; I like to use a wooden surface, but any will do. Make a well in the middle of the dome with your fist and pour in all the egg yolks and whole eggs.

I start by using my index finger and stirring the mixture until it requires 2 fingers, then 3 and so on, until you have a paste that is workable as dough.

Knead this 'paste' or (in Italian) 'pasta' for 20 minutes until it begins to feel like silk and satin. Sometimes I can feel velvet in mine. Just get those elbows and wrists working. It's a great work-out, and I use it to condition my upper body as I work. Ha, who needs to go to the gym?

Then roll the pasta until it is thin enough that you can see your palm through it, either by machine or hand (do so in batches), and then cut into the shapes you require. Dry briefly, then cook for the time specified, usually minimal. If rolling or using in batches, keep covered to prevent drying out. You could keep it in the fridge for up to 3 days.

Béchamel Sauce

This is a basic white sauce, which is useful in a number of ways, particularly in the lasagne on page 220.

For 6

70g butter
70g plain flour
650ml milk, warmed
sea salt and freshly ground black pepper & a pinch of freshly grated nutmeg

Melt the butter in a pan over a medium heat, sift in the flour and then whisk for 3-5 minutes, allowing the flour to start cooking. Pour in the milk and stir constantly until the mixture thickens, about 20 minutes I would say. The sauce must not taste of flour, it should be smooth and of a thick double cream consistency. Season and add the nutmeg if you like.

House Dressing

This is the basic dressing used at the restaurant and at my home. It's delicious, but to make it even more so, you could use 2 parts olive oil to 1 part hazelnut oil.

Makes about 6 tablespoons

3 tbsp extra virgin olive oil
2 tbsp white wine vinegar (Volpaia is the best)
1 tbsp Dijon mustard, sea salt and freshly ground black pepper

Mix the vinegar together with the mustard and seasoning to taste in a small bowl. Add the oil and whisk until emulsified.

Tahini Dressing

I use this with French beans with sesame seeds, and with broccoli with ginger. It's as versatile as my house dressing, but there is no oil in it.

Makes about 600ml

200g Fairtrade tahini (sesame paste)
50ml white wine vinegar
400g natural yoghurt
1 tsp each of paprika, cumin seeds, toasted and ground and caster sugar
sea salt and freshly ground black pepper

Put everything into the food processor and blitz until it comes together to make a dressing. Taste for seasoning.

Bagna Cauda

This makes rather a lot, but an average processor likes quantities such as this. Just keep it in the fridge, and treat it like a homemade mayonnaise. Halve the recipe if using a smaller or hand mixer.

Makes about 1 litre

6 garlic cloves, peeled
500ml milk
20 salted anchovies, soaked and cleaned (see page 90)
sea salt and freshly ground black pepper
40ml red wine vinegar
about 500ml light olive oil

Place the garlic in a small pan with the milk and simmer over a very low heat until the garlic is very soft, about 30-40 minutes. The milk will eventually start to expose the garlic: at this stage, the garlic will probably be cooked, so take off the heat, and reserve the milk as it will help you to form the mayonnaise.

Place the anchovies into your food processor, and blend until smooth. Pour in 75ml of the milk, plus the garlic, lots of black pepper and the vinegar, and continue to blend until you have a smooth paste.

With the machine running, begin to drizzle in the olive oil, and continue until you have created a mayonnaise consistency. You might not need all the oil, or you might need a touch more. Adjust the seasoning to taste.

Vanilla Custard/Ice-cream

It's taken me 20 years to confidently make ice-cream. I remember the first time I made an ice-cream base: I had 80 egg yolks, 6 litres of double cream, and loads of milk, and I split it all. Everything — it was sweet scrambled eggs — went into the bin, and I have been justifiably nervous ever since. But this is the recipe I use now, and I only make it in smaller batches...

For 8

850ml double cream
225ml milk
2 vanilla pods, split
1 cardamom pod, crushed
7 medium egg yolks
310g caster sugar

Put the cream, milk, vanilla and cardamom in a pan and bring to the boil.

Put the egg yolks and sugar in a bowl, and whisk until thick and pale. Pour half of the hot cream mixture on top of the egg yolks, and stir vigorously, then pour that mixture back into the same pan the cream came from. Lower the heat and stir, patiently, for 15-20 minutes. As it begins to thicken, pour into a bowl sitting over ice, which will stop the temperature going too far and overcooking the eggs.

Leave to cool, and reheat if using as a custard. If making ice-cream, turn the mixture into an ice-cream machine and churn until ready, or freeze in suitable containers, mixing every now and again.

DIRECTORY

This does not include every single name, address or telephone number that might be applicable, just a few names and websites that might start you off in the right direction.

GENERAL
British Nutrition Foundation — www.nutrition.org.uk
The Caroline Walker Trust — www.cwt.org.uk
Compassion in World Farming — www.ciwf.org.uk
Food Commission — www.foodcomm.org.uk
Food for Life — www.foodforlife.uk.org
Food Standards Agency — www.food.gov.uk
Friends of the Earth — www.foe.co.uk
Greenpeace — www.greenpeace.org.uk
Health Education Trust — www.healthedtrust.com
National Consumer Council — www.ncc.org.uk
The School Food Trust — www.schoolfoodtrust.org.uk
The Soil Association — www.soilassociation.org
Sustain — www.sustainweb.org
UK Biodiversity Action Plan — www.ukbap.org.uk
WRAP (Waste Resources and Action Programme) — www.wrap.org.uk

ENERGY
British Wind Energy Association — www.bwea.com
Centre for Alternative Technology — www.cat.org.uk
EarthEnergy — www.earthenergy.co.uk
Ecotricity — www.ecotricity.co.uk
Energywatch — www.energywatch.org.uk
Energy Saving Trust — www.saveenergy.co.uk
Good Energy — www.good-energy.co.uk
Green Energy UK — www.greenenergy.uk.com
National Energy Foundation — www.natenergy.org.uk, www.nef.org.uk

SavaPlug — www.savawatt.com
Solar Trade Association — www.solartradeassociation.org.uk
Windsave — www.windsave.com

WILDLIFE
The Bumblebee Conservation Trust — www.bumblebeeconservationtrust.co.uk
Royal Society for the Protection of Birds (RSPB) — www.rspb.org.uk
The Wildlife Trusts — www.wildlifetrusts.org
The World Wildlife Fund — www.wwf.org

TRANSPORT
Aviation Environment Federation — www.aef.org.uk
Environmental Transport Association (ETA) — www.eta.co.uk
Green Car Guide — www.green-car-guide.com
Liftshare — www.liftshare.org
School-run-org — www.school-run.org
Campaign for Better Transport — www.bettertransport.org.uk
Vehicle Certification Agency — www.vcacarfueldata.org.uk

REDUCE CARBON FOOTPRINT
Carbon Clear — www.carbon-clear.com
The Carbon Trust — www.carbontrust.co.uk
People and the Planet — www.peopleandplanet.net

FOOD GROWING AND DISTRIBUTION
British Association for Fair Trade Shops — www.bafts.org.uk
Fairtrade Foundation — www.fairtrade.net
Foundation for Local Food Initiatives
FLAIR (Food and Local Agriculture Information Resource)
— www.localfood.org.uk
National Farmers' Retail and Markets Association (FARMA)
— www.farmersmarkets.net
National Society of Allotment and Leisure Gardeners Ltd
— www.nsalg.org.uk
Waterscape — www.waterscape.com

ORGANIC ORGANISATIONS/SHOPS

Fresh and Wild — www.freshandwild.com
Garden Organic (Henry Doubleday Research Association)
— www.gardenorganic.org.uk
Organic Farmers and Growers — www.organicfarmers.uk.com
The Organic Food Federation — www.orgfoodfed.com
Planet Organic — www.planetorganic.com
Sunnyfields Organics — www.sunnyfields.co.uk
The Soil Association — www.soilassociation.org

COMPOSTING

Community Composting Network — www.communitycompost.org
Compost Guide — www.compostguide.com
Compost Information — www.compostinfo.org
Green Gardener — www.greengardener.co.uk
Living Soil (Bokashi) — www.livingsoil.co.uk
Wiggly Wigglers (wormeries) — www.wigglywigglers.co.uk

VEGETARIAN

Fruitarian Foundation — www.fruitarian.com
The Vegan Society — www.vegansociety.com
The Vegetarian Society — www.vegsoc.org

FISH AND FISHERIES

The Centre for Environment, Fisheries and Aquaculture Science
— www.cefas.co.uk
DEFRA (Department for the Environment, Food and Rural Affairs)
— www.defra.gov.uk
Fishonline — www.fishonline.org
Loch Duart — www.lochduart.com
The Marine Conservation Society (MCS) — www.mcsuk.org
Marine Stewardship Council (MSC) — www.msc.org
Seafish Industry Authority — www.seafish.org
WWF (World Wildlife Fund) — www.wwf.org.uk/fishforthefuture
www.wwf.org.uk/orca, www.panda.org/stopoverfishing

CONSERVATION

English Nature/Natural England — www.englishnature.org.uk
www.naturalengland.org
Forest Stewardship Council — www.fsc-uk.info
Millennium Seed Bank Project — www.kew.org/msbp
The National Trust — www.nationaltrust.org.uk
Plantlife International — www.plantlife.org.uk
Royal Horticultural Society — www.rhs.org.uk
Worldwatch Institute — www.worldwatchinstitute.org

RECYCLING

Aluminium Federation — www.alfed.org.uk
Aardvark Recycling — www.aardvarkrecycling.org
British Glass — www.britglass.org.uk
British Plastics Federation — www.bpf.co.uk
Waste Online — www.wasteonline.org.uk
Confederation of Paper Industries — www.paper.org.uk
Environment Agency — www.environment-agency.gov.uk
letsrecycle.com — www.letsrecycle.com
Mailing Preference Service (MPS) — www.mpsonline.org.uk
Recyclenow — www.recyclenow.com
British Glass — www.recyclingglass.co.uk
Steel Can Recycling Information Bureau (SCRIB) — www.scrib.org
Waste Aware Scotland — www.wasteawarescotland.org.uk

HOUSEHOLD PRODUCTS

Bio-d — www.biodegradable.biz
Ecover — www.ecover.com
Natural Collection — www.naturalcollection.com
Natural House — www.natural-house.co.uk
Vegiwash — www.vegiwash.com

Acknowledgements

OK, this is where I keep it real, and send love out to all who have helped me to get this far.

THE PLANET — *To Gaia, I send my deepest love for allowing me the chance of life. I am connected deeply to you.*

THE FAMILY — *To mum, for carrying me, and all your love. To my father Chris, deep love and respect for all your support through the past thirty years. To my dad for showing me the ways of the world. To my brothers Julian, Jon, Robert and Demetri, I am always here for you, boys. To Isaac, Ty, Neo, Aron, Thelonious, India, Brandon, Tuula and the Bump for being the future of our family. To Gill, Alexander, Albert and Eugenie, come and see me more. To Mary, Alan, John, David, Sally, Louise, Rosie, Alice, Joshua, Jo, Anna, Nicola. To Mick Jagger for your continued support in my life, to Jade for your inspiration, love to Assisi and Amber, big shout to Dan Williams. To Jerry, Elizabeth, James, Georgia and Gabrielle, you are welcome any time. To the Hillman (Brady Bunch) family, Lori, John, Francesca, John Jr, Laura, Paloma for your love and healing, Carmen, Alex, Kike, Sadie, Cherokee, for making me feel welcome. To the Marcuson family, Gill, Alan, Jake and Zoe, Josh, Sam, Lila Rose and Rudy Valentine, it's all in the history, thanks for being there.*

THE CHEFS — *To Rowley (Rolls Royce) Leigh, you started me off in all this. To Albert and Michel Roux for setting me in the right direction. To Sue (crazy hair) Miles for picking me back up. To Robert (back door) Cousins, you are still looking over my shoulder. To Max (Cadillac) Chiomento for all the wicked times. To Pierre Koffmann for showing me how to treat people. To Colin Westal for ghosting me, Kathy Gradwell for the meanest stare in the business, Jyanni Krystiasis, for perfection in the recipe. To Rose Gray for nurturing me, Ruth Rogers, for your continuing support and love in my career, Jamie (hots 2) Oliver, never will there be another, you got crazy skillz, Hugh Fearnley-Whittingstall for living it true and writing the best books, Theo (River Cafe) Randall, always a pleasure, April (Michelin star) Bloomfield, well deserved, babe. To Pete (da professor) Begg, Gary (dirty dog) Wilson, Celia (whatever) Harvey, Gregory (big apple) Merchand, Ben (Espanola) Hayes, Ben O'Donohue, Ashley (black eye) Hughes, The Trubshaw, Clare (got nice hair) Mitchell, Mr Matt 'shit kicker' Bond, Mario (green knife) George, Dane (the virgin) Wilson, and all you chefs I have worked with over the past 21 years, wicked times.*

THE BUSINESS HEADS — *To Nick Smallwood, you gave me my first chance and have given me the best advice every time I asked, thank you so much. To Ossie Gray, for the university dayz at the Cafe, Michael (da boss) Pyner, Andy Munro, Jack (flash) Gordon, Nick (da house) Jones, for teaching me more than you know. To Liam (big man) Black. To Vince Powers, for giving me my first head chef post, wicked stuff. To Steven Sweeney for rockin' it, and Jo and Ronnie Wood for showing me how to do it. To Patricia Michelson, you are who I look to. To Claire Hartten, and Geoff Crook, you made all the difference.*

THE TEACHER — *To Steven (Dragon Hall) Girard, the best teacher I could ever hope to find, my deepest respect and thanks, one love.*

THE BUSINESS PARTNER — *To Jamie Grainger-Smith, just the start, mate.*

THE PUBLISHERS — *To Zelda, Judith and Cecilia and the Hodder team for their support. To Susan (up all night) Fleming, this book would not have been written without you, thanks for putting up with me. To David (complementary designer) Lane, thanks for all the innovation.*

ALL THE REST — *To the Dragon Hall family for keeping it real, The Dirt Café team for keeping it underground, the River Cafe team, the Moro team, the Fifteen team, the Terrence Higgins Trust team, the Shoreditch Trust team, the Waugh Thistleton team, the La Fromagerie Team, and the Aardvark team (you ARE rubbish!). To Andreas (go to bed) Georgiou and your team, Paul (worm man) Richens, David (the hatchet) Matchet. To Marcus (suntan) Foley, ah, the good times, and all your great advice, Alexi (country girl) Robinson, Roger (cider barn) Wilkins, Elle (up a tree) Pickering. David (the wineo) Gleave, To the Acorn House Restaurant team, the Water House Restaurant team, the Eat Green team, it's all about the future. To the Market Kitchen crew and all the Jedi Warriors out there.*

Peace, one love.

INDEX

Recipes are shown in *italic*